SOCIAL WORK IN PRACTICE series

Series editors: **Viviene Cree**, University of Edinburgh and
Steve Myers, University of Salford

"This series combines all the elements needed for a sound basis in 21st-century UK social work. Readers will gain a leading edge on the critical features of contemporary practice. It provides thoughtful and challenging reading for all, whether beginning students or experienced practitioners."
Jan Fook, Professor in Social Work Studies, University of Southampton

This important series sets new standards in introducing social workers to the ideas, values and knowledge base necessary for professional practice. Reflecting the current curricula of the new social work degree and post-qualifying programmes and structured around the National Occupational Standards, these core texts are designed for students undertaking professional training at all levels as well as fulfilling the needs of qualified staff seeking to update their skills or move into new areas of practice.

Editorial advisory board:
Suzy Braye, University of Sussex
Jim Campbell, Queen's University Belfast
Ravi Kohli, University of Bedfordshire
Jill Manthorpe, King's College London
Kate Morris, University of Birmingham
Lyn Nock, BASW
Joan Orme, University of Glasgow
Alison Shaw, The Policy Press

Other titles in the series:
Social work: Making a difference by Viviene Cree and Steve Myers

Social work and multi-agency working: Making a difference
edited by Kate Morris

Youth justice in practice: Making a difference by Bill Whyte

Radical social work in practice: Making a difference by Iain Ferguson and Rona Woodward

Religion, belief and social work

Making a difference

Sheila Furness and Philip Gilligan

BASW
BRITISH ASSOCIATION
OF SOCIAL WORKERS

First published in Great Britain in 2010 by

The Policy Press
University of Bristol
Fourth Floor
Beacon House
Queen's Road
Bristol BS8 1QU
UK

tel +44 (0)117 331 4054
fax +44 (0)117 331 4093
e-mail tpp-info@bristol.ac.uk
www.policypress.co.uk

North American office:
The Policy Press
c/o International Specialized Books Services (ISBS)
920 NE 58th Avenue, Suite 300
Portland, OR 97213-3786, USA
tel +1 503 287 3093 • fax +1 503 280 8832 • e-mail info@isbs.com

British Library Cataloguing in Publication Data
A catalogue record for this book is available from the British Library.

Library of Congress Cataloging-in-Publication Data
A catalog record for this book has been requested.

ISBN 978 1 86134 981 1 paperback
ISBN 978 1 86134 982 8 hardcover

Cover design by The Policy Press.
Front cover: image kindly supplied by www.JohnBirdsall.co.uk
Printed and bound in Great Britain by TJ International, Padstow.

Contents

Acknowledgements

This book has been greatly enriched by the contributions of many other individuals whom we would like to thank for their help. First, we very much appreciate the time generously given by all those who agreed to share their practice experiences with us and who have given permission for these to be used as case studies within the book. We also acknowledge the valuable contribution made by our students who have engaged readily with the topics discussed and shown a willingness to explore both their beliefs and the impact of these. In particular, they have provided feedback about the Furness/Gilligan Framework as a tool for the analysis of practice. The anonymous reviewers provided a critique that has helped us to improve the final version of the book, while the staff at The Policy Press have worked hard to make it a reality. Finally, but by no means least, we must thank our partners, Jack and Patricia, for their enduring patience and support while we have been writing this book.

Introduction

> … people … have knowledge that is important in defining their situations – the problematic aspects as well as potential and actual solutions. (Early and GlenMaye, 2000: 119)

In writing this book, we note that religion and belief often play a very significant role in determining the ways in which people interpret events, resolve dilemmas, make decisions and view themselves, their own actions and the actions of others. Thus, we would argue that social workers will only be competent to engage with people if they, also, engage with these important aspects of many individuals' lives.

Those people who wish to train as social workers have always expressed and demonstrated a variety of motivations. These include the wish to help others in both practical and emotional ways; to improve people's lifestyles and control their behaviours; to transform society and achieve social justice; to pursue personally rewarding careers; to apply what they perceive as their aptitude for the role; and to serve a range of religious, political and ideological beliefs (Cree, 2003; Furness, 2007; Gilligan, 2007; DH, 2008). Values shape individual conduct in both professional practice and other aspects of life. However, individuals often remain unconscious of the relationship between their values and their actions. Discussions and work with both student social workers and practitioners over several years has demonstrated that some remain unaware of their own values while others struggle to disclose their values and beliefs. They fear that doing so will cause others to perceive them as oppressive or prejudiced, or that it will lead to conflict or ridicule. In their training, students are encouraged to develop skills in critical thinking and reflexivity, to share their views and to both respect and gain an understanding of different perspectives. In order for an institute of higher education to be accredited to offer professional social work qualifications it must satisfy the regulatory bodies for England, Scotland, Wales or Northern Ireland that the education and training offered will meet specified standards and requirements. These are informed by the Quality Assurance Agency for Higher Education benchmark statements for social work (QAA, 2000, 2008), the National Occupational Standards (DH, 2002) and the General Social Care Council (GSCC) code of practice (GSCC, 2002). In particular, honours graduates are expected to "acquire, critically evaluate, apply and integrate knowledge and understanding" in five core areas (QAA, 2008: 8). The curriculum should include explanations of matters such as religious belief and the nature and application of social work values, and make links between them and the ethical dilemmas that so often face social workers when making decisions. As social work educators, our intention in writing this book is to provide an accessible text that not only helps readers to engage with these issues, but also enables them to become more sensitised and committed to learning about religion and belief. We, therefore, aim to provide a framework that can be used to explore these issues within day-to-day practice. (This is detailed in Chapter Three.) We, also, seek to address three particular matters:

- the relevance and impact of religion and spiritual belief on the users and practitioners of social work in the UK;
- the extent to which social work (in its practices, policies and professional training) takes account of such beliefs in its pursuit of culturally sensitive and competent practice;
- the consideration of specific issues, settings, communities and stages in the life course which require social workers to give particular attention to issues of religion and belief in the context of their professional practice and social policy debates which are relevant to the UK in the early 21st century.

Strengths-based approach

Our approach to the role of religion and belief – and to social work in general – is underpinned by a broadly strengths-based perspective (see Saleeby, 2008) with an emphasis on the need for collaboration and partnership between practitioners and service users. We identify religion and religious and spiritual beliefs as potentially significant resources and targets for intervention. They may provide what Sullivan (1992) described as a 'helping environment' and Taylor (1997) as 'enabling niches' where the resilience of individuals, families and groups is built or enhanced. However, we also recognise that religion may be of no significance to some people or, at the other extreme, may significantly heighten or even play a part in causing the difficulties faced.

In common with other humanist approaches, the strengths perspective assumes that individuals have capacity for growth and change (Smalley, 1967; Weick, 1992). For many people, religion and beliefs contribute to the range of experiences and characteristics that contribute to who they are. They are likely to be among the systems in which individuals and groups are embedded, and to contribute to their strengths and resilience. At the same time, as Early and GlenMaye (2000: 119) remind us, service users have knowledge that is crucial to understanding their situations, including both the problematic aspects and the potential and actual solutions. They have usually managed to survive many adversities before the intervention of professionals, who need to encourage them to define and ascribe meaning to their situations, to listen to them and to accept and acknowledge their 'expertness' and internal knowledge of their situation (Weick, 1983; Weick and Pope, 1988).

Such awareness of people's 'expertise' about themselves complements our recognition that social workers need to be particularly aware of the power they have within relationships with service users and that self-awareness is a crucial component of culturally competent practice. Practitioners (whether they have specific religious or spiritual beliefs or none) need to recognise the potential impact of their reactions to people who espouse beliefs that differ from their own. They need to be particularly alert to the risk that they may devalue, or even demonise, the belief systems of others, while continuing to view their own as 'normal' or superior (see Weaver, 2008).

'Religion' and 'belief'

Those considering the subjects of 'religion' and 'belief' face considerable challenges around definitions and these challenges are greatly increased where individualised and occasional expressions of religious feeling and spiritual belief are included. We have, therefore, adopted a pragmatic and largely phenomenological/interpretive approach to definition. We have followed Beckford (1992, 2001) in defining 'religion' as largely what individual believers or communities say it is, rather than imposing narrower 'substantive' or 'functionalist' approaches (see Hunt, 2005: ch 1). In doing so, we recognise that meanings will be varied, inconsistent and changeable, but would suggest that this both reflects actual experiences and ensures that what individuals see as 'religious' or 'spiritual' beliefs and as practices significant to them are recognised as such. These will include a very wide spectrum of beliefs and practices, which will range from those dictated by several millennia of tradition and followed by whole communities to the perhaps relatively fleeting belief or practice of an isolated individual in crisis. (For example, those facing their own imminent death or responding to an immediate trauma.) What they have in common is that they are of importance to someone *as religious or spiritual beliefs or practices* and are likely to have an impact on the behaviour, responses and understanding of individuals, and on what those individuals need from social workers.

Thus, as well as mainstream world religions, such as Christianity, Hinduism, Islam, Judaism and Sikhism and the many variations within them, we recognise that there are, also, an unlimited number of smaller groupings. These are as different as the Church of Christ and Latter Day Saints ('Mormons') and

'New Age' movements such as 'goddess spirituality'. They are divergent in their doctrines and ideas, but all have the capacity to impact significantly on the lives of individuals. We also recognise that, for many people, religious and spiritual beliefs and the actions that arise from them are unique to them as individuals and, perhaps, to particular moments in time.

We are equally aware that for many people 'non-religious' or 'secular' spirituality is of central importance in determining worldviews, behaviour and responses. We are, therefore, conscious of providing little specific discussion of such 'non-religious' beliefs. This is not because we fail to recognise the potential significance of 'secular spirituality', but rather because adequate discussion of its role and importance would have required a book of at least twice the length of this one. Many writers (Bullis,1996; Becvar, 1998; Canda and Furman, 1999; Lindsay, 2002; Nash and Stewart, 2002; Coholic, 2003; Henery, 2003; Hodge, 2005, 2007; Moody, 2005; Moss, 2005; Derezotes, 2006; Coates et al, 2007; Holloway, 2007; Crisp, 2008; Gray, 2008; Mathews, 2009) have, in recent years, made important contributions to research and thinking about the relationship between both religious and non-religious 'spirituality' and social work. Some have done so without making any distinction between types of spirituality, starting, as we do, with regard to 'religion' from the perspective that 'spirituality' is largely what individual believers or groups say it is. We would encourage readers to also access this literature.

'Secularisation' and the 'death of God'?

We start from the premise that, in early 21st-century Britain, as elsewhere, social work is practised in a richly diverse, multi-ethnic and multi-faith society – a society in which religious and other beliefs are of crucial importance to many and play some role in shaping the worldview of most. We are convinced that, in such a context, there are many reasons why all social workers need to develop a working knowledge and understanding of the religious beliefs and practices of service users – that, without such knowledge and understanding, they cannot adequately perform their statutory duties or meet their professional responsibilities and cannot begin to claim that their work is culturally competent.

We would argue that those involved in a profession such as social work need to recognise the likely, but not always obvious, significance of religion and belief to many service users and colleagues. We suggest that social workers need to be ready and open to explore these subjects with people and to recognise that they may be significant sources of personal values, of serious dilemmas, of motivation and support, and of anxiety in relation to issues very relevant to social work practice.

Such views will no doubt be somewhat surprising to those readers who have accepted previous modernist orthodoxies within social science, which for several decades taught professionals that they were living and practising in a 'secular', 'post-religious' or at least 'post-Christian' era (see, for example, Wilson, 1966, 1976). As Hunt (2005) explains, writers on the sociology of religion built on the theories of Marx and Engels (1957), Durkheim (1915) and Weber (1904/1930) to reach the apparently obvious conclusion that, in the face of 'rationalism' and 'science', religion and religious beliefs in the late 20th century faced inevitable decline and would eventually disappear. Berger (1970: 13), for example, told us, "[i]f commentators on the contemporary situation of religion agree about anything, it is that religion has departed from the world", while Ammerman (1987: 2) predicted, even in a US context, that religion would become a "shrunken, emasculated apparition at the periphery of modern society". On the contrary, this prediction has failed to come to fruition and, in fact, there are real signs of a resurgence of interest in the study of religion (Hunt, 2005; McIntosh, 2007; Macionis and Plummer, 2008).

For readers who are particularly interested in finding out more about the historical and current debates within the field of religion, we would recommend reference to Davie (1994, 2007). She reminds us that: "The sociology of religion aims to discover the patterns of social living associated with religion in all its diverse forms, and to find explanations for the data that emerge" (Davie, 2007: 6). She also argues that more attention should be given to 'lived religion' rather than to the categories imposed by the social researcher. The challenge, for both researchers and practitioners, is to understand worldviews that are underpinned by, and give rise to, values that are different – sometimes very different – to their own.

Have social workers considered issues of religion and belief?

We would argue that anyone involved in social work practice or in the management, training or education of social workers will need, at many points in their career, to address questions around the impact of religion and belief. Unless they do so, they cannot fully deliver on their responsibility "to protect the rights and to promote the interests of service users and carers", while "treating each person as an individual", and "respecting diversity and different cultures and values" (GSCC, 2002: 14-15). Individual social workers also need to include such questions within their reflections on and in action (Schön, 1983). However, during the final decades of the 20th century, there was little to suggest that such issues were given any priority in the education and training of social workers in Britain and much to suggest that discussion of religion, in particular, had declined. Relevant literature available in British journals tended to deal with very specific issues, with particular groups, with issues in other countries or with history (Runnymede Trust and Wood, 1996; Smyth and Campbell, 1996; Lloyd, 1997; Bowpitt, 1998; Kirton, 1999; Garr and Marans, 2001; Pacheco et al, 2003).

This was, of course, in apparent contrast to an earlier rekindling of interest in the role of religion in both social work education and practice in the USA (Loewenburg, 1988; Canda, 1989; Netting et al, 1990; Amato-von Hemert, 1994; Sermabeikian, 1994; Sheridan and Amato-von Hemert, 1999) and to more confident explorations of the role of spirituality by some therapists and other practitioners in particular types of health settings in Britain (Bragan, 1996; Cobb and Robshaw, 1998; Speck, 1998; Brandon, 1999). However, while US social workers appeared, sometimes, more sympathetic to religious or spiritually sensitive interventions than their British counterparts (Sheridan and Amato-von Hemert, 1999; Gilligan and Furness, 2006), studies conducted in the 1990s suggest that around two thirds of social work students in the USA also reported that they received very little input related to religion and spirituality in their graduate social work classes (Derezotes, 1995; Sheridan and Amato-von Hemert, 1999). Cree (1996), nevertheless, argues that professional social work has effectively 'rebranded' central themes from the Judaeo-Christian tradition and used them in a secular way.

Ahmad (1996: 190) reminds practitioners that:

> Cultural norms provide guidelines for understanding and action, guidelines which are flexible and changing, open to different interpretations across people and across time, structured by gender, class, caste, and other contexts, and which are modulated by previous experiences, relationships, resources and priorities.

There are no reasons to think that this is not as true for social work practitioners and those who use their services as for anyone else. However, even in reflecting on their own professional development, social workers have often needed reminding that learning cannot be separated from the influence of context and culture, including religion and beliefs (Boud et al, 1993).

Research conducted by the authors in 2002 (Furness, 2003; Gilligan, 2003), 2004 (Gilligan and Furness, 2006) and 2006-07 (Gilligan, 2009), like that conducted by Furman et al (2005), demonstrates that a very large number of social workers in Britain have been brought up with religious or spiritual beliefs and that many continue to hold these. However, such research has also found that, for many years, social work professionals received very little and inconsistent preparation around either how to respond to the needs of those individuals and groups for whom religious or spiritual beliefs are of central importance or how to resolve the dilemmas that may arise from their own beliefs.

Analysis of semi-structured interviews with practice teachers and social work students, undertaken during the winter of 2002–03, suggested that, even among those who are explicitly sympathetic to religion and/or spirituality and who are aware of its potential significance to their own practice in social work, there was a pervading sense of them seeing these subjects as too dangerous, too personal, too embarrassing, too old-fashioned, too uncertain or just too difficult to discuss (Gilligan, 2003). One interviewee commented straightforwardly, regarding religion in the context of social work practice, "It isn't discussed".

The picture that emerged might, perhaps, have been expected. Several American authors (Canda, 1989; Sheridan et al, 1994; Canda and Furman 1999; Canda et al, 2004) indicate that social work professionals have been inadequately prepared to undertake competent work in the field of religion, spirituality and social work, and advocate the inclusion of relevant material within the social work curriculum. At the same time, they have not necessarily reached agreement about the content or the means by which relevant materials should be included (Sheridan and Amato-von Hemert, 1999; Gilbert, 2000; Praglin, 2003). Moreover, a similar, if more recent, debate in Britain has not yet achieved much consensus around how to actually achieve 'spiritually competent' social work practice. This is, perhaps, in part because of differing views around the extent to which this should focus on offering religious and spiritual interventions or simply take account of religion and spirituality where these are significant to service users.

In 1998, the Central Council for Education and Training in Social Work (CCETSW), as the awarding and regulatory body for social work education in Britain, published a range of literature to promote equal opportunities and antiracism in social work. As part of this series, consideration was given to the implications of the beliefs and practices of minority faiths for social work practice (see Furness, 2003). Patel et al (1998: ii), reporting on this, emphasised that "religious cultural practices, group and individual spirituality, religious divisions and religion as therapy have had no place in social work education and practice", but argued for a more informed understanding of religious differences and ethnic influences to better prepare social workers for a plural society. More recently, Moss (2003) reported on the provisional findings of a survey he had carried out with British higher education institutions offering professional social work courses to find out the extent to which issues of religion and spirituality were included within the curriculum. His findings indicated a very wide variation between individual programmes. Meanwhile, the question of how qualified workers can be challenged to effectively address such issues has, until recently, received even less consistent attention.

Crompton (1996: sec 4, p 1) reported the view that training in Britain encourages social workers to hold back on their beliefs and quoted social workers in one agency as stating, "We find that it often depends on the views and beliefs of an individual social worker, whether religion is given any importance or not". She concluded, in the context of little published material specifically aimed at social workers either on spirituality or on different religions, that, "To talk about religion and spirituality is for many people as embarrassing as talking about sex, death and money".

It is our intention that the following chapters will provide frameworks and insights that will help readers to overcome any such embarrassments and, at the same time, to become more aware of their own and others' systems of belief and their impact and significance.

Chapters Two to Eleven

Chapters Two and Three outline the context for the reader. We explore the reasons why we believe issues arising from religion and belief are relevant to social work practice and why it is essential for all social work practitioners to develop confidence and competence in responding to them. The responsibilities of social workers to take appropriate account of the religious and spiritual beliefs of service users will be located in the context of relevant legislation, policies and procedures. Models to promote and develop cultural competence in health and social care practice will be presented and a suggested framework introduced and explained.

This 'Furness/Gilligan' framework is applied to real-life case examples in subsequent chapters. All the case examples are based on semi-structured interviews with current social work practitioners and managers working in different localities. Interviews were audio-recorded and transcribed. Transcripts were, subsequently, read and, where necessary, corrected by interviewees. All names and some other details have been changed to protect identities.

Chapter Four explores the potential significance of religion and spiritual beliefs in the lives of 'looked after' children and of children and young people in need and in the lives of their parents and carers. It discusses dilemmas arising from situations such as those where the religious and spiritual needs of a young person cannot be met directly by the placements available for them and explores issues such as the need to give young people opportunities to discuss their religious and spiritual beliefs and to listen to what they say about their religious needs and beliefs.

Chapter Five explores the religious and spiritual needs of older people. We consider how people make transitions at critical periods of the life course and a range of coping and support mechanisms available to them. Consideration is given to dealing with death and dying and the importance of respecting different forms of cultural expressions of grief.

Chapter Six explores several issues around the potentially crucial impact of religion and belief in relation to child and adult abuse and the dilemmas faced by practitioners in this context. It highlights the potential importance of religion and belief to factors such as resilience and pays particular attention to both 'clerical' abuse and safeguarding systems within faith communities and abuse linked to beliefs in 'spirit possession'.

Chapter Seven considers the cultural differences and assumptions made about others' mental health that have resulted in the misdiagnosis and mistreatment of a significant number of those experiencing mental distress. It will also explore the role of religious-based groups and spiritual interventions as potential resources for social workers offering services in this field.

Chapter Eight considers the needs and experiences of people with learning disabilities in relation to religion and belief. In particular, it discusses evidence that the birth of a child with learning disabilities tends to stimulate either a greater faith or results in a complete loss of faith by parents, and the issue of some parents believing that they are being punished for their sins. It explores suggestions that the religious experiences of people with disabilities are, too often, ones of exclusion and marginalisation, and the particular vulnerability of people with learning disabilities to forced marriages.

Chapter Nine explores issues of particular relevance to social work with migrants, refugees and asylum seekers newly arrived in Britain. It highlights the role of faith organisations in supporting people who have recently arrived in, or are threatened with deportation from Britain and the potential importance of religion and belief as sources of emotional and social support to people in diasporic communities.

Chapter Ten discusses the characteristics of different faith-based approaches to social work, together with issues that are likely to bring agencies and individuals into conflict with accepted social work values, official guidance or legislation. It considers some means by which these conflicts or dilemmas might be resolved or avoided. In particular, it gives attention to issues around adoption by same-sex couples and to the impact of recent equality and adoption legislation on individual practitioners and faith-based organisations opposed to this.

The final chapter identifies recurring themes and makes recommendations for best practice in culturally competent and sensitive social work practice.

An appendix provides some brief outlines of what we and other people understand to be characteristics and key practices and traditions of the six major world religions that appear most relevant to Britain. Such information can never be comprehensive nor provide an adequate substitute for dialogue with individuals about their actual beliefs and practices or their experience of what aspects of these are significant to them. It also provides information about what we have found to be the most useful sources of further information regarding specific religions and beliefs.

Key question

(1)   What do you hope to learn by reading this book?

References

Ahmad, W.I.U. (1996) 'The trouble with culture', in D. Kelleher and S. Hillier (eds) *Researching cultural differences in health*, London: Routledge, pp 190–219.

Amato-von Hemert, K. (1994) 'Should social work education address religious issues? Yes!', *Journal of Social Work Education*, **30**(1), 7–11.

Ammerman, N. (1987) *Bible believers*, New York: Rutgers University Press.

Beckford, J. (1992) 'Religion, modernity and post-modernity', in B. Wilson (ed) *Religion: Contemporary issues*, London: Bellew Publishing, pp 11–23.

Beckford, J. (2001) 'The construction and analysis of religion', *Social Compass*, **48**(3), 439–41.

Becvar, D.S. (1998) *The family, spirituality, and social work*, New York: Haworth Press.

Berger, P. (1970) *A rumour of angels: Modern society and the rediscovery of the supernatural*, London: Allen Lane.

Boud, D., Cohen, R. and Walker, D. (eds) (1993) *Using experience for learning*, Buckingham: Society for Research into Higher Education and Open University Press.

Bowpitt, G. (1998) 'Evangelical Christianity, secular humanism, and the genesis of British social work', *British Journal of Social Work*, **28**(5), 675–93.

Bragan, K. (1996) *Self and spirit in the therapeutic relationship*, London: Routledge.

Brandon, D. (1999) 'Melting straitjackets', *Journal of Psychiatric and Mental Health Nursing*, **6**(4), 321–6.

Bullis, R.K. (1996) *Spirituality in social work practice*, Washington, DC: Taylor & Francis.

Canda, E.R. (1989) 'Religious content in social work education: a comparative approach', *Journal of Social Work Education*, **25**(1), 36–45.

Canda, E. and Furman, L. (1999) *Spiritual diversity in social work practice: The heart of helping*, New York: Free Press.

Canda, E.R., Nakashima, M. and Furman, L.D. (2004) 'Ethical considerations about spirituality in social work: Insights from a national qualitative survey', *Families in Society*, **85**(10), 1-9.

Coates, J., Graham, J., Swartzentruber, B. and Ouelette, B. (2007) *Spirituality and social work: Selected Canadian readings*, Toronto: Canadian Scholars Press.

Cobb, M. and Robshaw, V. (eds) (1998) *The spiritual challenge of health care*, London: Churchill Livingstone.

Coholic, D. (2003) 'Incorporating spirituality in feminist social work perspectives', *Affilia*, **18**(1), 49-67.

Cree, V.E. (1996) *Social work: A Christian or secular discourse?* (Waverley Paper), Edinburgh: University of Edinburgh.

Cree, V.E. (ed) (2003) *Becoming a social worker*, London: Routledge.

Crisp, B.R. (2008) 'Social work and spirituality in a secular society', *Journal of Social Work*, **8**(4), 363-75.

Crompton, M. (1996) *Children, spirituality and religion: A training pack*, London: CCETSW.

Davie, G. (1994) *Religion in Britain since 1945: Believing without belonging*, Oxford: Blackwell.

Davie, G. (2007) *The sociology of religion*, London: Sage Publications.

Derezotes, D.S. (1995) 'Spirituality and religiosity: neglected factors in social work practice', *Arete*, **20**(1), 1-15.

Derezotes, D. (2006) *Spiritually orientated social work practice*, Boston, MA: Allyn and Bacon.

DH (Department of Health) (2002) *Requirements for social work training*, London: DH (www.dh.gov.uk/en/Publicationsandstatistics/Publications/PublicationsPolicyAndGuidance/DH_4007803).

DH (2008) *Evaluation of the new social work degree qualification in England: Volume 1: Findings*, London: DH.

Durkheim, E. (1915) *The elementary forms of religious life*, London: Allen and Unwin.

Early, T.J. and GlenMaye, L.F. (2000) 'Valuing families: social work practice with families from a strengths perspective', *Social Work*, **45**(2), 118-30.

Furman, L.D., Benson P.W., Canda E.R. and Grimwood C. (2005) 'A comparative international analysis of religion and spirituality in social work: A survey of UK and US social workers', *Social Work Education*, **24**(8), 813-39.

Furness, S. (2003) 'Religion and culturally competent practice', *Journal of Practice Teaching in Health and Social Work*, **5**(1), 61-74.

Furness, S. (2007) 'An enquiry into students' motivations to train as social workers in England', *Journal of Social Work*, **7**(2), 239-53.

Garr, M. and Marans, G. (2001) 'Ultra-orthodox women in Israel: a pilot project in social work education', *Social Work Education*, **20**(4), 459-68.

Gilbert, M.C. (2000) 'Spirituality in social work groups: practitioners speak out', *Social Work with Groups*, **22**(4), 67-84.

Gilligan, P. (2003) '"It isn't discussed". Religion, belief and practice teaching: missing components of cultural competence in social work education', *Journal of Practice Teaching in Health and Social Care*, **5**(1), 75-95.

Gilligan, P. (2007) 'Well motivated reformists or nascent radicals: how do applicants to the degree in social work see social problems, their origins and solutions?', *British Journal of Social Work*, **37**(4), 735-60.

Gilligan, P. (2009) 'Considering religion and beliefs in child protection and safeguarding work: is any consensus emerging?', *Child Abuse Review*, **18**(2), 94-110.

Gilligan, P. and Furness, S. (2006) 'The role of religion and spirituality in social work practice: views and experiences of social workers and students', *British Journal of Social Work*, **36**(4), 617-37.

Gray, M. (2008) 'Viewing spirituality in social work through the lens of contemporary social theory', *British Journal of Social Work*, **38**(1): 175-96.

GSCC (General Social Care Council) (2002) *Code of practice for social care workers and code of practice for employers of social care workers*, London: GSCC (www.gscc.org.uk/NR/rdonlyres/041E6261-6BB0-43A7-A9A4-80F658D2A0B4/0/Codes_of_Practice.pdf).

Henery, N. (2003) 'The reality of visions: contemporary theories of spirituality in social work', *British Journal of Social Work*, **33**(8), 1105-13.

Hodge, D.R. (2005) 'Spirituality in social work education: a development and discussion of goals that flow from the profession's ethical mandates', *Social Work Education*, **24**(1), 37-55.

Hodge, D.R. (2007) 'The Spiritual Competence Scale: a new instrument for assessing spiritual competence at the programmatic level', *Research on Social Work Practice*, **17**(2), 287-295.

Holloway, M. (2007) 'Spiritual need and the core business of social work', *British Journal of Social Work*, **37**(2), 265-80.

Hunt, S. (2005) *Religion and everyday life*, Abingdon: Routledge.

Kirton, D. (1999) 'Perspectives on "race" and adoption: the views of student social workers', *British Journal of Social Work*, **29**(5), 779-96.

Lindsay, R. (2002) *Recognising spirituality: The interface between faith and social work*, Crawley, WA: University of Western Australia Press.

Lloyd, M. (1997) 'Dying and bereavement, spirituality and social work in a market economy of welfare', *British Journal of Social Work*, **27**(2), 175-90.

Loewenburg, F.M. (1988) *Religion and social work practice in contemporary American society*, New York: Columbia University Press.

McIntosh, T. (2007) 'Believing religion', in S. Matthewman, C. Lane West-Newman and B. Curtis (eds) *Being sociological*, Basingstoke: Palgrave Macmillan, pp 275-93.

Macionis, J.J. and Plummer, K. (2008) *Sociology: A global introduction* (4th edn), Harlow: Pearson Education.

Mathews, I. (2009) *Social work and spirituality*, Exeter: Learning Matters.

Marx, K. and Engels, F. (1957) *On religion*, Moscow: Progress Publishers (www.marxists.org/archive/marx/works/subject/religion/index.htm).

Moody, H.R. (ed) (2005) *Religion, spirituality, and aging: A social work perspective*, New York: Haworth Press.

Moss, B. (2003) 'Research into practice', CommunityCare.co.uk, 23 October, (www.communitycare.co.uk/Articles/2003/10/23/42593/research-into-practice.html).

Moss, B. (2005) *Religion and spirituality*, Lyme Regis: Russell House Publishing.

Nash, M. and Stewart, B. (2002) *Spirituality and social care: Contributing to personal and community well-being*, London: Jessica Kingsley.

Netting, F.E., Thibault, J.M. and Ellor, J.W. (1990) 'Integrating content on organized religion into macropractice courses', *Journal of Social Work Education*, **26**(1), 15-24.

Pacheco, E.R., Plaza, S.H., Fernández-Ramirez, B. and Andrés, P.C. (2003) 'The implications of immigration for the training of social work professionals in Spain', *British Journal of Social Work*, **33**(1), 49-65.

Patel, N., Nalk, N. and Humphries, B. (1998) *Visions of reality: Religion and ethnicity in social work*, London: CCETSW.

Praglin, L.J. (2003) 'Spirituality, religion and social work: an effort toward interdisciplinary conversation', *Journal of Religion and Spirituality in Social Work*, **23**(4), 67-84.

QAA (Quality Assurance Agency for Higher Education) (2000) *Subject benchmark statements: Social policy and administration and social work*, Gloucester: QAA (www.qaa.ac.uk/academicinfrastructure/benchmark/honours/socialwork.pdf).

QAA (2008) *Social work*, Mansfield: QAA (www.qaa.ac.uk/academicinfrastructure/benchmark/statements/socialwork08.pdf).

Runnymede Trust and Wood, J. (1996) 'Jewish issues in social work education', in N. Patel, N. Nalk and B. Humphries (eds) *Visions of reality: Religion and ethnicity in social work*, London: CCETSW, pp 69-83.

Saleeby, D. (2008) *The strengths perspective in social work practice* (5th edn), Boston, MA: Allyn & Bacon.

Schön, D. (1983) *The reflective practitioner*, London: Basic Books.

Sermabeikian, P. (1994) 'Our clients, ourselves: the spiritual perspective and social work practice', *Social Work*, **39**(2), 178-83.

Sheridan, M.J. and Amato-von Hemert, K. (1999) 'The role of religion and spirituality in social work education and practice: a survey of student views and experiences', *Journal of Social Work Education*, **35**(1), 125-41.

Sheridan, M.J., Wilmer, C.M. and Atcheson, L. (1994) 'Inclusion of content on religion an spirituality in the social work curriculum: a study of faculty views', *Journal of Social Work Education*, **30**, 363-76.

Smalley, R.E. (1967) *Theory for social work practice*, New York: Columbia University Press.

Smyth, M. and Campbell, J. (1996) 'Social work, sectarianism and anti-sectarian practice in Northern Ireland', *British Journal of Social Work*, **26**(1), 77-92.

Speck, P. (1998) 'The meaning of spirituality in illness', in M. Cobb and V. Robshaw (eds) *The spiritual challenge of health care*, London: Churchill Livingstone, pp 21-33.

Sullivan, W.P. (1992) 'Reclaiming the community: the strengths perspective and deinstitutionalization', *Social Work*, **37**(3), 204-09.

Taylor, J.B. (1997) 'Niches and practice: extending the ecological perspective', in D. Saleebey (ed) *The strengths perspective in social work practice* (2nd edn), White Plains, NY: Longman, pp 217-27.

Weaver, H.N. (2008) 'Spirituality in cross-cultural contexts: implications for practice and research', presented at the Third North American Conference on Spirituality and Social Work, June (http://w3.stu.ca/stu/sites/spirituality/documents/HilaryWeaver-SpiritualityinCross-CulturalContexts_000.pdf).

Weber, M. (1904) *Die protestantische Ethik und der 'Geist' des Kapitalismus*, trs M. Talcott-Parsons, 1930, as *The protestant ethic and the spirit of capitalism*, London: Allen and Unwin (www.ne.jp/asahi/moriyuki/abukuma/weber/world/ethic/pro_eth_frame.html).

Weick, A. (1983) 'Issues in overturning a medical model of social work practice', *Social Work*, **28**(6), 467-71.

Weick, A. (1992) 'Building a strengths perspective for social work', in D. Saleebey (ed) *The strengths perspective in social work practice*, White Plains, NY: Longman, pp 18-26.

Weick, A. and Pope, L. (1988) 'Knowing what's best: a new look at self-determination', *Social Casework*, **68**(1), 10-16.

Wilson, B. (1966) *Religion in a secular society*, London: Weidenfeld and Nicolson.

Wilson, B. (1976) *Contemporary transformations of religion*, London: Oxford University Press.

2

The requirement to consider religion and spiritual beliefs

> ... while religion as a social identity has declined significantly, it continues to be strongly related to the views of the minority who attend religious services or feel they belong to a religion. (NCSR, 2007: 2)

How is religion significant?

O'Beirne (2004) notes that, at least until the 1990s, there was very little quantitative research that could provide demographic information about those affiliated even to the major faith communities or about the influence of religion on social attitudes or life experiences. However, the 2001 Census and Social Trends series provides a useful source of data about religious affiliation and practice (see Table 2.1).

The 2001 Census reported over 75% of households in England and Wales as having a religion. The Census also demonstrated that populations adhering to the larger minority religions are concentrated in particular localities and include very high proportions of individuals under 25 years – young people who appear to be actively maintaining and interpreting the cultural and religious values of their parents (Drury, 1996; Anwar, 1998; Jacobson, 1998; Ghuman, 1999; Darr, 2001; Lewis, 2002). Muslims accounted for 2.7% of the total UK population in 2001, but for 36% of the population of Tower Hamlets, 24% of Newham and 16% of Bradford, while 38% of British Muslims lived in London, 14% in the West Midlands, 13% in the North West and 12% in Yorkshire and the Humber. Hindus accounted for 1% of the total UK population in 2001, but for 15% or more of the populations of Brent (17%), Harrow (20%) and Leicester (15%), while 74% of British Hindus lived in London and the East and West Midlands. Sikhs accounted for 0.6% of the total UK population in 2001, but for 7% or more of the populations of Ealing (10%), Hounslow (10%), Sandwell (7%), Slough (10%) and Wolverhampton (8%), while 31% of British Sikhs lived in the West Midlands. Jewish people accounted for 0.5% of the total UK population

Table 2.1: UK population by self-identified religion or belief (2001 Census)

Religion or belief	England	Scotland	Wales	Northern Ireland	UK (total)	UK (%)
Christian	35,251,244	3,294,545	2,087,242	1,446,386	42,079,417	71.6
No religion	7,171,332	1,394,460	537,935	*	9,103,727	15.5
Muslim	1,524,887	42,557	21,739	1,943	1,591,126	2.7
Hindu	546,982	5,564	5,439	825	558,810	1.0
Sikh	327,343	6,572	2,015	219	336,149	0.6
Jewish	257,671	6,448	2,256	365	266,740	0.5
Buddhist	139,046	6,830	5,407	533	151,816	0.3
Other religion	143,811	26,974	6,909	1,143	178,837	0.3
Total religion or belief	45,362,316	4,783,950	2,668,942	1,451,414	54,266,622	92.3
Not stated*	3,776,515	278,061	234,143	233,853	4,522,572	7.7
Total	49,138,831	5,062,011	2,903,085	1,685,267	58,789,194	100.0

* 'Not stated' includes 'No religion' in Northern Ireland

in 2001, but for 15% of the population of Barnet, while 56% of the Jewish population of Great Britain lived in London. 'Place' thus has important implications for policy makers.

The Census also demonstrated that there are significant correlations between a household's declared religion and other significant issues. For example:

> Families headed by a Muslim are more likely than other families to have children living with them. Nearly three quarters (73 per cent) had at least one dependent child in the family in 2001, compared with two fifths of Jewish (41 per cent) and Christian (40 per cent) families.
>
> Muslim families also had the largest number of children. Over a quarter (27 per cent) of Muslim families had three or more dependent children, compared with 14 per cent of Sikh, 8 per cent of Hindu, and 7 per cent of Christian families. (National Statistics, 2005)

The National Centre for Social Research reports from the findings of the 2006 British Social Attitudes Survey (NCSR, 2007: 3-4) that 31% of the people questioned belonged to a religion or attended religious services, and that:

> ... this group has markedly different attitudes towards pre-marital sex and abortion than people who do not have a religious identity – and the difference between the two groups has actually widened over time.

And:

> Religion makes a difference: people who regularly attend a religious service are far less likely to support euthanasia than people who never attend. People who attend once a week or more support euthanasia in an average of 1.4 out of 5 scenarios; the equivalent figure for those who never or practically never attend is 2.8.

Regarding self-identity, O'Beirne (2004) reports that, especially for members of minority communities, 'religion' is of central importance for 'self-identity'. Her analysis of data from the 2001 Home Office Citizenship Survey demonstrates that, while 'religion' was ranked only ninth by the whole sample among those factors of importance to their identity (that is, behind 'family', 'work', 'education' and 'nationality'), it was considered more important for identity than 'skin colour' or 'ethnic or cultural group'. Seventeen per cent of white respondents said that 'religion' was important to their self-identity, as did 44% of black and 61% of Asian respondents. White respondents ranked 'religion' tenth on the list of 15 items and respondents of mixed ethnicity ranked it seventh, but Asian and black respondents ranked 'religion' among the top three factors of importance in their personal descriptions. All ethnic groups ranked 'family' highest (see O'Beirne, 2004: 18-19).

O'Beirne also notes significant variations across the six main faith communities. For those affiliated to the Muslim, Hindu and Sikh faiths, 'religion' was ranked second only after 'family'. Jewish respondents ranked 'religion' highest. Christian respondents ranked it seventh. However, black Christian respondents ranked 'religion' second after only 'family' (O'Beirne, 2004: 19-20).

Patel et al (1998: 10) concluded that, for a large and increasing number of service users, "Religion is a basic aspect of human experience, both within and outside the context of religious institutions", while Modood et al (1997: 297) report that "religion is central in the self-definition of the majority of South Asian people".

In a more recent study focused on British-born 'Pakistani' men aged 16 to 25 years, Alam and Husband (2006) note that, for them, Islam remains an integral aspect, not only in their spiritual, but also in their personal-political, lives, even when they did not profess to be practising Muslims. Moreover, becoming more religious was a relatively common aspiration and there was little or no conflict regarding the juxtaposition of 'Britishness' and 'Muslimness'.

Religious affiliation may also be of significance in relation to very specific issues and, as a result, may need to be given particular emphasis and consideration in formulating policies and procedures. For example, Douds et al (2003) note that, in places where there are large numbers of men from religious traditions that prohibit the consumption of alcohol, there is likely to be a lower incidence of alcohol misuse. Jayakody et al (2005: 1), in the context of exploring ways to prevent teenage pregnancy in Britain, report that, while young men claiming higher religious observance were less likely to have started sex, once they had started having sex, they were more likely to have unprotected sex than young men who had never attended a religious meeting. Thus, they conclude that the provision of relevant information within an appropriate and acceptable religious context may be essential to help to reduce risks of both unplanned pregnancies and sexually transmitted diseases (Jayakody et al, 2005: 8-9). 'Religion' is also, increasingly, a subject within political discourse and debate, leading Cooper and Lodge (2008: 3) in their introduction to a book whose contributors include Prime Minister Gordon Brown and a significant group of faith leaders to emphasise "the increasing salience of a number of moral questions and policy issues that relate intimately to religious convictions and commitments".

All cultures have mechanisms, including religion, that regulate matters such as sexual behaviour. Indeed, Durkheim (1915) argued that the three main functions of religion were: to maintain social cohesion through shared symbols, values and norms; to ensure social control by conferring legitimacy on the political system and cultural norms such as marriage and reproduction; and to provide meaning and purpose (Macionis and Plummer, 2008: 611).

Essentialist thinking holds the notion that sexuality is an essential, innate and fixed part of our human nature, and faith-based essentialism tends to define some sexual practices as 'natural' and others as 'against nature' and/or as transgressions of God's law (Scott and Jackson, 2006: 236). To give one example, some strands of Christian teaching and thought have held a largely negative attitude to the body and sexuality. The body is seen as the site of sin and corruption. Eve tempted Adam in the Garden of Eden and is responsible for humanity's fall from grace into the state of sin (Stevens, 2007: 216). In some contexts, women are still blamed for 'luring men into temptation' and this adds to the phenomenon of men either escaping punishment or being given relatively lenient sentences by the judiciary when convicted of domestic violence and rape (see, for example, Myhill and Allen, 2002). The Roman Catholic Church teaches that sexual intercourse is primarily for the purpose of procreation within the bounds of marriage. Artificial forms of contraception are forbidden and other sexual acts, such as same-sex sexual intercourse, are seen as 'sinful'. Social constructionist thinking, on the other hand, sees sexuality as being determined by social and historical forces within society, including religious thinking and beliefs. For example, male identified heterosexuality is seen as being institutionalised as the only 'normal' form of sexuality, while other forms are portrayed as deviant and in need of correction (see Scott and Jackson, 2006). In this context, men and women are encouraged to question how societal and religious expectations can lead them into gendered sexual roles that ignore their sense of agency and thus perpetuate oppressive and abusive practices. Consideration of such contrasting theoretical positions helps practitioners and theorists to question how far 'experience' is a product of factors such as culture, religion and belief and of the particular perceptions of reality that arise from them (Stevens, 2007: 223).

Relevant general legislation

The emphasis in relevant general legislation is very much on the prevention of discrimination, but, in recent years, the UK parliament has passed a variety of laws that include some attempt to protect 'religious freedom'. These include the:

- Human Rights Act 1998
- Employment Equality (Religion or Belief) Regulations 2003
- Racial and Religious Hatred Act 2006
- Equality Act 2006.

Such legislation applies throughout the UK, while Local Authority Circular (2000)17 (DH, 2000a) alerted all local authorities and directors of social services in England, for example, to the implementation of the Human Rights Act 1998 from 2 October 2000 and, therefore, to the need for social services to maintain best practice so as not to act incompatibly with the European Convention on Human Rights (ECHR) (Council of Europe, 1966). Thus, it reminded them that:

> Everyone has the right to freedom of thought, conscience and religion; this right includes freedom to change his religion or belief, and freedom, either alone or in community with others and in public or private, to manifest his religion or belief, in worship, teaching, practice and observance. (ECHR, Article 9[1])

And that:

> The enjoyment of the rights and freedoms set forth ... shall be secured without discrimination on any ground such as sex, race, colour, language, religion, political or other opinion, national or social origin, association with a national minority, property, birth or other status. (ECHR, Article 14)

Since 2 December 2003 it has been unlawful to discriminate against somebody in the workplace on grounds of their religious or other belief. Religion or beliefs are defined as meaning any religion, religious belief or similar philosophical belief. The broad definition means that, as well as including all major religions, the law is also likely to cover paganism, atheism and humanism. It may also include pacifism and vegetarianism.

Under the Equality Act 2006, it is unlawful to discriminate against someone because of their religion or belief (or because they have no religion or belief):

- in any aspect of employment;
- when providing goods, facilities and services;
- when providing education;
- in using or disposing of premises;
- when exercising public functions.

Part 2 of the Equality Act came into force on 30 April 2007 and deals, among other things, with the prohibition of discrimination on grounds of religion or belief when providing services and education or exercising public functions, such as providing social work services.

The Department for Communities and Local Government (DCLG, 2007) gives specific guidance on Part 2 of the Equality Act 2006 and sets out the effect of the law and the exceptions provided. (The significant exceptions allow charities and other organisations whose purpose is related to religion or belief to serve particular communities or relate to issues such as 'national security'.) DCLG (2007: 13-14) is explicit on a number of points that are particularly relevant to the provision of social work and related services.

Public authorities, such as local authorities, must ensure that all their services of any particular kind are provided in such a way that no one entitled to use any service is disadvantaged in receiving it by reason of religion or belief. They should ensure that their employees and agents also do so, using contractual or other controls as appropriate to achieve that result.

Even when public authorities are not specifically exempt, they should not stop working with religious organisations because of a fear that working with such organisations might be perceived as discriminatory under the religion or belief provisions of Part 2. Nothing in Part 2 has such an effect. For example:

■ If a local authority considers that it cannot provide meals on wheels to meet particular religious dietary requirements through its own direct provision, there is nothing to prevent it funding a separate provider or providers to do so. Even where there is no strict religious requirement for it, there is nothing to prevent an authority funding one provider that offers a service restricted on religious grounds and others that are not restricted, provided that decisions are made in a non-discriminatory way and that their provisions overall meet the needs of other users.
■ There is nothing to prevent a local authority from funding a religious group to run care homes for people of their own religion, so long as there are care homes available to people who are not of that religion.

Children and young people

Legislation such as the Children Act 1989, the Children (Scotland) Act 1995   X
and the Children (Northern Ireland) Order 1995 gives explicit instructions to social workers and others as to how they should respond to the religious needs of children and young people, and Crompton (1996, 1998), like others, notes the need for social workers in this field to give explicit attention to religion, if they are to perform their statutory duties competently. X

Seden (1995) emphasises the fact that the 1989 Act follows the spirit of the United Nations Convention on the Rights of the Child (UNICEF, 1995) in giving explicit directions to local authorities to give "due consideration ... to the child's religious persuasion, racial origin, cultural and linguistic background" (section 22(5)(c)) when placing them, and in requiring that they "shall not cause the child to be brought up in any religious persuasion other than that in which he would have been brought up if the order had not been made" (section 31) (DH, 1989a). However, she goes on to emphasise that, in assessing the significance of religious persuasion, it is important to look beyond the mere preservation of the parents' right to specify creed (that is, a set of beliefs or religious system) and to look at what being brought up in a particular religious persuasion actually means.

DH Guidance to the Act stresses that:

> The importance of religion as an element of culture should never be overlooked: to some children and families it may be the dominant factor so that the religion of a foster parent, for example, may in some cases be more important than their ethnic origin. (DH, 1989b: para 2.41)

Similarly, the practice guidance for assessing children in need and their families (DH, 2000b) emphasises that:

> Religion or spirituality is an issue for all families whether white or black ... For families where religion plays an important role in their lives, the significance of their religion will also be a vital part of their cultural traditions and beliefs. (para 2.69)

However, it also notes that "there is some evidence to suggest that information about a child's or family's religion is not always recorded in case files" (DH, 2000b: para 2.68).

Scottish Office guidance on the Children (Scotland) Act 1995 and the Adoption (Scotland) Act 1978 suggests that, in making decisions about a looked after child, the child's views regarding religious persuasion should be given priority, while, according to paragraph 2.38 of Northern Ireland Office (1995):

> A child's religious and cultural background and ethnic origins are important factors for consideration in any placement decision. It may be taken as a guiding principle of good practice that, for example, in any placement decision, placement with a family of similar religious or ethnic background is most likely to meet a

child's needs as fully as possible and to safeguard his welfare most effectively.

DH (2001a), in the context of the Children (Leaving Care) Act 2000, requires that:

> All preparation for leaving care and provision of aftercare must take account of the religious persuasion, racial origin, cultural and linguistic background and other needs of young person (section 22(5)(c)) (p 27)

> The befriender will need to be 'matched' with the young person, eg he or she should preferably be from the same cultural, linguistic, racial and religious background. (p 33)

> Young people from ethnic minorities may need help – preferably from someone with the same background – to help them to understand their racial, cultural, linguistic and religious background and to take a pride in themselves. (p 34)

Moreover, "Cultural/religious needs" are listed among the "Items to be considered a priority for funding" (p 63).

Remarkably, neither *Every child matters* nor the government's response to Lord Laming's report into the death of Victoria Climbié made reference to 'religion', 'religious belief' or to 'spirituality' (see HM Treasury, 2003; and DfES et al, 2003). However, the Children Act 2004 left all relevant requirements of the 1989 Act unchanged and they remain current.

DfES (2006: 28) suggests that practitioners undertaking a Common Assessment Framework (CAF) assessment will need in assessing "Identity, including self-esteem, self-image and social presentation" to include consideration of "race, religion, age, gender, sexuality and disability", and notes that these "may be affected by bullying or discriminatory behaviour".

Such guidance is, of course, not confined to the UK. In New Zealand, for example, in setting out key factors that courts must consider when deciding what is best for children, the Care of Children Act 2004 includes the requirement that "the child's identity, including their culture, language and religion, should be preserved and strengthened" (Ministry of Justice/ Tahu o te ture, 2006). At the same time, it seems pertinent to ask how much priority social workers will give to children's religious needs, in the context of competing priorities and a lack of emphasis on such issues in social work training and education. In the context of both limited resources and awareness, it seems likely that budgets rather than needs will, in fact, determine whether a Muslim child has an opportunity to attend mosque and madrasa or a Catholic child to attend Sunday mass.

Adults

The National Health Service (NHS) and Community Care Act 1990 and similar legislation make relatively little reference to religion and belief. However, many local authorities in guidance to service users and practitioners are explicit in requiring that religious needs are considered in assessments and in the planning and commissioning of services and interventions. Worcestershire County Council (2006: 1), for example, states:

> The main aim of our work is to encourage and help people to remain as independent as possible, recognising differences in individual need by taking account of race, culture, religion, disability, gender, sexuality and age.

The government's 2005 Green Paper (DH, 2005: 16) appeared to make it clear that services in adult social care "should be tailored to the religious, cultural and ethnic needs of individuals", while the subsequent White Paper (DH, 2006: 17, para 1.27) is explicit in stating:

> ... we are committed to a health and social care system that promotes fairness, inclusion and respect for people from all sections of society, regardless of their age, disability, gender, sexual orientation, race, culture or religion, and in which discrimination will not be tolerated.

However, despite this apparent emphasis, it should also be noted that there are no other references to 'religion' or 'religious belief' in either of these documents. The Department of Health's more recent 128-page report drawing on 11 research studies commissioned by the Department of Health's Policy Research Programme between 2003 and 2007, and assessing what it describes as "the progress and outcomes" of the process of modernisation initiated in two Green Papers (DH, 1998, 2005) and the most recent White Paper (DH, 2006a), makes no reference whatsoever to 'religion', 'religious belief' or to 'spirituality (see DH, 2007).

Older people

Documentation relating to the Single Assessment Process (see, for example, DH, 2001b, 2002) requires practitioners not only to note the subject's religion, but also to comment on their personal fulfilment, spiritual fulfilment, personal relationships and lifestyle choices.

DH (2001b) states clearly that:

- The objective of providing person-centred care requires managers and professionals to, among other things, "recognise individual differences and specific needs including cultural and religious differences" (p 23).
- Service users and their carers should be able to expect that "procedures are in place to identify and, where possible, meet any particular needs and preferences relating to gender, personal appearance, communication, diet, race or culture, and religious and spiritual beliefs" (p 25).
- Health promotion activity should take account of differences in lifestyle and the impact of cultural/religious beliefs (p 108).
- Services provided by the NHS and local authorities to "ensure that older people have fair access to programmes of disease prevention and health promotion, including cancer screening, blood pressure management, smoking cessation, advice about lifestyle including nutrition and physical activity, and falls prevention ... should take account of the impact of cultural and religious beliefs and lifestyles" (p 113).

It recognises that:

> Good assessment also requires that the needs and circumstances of older people from black and minority ethnic communities are assessed in ways that are not culturally biased and by staff who are able to make proper sense of how race, culture, religion and needs may impact on each other. (p 31, para 2.31).

Mental health

In relation to modern standards and service models for mental health, DH (1999: 10) noted that:

> ... key skills and competencies are required throughout mental health services to ensure services are non-discriminatory, and sensitive to the needs of all service users and care regardless of age, gender, race, culture, religion, disability, or sexual orientation.

In the particular context of providing community development workers (CDWs) for black and minority ethnic (BME) communities in meeting mental health needs, DH (2006b) advises such workers to do several things in order to help them fulfil their strategic role. In relation to faith/religious communities, these include addressing the following questions:

- What communities exist locally?
- Where are they?
- Which groups or parts of society/their faith/religion do they cover?
- Are they aware of the initiative – and the role of the BME CDW?
- What are their hopes and expectations of the CDW?
- Do they recognise mental illness?
- What is their understanding of mental illness?
- What education and training do they receive in respect of mental illness?
- What is their attitude to mental illness?
- From their contacts, do they recognise any common threads or themes for those people they come across from the BME community? If so, what are they and what do they believe the options/solutions might be to tackle these? Who would be best placed to offer a solution?
- What support do they provide to members of their community (and their families/carers) who suffer from a mental illness?
- How do/should members of their community ask for support from them?
- What support do *they* need to help provide support to members of their community (and their families/carers) who suffer from a mental illness? For example, would talks to Asian community groups at different places of worship help such as gurdwaras, mosques and temples? (p 34)

Learning disabilities

The government's White Paper *Valuing people: A new strategy for learning disability for the 21st century* (DH, 2001c) notes that the needs of people with learning disabilities from minority ethnic communities were too often overlooked and that, in particular, "agencies often underestimate people's attachments to cultural traditions and religious beliefs", while DH (2001d: 30) notes that "fears about the type of care and support that would be provided away from the family home, whether this care and support would be appropriate in relation to the family's culture or religion, and worries about possible sexual impropriety and vulnerability" are issues that "need to be addressed as part of the context in which people with learning difficulties must negotiate independence".

The *Community care and primary care training set* (Stanley et al, 2007: 20) advises practitioners assessing capacity that they must always "Be aware of any cultural, ethnic or religious factors which may have a bearing on the individual", and "Consider whether an advocate ... or someone else could assist, eg a member of a religious or community group to which the person belongs".

Asylum seekers and refugees

A variety of official procedures and guidance exist that clearly acknowledge the potential significance of religion to refugees and asylum seekers and to the reasons for their need to seek asylum.

Home Office (2004: 4), for example, states unequivocally with regard to religion:

> 8.1 When considering whether it is appropriate to allocate dispersed accommodation caseworkers should give consideration to Article 9 of the European Convention on Human Rights which provides that everyone has the right to freedom of thought, conscience and religion. This right includes freedom to change religion or belief and freedom, either alone or in community with others and in public or private, to manifest his/her religion or belief in worship, teaching, practice and observance.

> 8.2 Caseworkers should therefore examine each case on its own merits. If an applicant states, and it is accepted, that they should be allocated accommodation in a certain area because it is the only place they can worship, then the request may be granted (subject to due regard to cost of accommodation in the area). Such cases, which are likely to be very rare, should be referred to HEO level with a written proposal.

> 8.3 If there is only one place of worship, and asylum seekers of the same religion have already been dispersed, it is likely to be possible for a new asylum support applicant to be able to practise their religion with others in the dispersal area.

> 8.4 Further investigation may be required. It may be necessary for the caseworker to write to the applicant for further details about the religious group or the place of worship.

And, regarding gender-related persecution and religion, Home Office (2006: 7-8) instructs case owners in the UK Border Agency that:

> A woman may face harm for her adherence to, or rejection of, a religious belief or practice. Religion as the ground of persecution may include but is not limited to, the freedom to hold a belief system of one's choice or not to hold a particular belief system and the freedom to practise a religion of one's choice or not to practise a prescribed religion.
>
> Where the religion assigns particular roles or behavioural codes to women, a woman who refuses or fails to fulfil her assigned role or abide by the codes may have a well founded fear of persecution on the ground of religion. For example a woman who does not adhere to certain dress codes, such as wearing a veil, may be subject to discrimination and harassment amounting to persecution.
>
> Failure to abide by the behavioural codes set out for women may be perceived as evidence that a woman holds unacceptable religious opinions regardless of what she actually believes about religion.
>
> A woman's religious identity may be perceived to be aligned or shared with that of other members of her family or community. Imputed or attributed religious identity may therefore be important.

Professional codes of practice

Social work training and education in Britain must include "aspects of philosophical ethics relevant to the understanding and resolution of value dilemmas and conflicts in both interpersonal and professional contexts" (QAA, 2008: 9).

In the US, the National Association of Social Workers' *Code of ethics* (NASW, 1999: 3) makes very specific mention of individuals' religious beliefs and practices:

> Social workers also should be aware of the impact on ethical decision making of their clients' and their own personal values and cultural and religious beliefs and practices. They should be aware of any conflicts between personal and professional values and deal with them responsibly.

It, also, states very clearly that:

> Social workers should not take unfair advantage of any professional relationship or exploit others to further their personal, religious, political, or business interests. (NASW, 1999: 9)

In contrast, in Britain, such imperatives, while implicitly present, are notable for their lack of specificity regarding religion and beliefs. As a result, they are open to interpretation to an extent that some would argue they are insufficient. The British Association of Social Workers' code of practice (BASW, 2002), for example, recognises that, among many other things, social workers have a duty to:

> Show respect for all persons, and respect service users' beliefs, values, culture, goals, needs, preferences, relationships and affiliations. (p 4)

> Place service users' needs and interests before their own beliefs, aims, views and advantage, and not to use professional relationships to gain personal, material or financial advantage. (p 7)

And:

> Be alert to the possibility of any conflict of interest, which may affect their ability to exercise professional discretion or bias their judgement. (p 10)

However, it makes no specific mention of religious beliefs or practices.

At the same time, the General Social Care Council's *Code of practice for social care workers and code of practice for employers of social care workers* (GSCC, 2002), which have been adopted across the UK, display a similar lack of specificity as regards religion and belief, but provide a broader framework in which culturally competent practice in relation to them can be accommodated, if not specifically required. GSCC (2002) requires that all social care workers protect the rights and promote the interests of service users and carers by:

> 1.1 treating each person as an individual;

> 1.2 respecting and, where appropriate, promoting the individual views and wishes of both service users and carers;

> 1.3 supporting service users' rights to control their lives and make informed choices about the services they receive;

1.4 respecting and maintaining the dignity and privacy of service users;

1.5 promoting equal opportunities for service users and carers;

1.6 respecting diversity and different cultures and values.

It also tells social care workers that they must strive to establish and maintain the trust and confidence of service users and carers by:

2.6 Declaring issues that might create conflicts of interest and making sure that they do not influence your judgement or practice.

Key questions

(1) Think of the last service user you spoke to.
  • List what you know about their cultural background and their religious/spiritual beliefs.
  • Is this more or less than you usually know about a service user's cultural background and religious/spiritual beliefs? *Why is this the case?*
  • Did this service user need you to know more?
(2) Do you know which religions and beliefs are likely to be significant to your service users?
(3) What do you know about these religions and beliefs?
(4) If you needed to know more, how would you achieve this?
(5) Are religion and beliefs significant to you? If so, how do they impact on your practice?
(6) Are religion and beliefs significant to your colleagues? If so, how do they impact on their practice?

References

Adoption (Scotland) Act 1978, Edinburgh: HMSO (www.opsi.gov.uk/ RevisedStatutes/Acts/ukpga/1978/cukpga_19780028_en_11).

Alam, M.Y. and Husband, C. (2006) *British-Pakistani men from Bradford: Linking narratives to policy*, York: Joseph Rowntree Foundation (www.jrf. org.uk/bookshop/eBooks/1585-pakistani-men-bradford.pdf).

Anwar, M. (1998) *Between cultures: Continuity and change in the lives of young Asians*, London: Routledge.

BASW (British Association of Social Workers) (2002) *Code of ethics for social work* (http://basw.co.uk/Portals/0/CODE%20OF%20ETHICS.pdf).

Children Act 1989, London: HMSO (www.opsi.gov.uk/acts/acts1989/Ukpga_19890041_en_1.htm).

Children Act 2004, London: HMSO (www.opsi.gov.uk/acts/acts2004/pdf/ukpga_20040031_en.pdf).

Children (Scotland) Act 1995, Edinburgh: The Stationery Office (www.opsi.gov.uk/ACTS/acts1995/ukpga_19950036_en_1).

Children (Northern Ireland) Order 1995 (www.uk-legislation.hmso.gov.uk/si/si1995/uksi_19950755_en_1).

Cooper, Z. and Lodge, G. (eds) (2008) *Faith in the nation: Religion, identity and the public realm in Britain today*, London: Institute for Policy Research and Development.

Council of Europe (1966) *The European Convention on Human Rights*, Strasbourg: Council of Europe (www.hri.org/docs/ECHR50.html).

Crompton, M. (1996) *Children, spirituality and religion: A training pack*, London: CCETSW.

Crompton, M. (1998) *Children, spirituality, religion and social work*, Aldershot: Ashgate.

Darr, A. (2001) 'The underrepresentation of Asian students on nursing, radiography and physiotherapy courses', unpublished PhD thesis, Department of Applied Social Studies, University of Bradford.

DCLG (Department for Communities and Local Government) (2007) *Guidance on new measures to outlaw discrimination on grounds of religion or belief in the provision of goods, facilities and services*, London: DCLG (www.communities.gov.uk/documents/communities/pdf/325878).

DfES (Department for Education and Skills) (2006) *The Common Assessment Framework for children and young people: Practitioners' guide* (www.everychildmatters.gov.uk/caf; or search www.teachernet.gov.uk/publications using the ref: 0337-2006BKT-EN).

DfES, DH and Home Office (2003) *Keeping children safe: The government's response to the Victoria Climbié Inquiry Report and Joint Chief Inspectors' report Safeguarding Children* (http://publications.everychildmatters.gov.uk/eOrderingDownload/CM-5861.pdf.pdf).

DH (Department of Health) (1989a) *An introduction to the Children Act 1989*, London: HMSO.

DH (1989b) *Volumes of guidance on the Children Act 1989*, London: HMSO.

DH (1995) *Looking after children*, London: HMSO.

DH (1998) *Modernising social services: Promoting independence. Improving protection. Raising standards*, London: The Stationery Office.

DH (1999) *National service framework for mental health: Modern standards and service models* (www.dh.gov.uk/en/Publicationsandstatistics/Publications/PublicationsPolicyAndGuidance/DH_4009598).

DH (2000a) *Local Authority Circular (2000)17: Legislation: Human Rights Act 1998* (www.dh.gov.uk/en/Publicationsandstatistics/Lettersandcirculars/LocalAuthorityCirculars/AllLocalAuthority/DH_4003821).

DH (2000b) *Assessing children in need and their families: Practice guidance*, London: HMSO.

DH (2001a) *Children (Leaving Care) Act 2000: Regulations and guidance*, London: The Stationery Office (http://www.dh.gov.uk/en/Publicationsandstatistics/Publications/PublicationsLegislation/DH_4005283).

DH (2001b) *National service framework for older people*, London: The Stationery Office.

DH (2001c) *Valuing people: A new strategy for learning disability for the 21st century* (www.archive.official-documents.co.uk/document/cm50/5086/5086.pdf).

DH (2001d) *Learning difficulties and ethnicity report to the Department of Health* (www.dh.gov.uk/en/Publicationsandstatistics/Publications/PublicationsPolicyAndGuidance/DH_4002991).

DH (2002) *The single assessment process: Guidance for local implementation* (www.dh.gov.uk/en/Publicationsandstatistics/Publications/PublicationsPolicyAndGuidance/DH_4008389).

DH (2005) *Independence, well-being and choice: Our vision for the future of social care for adults in England* (Social Care Green Paper) (www.dh.gov.uk/en/Publicationsandstatistics/Publications/PublicationsPolicyAndGuidance/DH_4106477).

DH (2006a) *Our health, our care, our say: A new direction for community services* (www.dh.gov.uk/en/Publicationsandstatistics/Publications/PublicationsPolicyAndGuidance/DH_4127453).

DH (2006b) *Mental health policy implementation guide: Community development workers for black and minority ethnic communities: Final handbook* (www.dh.gov.uk/en/Publicationsandstatistics/Publications/PublicationsPolicyAndGuidance/DH_064110).

DH (2007) *Modernising adult social care – what's working* (www.dh.gov.uk/en/Publicationsandstatistics/Publications/PublicationsPolicyAndGuidance/DH_076203).

Douds, A.C., Cox, M.A., Iqbal, T.H. and Cooper, B.T. (2003) 'Ethnic differences in cirrhosis of the liver in a British city: alcoholic cirrhosis in South Asian men', *Alcohol and Alcoholism*, **38**(2), 148-50.

Drury, B. (1996) 'Sikh girls and the maintenance of an ethnic culture', *New Community*, **17**(3), 387-98.

Durkheim, E. (1915) *The elementary forms of religious life*, London: Allen and Unwin.

Employment Equality (Religion or Belief) Regulations 2003, London: HMSO (www.opsi.gov.uk/si/si2003/20031660.htm).

Equality Act 2006, London: HMSO (www.opsi.gov.uk/ACTS/acts2006/pdf/ukpga_20060003_en.pdf).

Ghuman, P. (1999) *Asian adolescents in the West*, Leicester: BPS Books.

GSCC (General Social Care Council) (2002) *Code of practice for social care workers and code of practice for employers of social care workers*, London: General Social Care Council (www.gscc.org.uk/NR/rdonlyres/041E6261-6BB0-43A7-A9A4-80F658D2A0B4/0/Codes_of_Practice.pdf).

HM Treasury (2003) *Every child matters*, London: HMSO (http://publications.everychildmatters.gov.uk/eOrderingDownload/CM5860.pdf).

Home Office (2004) *Asylum support policy bulletin 31: Dispersal guidelines* (www.bia.homeoffice.gov.uk/sitecontent/documents/policyandlaw/asylumsupportbulletins/dispersal/pb31?view=Binary).

Home Office (2006) *Gender issues in the asylum claim* (www.bia.homeoffice.gov.uk/sitecontent/documents/policyandlaw/asylumpolicyinstructions/apis/genderissueintheasylum.pdf?view=Binary).

Human Rights Act 1998, London: HMSO (www.opsi.gov.uk/ACTS/acts1998/19980042.htm).

Jacobson, J. (1998) *Islam in transition: Religion and identity among British Pakistani youth*, London: Routledge.

Jayakody, A., Sinha, S., Curtis, K., Roberts, H., Viner, R. and the Research with East London Adolescents Community Health Survey (2005) *Culture, identity, religion and sexual behaviour among black and minority ethnic teenagers in East London* (Paper 4 of four papers prepared for Teenage Pregnancy Unit), London: DfES (www.dfes.gov.uk/research/data/uploadfiles/RW42d.pdf).

Laming, Lord (2003) *The Victoria Climbié Inquiry: Report of an inquiry*, London: HMSO (www.victoria-climbie-inquiry.org.uk/finreport/finreport.htm).

Lewis, P. (2002) *Islamic Britain: Religion, politics and identity among British Muslims*, London: I.B. Tauris & Co.

Macionis, J.J. and Plummer, K. (2008) *Sociology: A global introduction* (4th edn), Harlow: Pearson Education.

Ministry of Justice/Tahu o te ture (2006) *An introduction to the Care of Children Act*, Christchurch: Ministry of Justice (www.justice.org.nz/family/pdf-pamphlets/courts002.pdf).

Modood, T., Bethoud, R., Lakey, J., Nazroo, J., Smith, P., Virdee, S. and Beishon, S. (1997) *Ethnic minorities in Britain: Diversity and disadvantage*, London: Policy Studies Institute.

Myhill, A. and Allen, J. (2002) *Rape and sexual assault of women: The extent and nature of the problem: Findings from the British Crime Survey* (Home Office Research Study 237), London: Home Office.

NASW (National Association of Social Workers) (1999) *Code of ethics* (www.socialworkers.org/pubs/code/default.asp).

National Statistics (2005) *Religion: Muslim families most likely to have children* (www.statistics.gov.uk/CCI/nugget.asp?ID=1168&Pos=1&ColRank=1 &Rank=326).

NCSR (National Centre for Social Research) (2007) *2006 British Social Attitudes Survey* (www.natcen.ac.uk/natcen/pages/news_and_media_docs/ BSA_%20press_release_jan07.pdf).

NHS and Community Care Act 1990, London: HMSO (www.opsi.gov.uk/ ACTS/acts1990/Ukpga_19900019_en_1.htm).

Northern Ireland Office (1995) *Children (NI) Order 1995. Regulations and guidance: Family placements and private fostering: Volume 3*, Belfast: The Stationery Office (www.dhsspsni.gov.uk/co-volume3-family-placements-private-fostering.pdf).

O'Beirne, M. (2004) *Religion in England and Wales: Findings from the 2001 Home Office Citizenship Survey* (Home Office Research Study 274) (www. homeoffice.gov.uk/rds/pdfs04/hors274.pdf).

Patel, N., Nalk, N. and Humphries, B. (1998) *Visions of reality: Religion and ethnicity in social work*, London: CCETSW.

QAA (Quality Assurance Agency for Higher Education) (2008) *Quality Assurance Agency for Higher Education subject benchmark statements for social work* (QAA 236 02/08), Mansfield: QAA (www.qaa.ac.uk/ academicinfrastructure/benchmark/statements/socialwork08.pdf).

Racial and Religious Hatred Act 2006, London: HMSO (www.opsi.gov.uk/ acts/acts2006/20060001.htm).

Scott, S. and Jackson, S. (2006) 'Sexuality', in G. Payne (ed) *Social divisions* (2nd edn), Basingstoke: Palgrave Macmillan, pp 233-50.

Seden, J. (1995) 'Religious persuasion and the Children Act', *Adoption and Fostering*, **19**(2), 7-17.

Social Work Services Group, Scottish Office Staff (1995) *The Children (Scotland) Act 1995 regulations and guidance*, Edinburgh: The Stationery Office (www.scotland.gov.uk/Publications/2004/10/20066/44707).

Stanley, N., Lyons, C., Manthorpe, J., Rapaport, P., Carrahar, M., Grimshaw, C., Voss, S. and Spencer, L. (2007) *Mental Capacity Act 2005: Community care and primary care training set*, London: Department of Health (www. dh.gov.uk/prod_consum_dh/idcplg?IdcService=GET_FILE&dID=139 831&Rendition=Web).

Stevens, M. (2007) 'Sexualizing', in S. Matthewman, C. Lane West-Newman and B. Curtis (eds) *Being sociological*, Basingstoke: Palgrave Macmillan, pp 213-31.

UNICEF (1995) *The Convention on the Rights of the Child (information kit)*, London: UNICEF.

Worcestershire County Council (2006) *A guide to assessments: What happens next?*, Worcester: Worcestershire County Council, Adult Services (www. worcestershire.gov.uk/home/wcc-social-aop-sp-guidetoassessments. pdf).

3

Frameworks and models to develop cultural competence in relation to religion and belief

> Probes about religious matters should become a routine part of assessment even for the client who does not spontaneously raise these issues. (Pargament, 1997: 374)

Introduction

The two preceding chapters have considered some of the reasons why it is important that social workers and others in the caring sector develop their understanding and awareness of issues of religion and belief. This chapter outlines a range of models that aim to help both social care and health professionals develop cultural competence in their work. We then present a framework of key principles, which we suggest can and should be applied at all stages of practice, and especially during assessments, to ensure that practitioners both identify when religion and belief are significant in their work and in the lives of those they are serving and take sufficient account of them where appropriate and necessary. Our model for ensuring cultural competence will be further explained and, where possible, applied to contemporary but anonymised case examples in the following chapters. The model seeks to assist workers to become more aware of their own values relating to religion and belief and to provide a useful base from which to build and develop a sound cultural framework for practice.

Canda (1989), in the US, emphasised that, regardless of any conflicts they may feel, social workers need to respond to a variety of religious and spiritual needs and to understand a variety of religious and spiritual issues. Otherwise, the service they provide is unlikely to be adequate to meet the needs of those for whom religion and spirituality have significance. Twenty years later, in Britain and elsewhere, there appears to be an increased willingness on the part of some professionals to recognise the need both to grapple with such issues and to explore ways in which this can be done more systematically and with greater effect (Furness, 2003; Furman et al, 2004; Gilligan and Furness, 2006; Crisp, 2008; Gray, 2008; Gilligan, 2009; Stirling et al, 2009). This book seeks to encourage this trend.

The need for a framework

Gerrish et al (1996) carried out research in England to find out the views of nursing students at three different educational institutions about their preparation for practice, particularly in respect of working with people from diverse backgrounds. In that study, students generally felt ill equipped to meet the needs of the local communities in which they worked. An enquiry carried out by Furness (2005) found that social work students held anxieties about a range of issues prior to assessed placements that included appearance/appropriate dress, arrangements for prayer and the attitude of service users towards them. Gilligan's (2005) study with practice educators (that is, those who assess social work students' practice competence on placement) indicated that little attention was given in supervision sessions to the exploration of religious views, even when the practice educator or student was known to be affiliated to a religion. He speculates that they might lack confidence in their skills to deal with such issues to the extent that they avoid them altogether, but emphasises that student social workers are unlikely to develop qualifying competence if they and their mentors ignore matters that shape their understandings of and responses to events and people. Inset 1, perhaps, illustrates the impact of such reluctance to address questions of religion more vividly.

Inset 1: Comments from social work manager

Every assessment comes through me or my job share partner. She was in the meeting as well and I was looking at her, going "We're not covering this". So we had a bit of a chat afterwards and she said, "You know, unless a family is really strict Muslim and it's obvious, the social workers aren't even asking, they're not even looking at it as a topic. I don't recall any other assessment work over the last month where we've even looked at religious support or anything about beliefs."

We looked at the assessments to double check and there was nothing, absolutely nothing. So I had a chat with the social workers and I said, "We're going to have to look at this because, if we're using the assessment framework

▶

and we're saying we're covering all these domains, we're actually fibbing because we really aren't and we're not asking the questions". And then it got us thinking about a couple of cases of families where there's some odd behaviours and we were thinking about it and we said, "This could be faith- or belief-led because that would explain an awful lot but we've not even explored it". My social workers said, "Can we ask that?". I think that they thought that it was too intrusive to ask somebody about religion, but I said, "We talk about relationships, mum and dad, what kind of relationship do they have, do they have time together, do they have time as a couple? So if we're talking about really personal things, I think we're going to be okay if we ask them about religion." I said, "It's going to open doors for families to talk about things and I think it's going to open doors for support".

One aspect of cultural competence is an appreciation and understanding by practitioners of the part that religion and spirituality plays in people's lives. Those affected by ill health and life crises may turn to their faith and belief systems as ways to support and comfort them in times of need, especially when conventional health treatment has failed to cure or aid recovery. Dissatisfaction with traditional health care responses and a search for more meaningful engagement that embraces individual belief and hope have been neglected areas of study. Both health and social care practitioners are beginning to realise that tapping into their religious or spiritual beliefs can contribute to helping individuals deal with serious health and social issues over the life course (MacKinlay, 2001; Purnell and Paulanka, 2003; Sue, 2006; Cox et al, 2007).

Cultural, transcultural, intercultural and cross–cultural competence are terms that are increasingly commonplace. They are often used interchangeably, but without precise definition, to denote inclusive approaches in response to diversity and difference in society (Furness, 2005). Powell (2001: 93), for example, reminds us that "social work, which operates primarily in the cultural rather than the economic domain of society, has much to contribute in the promotion of remedies to injustice based upon cultural respect and social recognition". It is important that social workers recognise these strengths and are able to share and develop the knowledge and expertise they gather from their professional education and practice experience if service users are to be understood and actively involved in their assessments and programmes of care.

Models for cultural competence

There is a welcome and growing body of literature written predominantly for health professionals and more recently for social workers about the importance of developing and incorporating cultural and spiritual sensitivity and awareness in their work with others (Leininger, 1978; Loewenberg, 1988; Campinha-Bacote,1994; Fernando, 1995; Canda and Furman, 1999; Henley and Schott, 1999; Hodge, 2001, 2005; Scales et al, 2002; Purnell and Paulanka, 2003; Sue, 2006; Gray et al, 2008; Laird, 2008; Stirling et al, 2009).

There are, also, a number of useful models that promote cultural competence, either directly or indirectly, and can complement the Furness/ Gilligan Framework, which will be described later in this chapter. These are predominantly of two types: *reflective models* that try to help the practitioner to develop professional competence and *assessment models* that try to aid in the collection of information. A selection of these models is outlined below.

Reflective models for professional development

Unconscious incompetence – conscious competence (Howell, 1982)

Howell developed a four-stage model for learning and motivation that can usefully be applied to developing cultural competence, especially in relation to practitioners' needs to reflect on their readiness to respond appropriately and effectively in new situations. Before practitioners acquire the knowledge and skills necessary to carry out a specific task they start from a premise of being 'unconsciously incompetent'. If they choose to learn how to carry out the task then they can move to a position of 'conscious incompetence'. By being persistent, having the opportunity to practise and receiving direction, encouragement and feedback they can become 'consciously competent'. This model is useful in helping social work students to appreciate their position as learners, particularly while on practice placements. Howell identifies the last stage to be 'unconscious competence'. However, there are real dangers of reverting back to 'unconscious incompetence' if the learner is not always actively engaged with the process. This can be clearly illustrated by the example of drivers who become overconfident and develop 'bad' motoring habits as driving becomes 'automatic'.

ASKED (awareness, skill, knowledge, encounter, desire) model (Campinha-Bacote, 1999)

Campinha-Bacote (1994, 1999) has developed the ASKED model, which is a process whereby individuals become aware and sensitive to their own values and beliefs and to the lifestyles of others (*awareness*). This exploration of values, prejudices and biases in a conscious, deliberate and reflective manner can help the practitioner to become aware of cultural differences. It is then important that the practitioner develops the *skills* and *knowledge* through encounters and active engagement in order to develop cultural competence. Assessments need to be conducted in an open, respectful and accepting way. The worker needs to be informed about other cultures and worldviews by actively seeking out opportunities to meet others (*encounters*). They also need to show a genuine desire and interest in finding out more about others, and to be open to modifying their own attitudes and beliefs in order to practise more effectively and inclusively (*desire*). This is a cyclical process that builds and develops on capacity for cultural competence.

The transactional model of cultural identity (Green, 1999)

Green (1999) seeks to move beyond categorical models of identity in which individuals are expected to possess a particular set of traits because they belong to a particular cultural or ethnic group. Green's model emphasises that diversity and the complexities of human identity lie in the dynamic interaction between people rather than within one person who is too often conceptualised as 'other'. The transactional model provides a method for examining how practitioners interact with service users. It attempts to avoid simply labelling the beliefs of those belonging to minority faiths and belief systems as 'different' from the presumed normality of the beliefs of (or an absence of belief among) dominant or majority groups, and requires practitioners to reflect on how their own backgrounds influence the way they interact with others.

Awareness and sensitivity to difference (Papadopoulos, Tilki and Taylor, 2006)

Papadopoulos et al (Papadopoulos, 2006) identify four stages of a process to help nursing students become more aware and sensitive to difference and improve their practice and interactions with others. This model can help practitioners to explore their own belief systems and those of others in order to understand the impact of religion on the lives of service users. The different stages are:

(1)   promoting cultural awareness;
(2)   gaining cultural knowledge;
(3)   becoming culturally sensitive;
(4)   demonstrating cultural competence.

Promoting cultural awareness. The first stage entails becoming more consciously open and aware and appreciative of how identity is formed and shaped by family life, social environment and interactions with others. Part of the process of socialisation entails learning to recognise similarities and differences, and categorising ourselves and others within social groups based on difference. The challenge is how to construct identity out of equal rather than dominant power relations (Singh, 1992). Stereotyping can lead to negative labels and outcomes for certain groups and this process needs to be recognised and avoided. Attention also needs to be given to unconscious and internalised values and beliefs that can be applied and used to judge others' behaviours and actions (Papadopoulos, 2006). This can be a difficult and challenging process, and practitioners have to work hard at listening to and responding to feedback, developing skills of reflection and actively engaging in working with others to improve their cultural understanding.

Gaining cultural knowledge. It is necessary for the individual to be interested and motivated to engage and find out about others' lifestyles, customs and traditions. There also needs to be an understanding of how certain types of knowledge gain respect, credence and acceptability. Dominant positions such as patriarchy, ethnocentrism, euro-centrism and heterosexuality have become the norm and have contributed to protecting the interests of dominant groups. This process excludes others not belonging to those groups from accessing and receiving the same societal benefits (Dominelli, 2002; Lyons et al, 2006; Llewellyn et al, 2008; Macionis and Plummer, 2008).

For social workers, it is important to question why different groups and individuals experience disparate life opportunities. Contacts with others can help practitioners to understand and gain some insight into their cultural traditions and ways of life. Certain localities may not offer significant opportunities for direct contact with people of different ethnicities but secondary sources such as television, film, the Internet and literature can also help to inform about others' experiences and allow for reflection and discussion.

Becoming culturally sensitive. Social work originated from charitable actions towards those with impoverished and destitute lives by well-meaning benefactors (Payne, 2005; Reamer, 2006). Early on in their history, social workers established themselves as the 'experts', as they had the training and knowledge to direct and guide clients to take the 'supposedly' best course of action (Hugman, 1991). This patriarchal and benevolent approach was criticised as creating a sense of dependency and as failing to challenge oppression and discrimination, despite claims that these are key aims of social work (Clark, 2000; Healy, 2005). Such social work is seen, at best, as colluding with the state and, at worst, as contributing to and perpetuating social inequalities (Dominelli, 2002; Mullaly, 2002). Meanwhile, both contemporary nursing and social work aim to demonstrate respect for all communities and groups, and to be working in equal partnerships with people rather than imposing values on them. This is not to say that any set of values and views should be accepted without question, especially where they promote behaviours and actions that are oppressive and damaging to self or others. Effective communication skills are vital not only to build up relationships but also to facilitate processes in which workers can really appreciate difference. They need to challenge themselves, to be open to challenge from others and to recognise the potential for possible misinterpretation. It might be helpful to break down communication into two components. The first requires an understanding of cultural values and rules, behavioural patterns and verbal and non-verbal cues to allow effective engagement and interaction with others. The second requires self-acknowledgement of anxieties and fears that may interfere with relations with others (Gerrish et al, 1996).

Demonstrating cultural competence. This stage requires an active engagement and application of gained awareness, knowledge and sensitivity (Papadopoulos, 2006: 18). Effective supervision by experienced colleagues, reflection on practice, ongoing training and professional development and feedback from service users and colleagues can all contribute to help the practitioner to develop culturally appropriate assessment skills, as well as the confidence to enable them to question and challenge areas of practice that they think are discriminatory or oppressive.

Models to aid cultural assessment

The models discussed below provide useful frameworks to help practitioners gain a greater understanding of the beliefs and practices of individuals and groups. However, it is essential that practitioners, following the person-centred and strengths-based approach required by the Furness/Gilligan Framework outlined below, ask appropriate open-ended questions in order to allow people to express themselves in the ways that they choose, that are familiar to them and that respect their expertise. It is also important to recognise that beliefs and practices will vary even among those adhering to the same religious persuasion. A variety of daily living activities may be profoundly influenced by a person's religious and spiritual beliefs and may, therefore, require exploration with them: modesty and privacy; clothing, jewellery and make-up; washing and hygiene; hair care; prayer; holy days and festivals; physical examination; birth; contraception; abortion; attitudes to death, dying and mourning; medication; healing practices; transfusions, organ donation and transplants (see 'Paula' in Chapter Four); last offices; post-mortem and funeral services (Husband and Torry, 2004). Religious worship and observance may be significant to the person, and give meaning to events and life experiences. Discussion of them may inform the assessment in significant ways (see 'Margaret' in Chapter Eight).

Bloch (cited by Isaacs and Benjamin, 1991) identified several areas that are relevant when carrying out a cultural assessment in order to better understand what shapes service users' ideas about their social situation and needs. Hogan-Garcia (2003) has also produced a table containing similar elements:

- language and communication processes;
- ethnic identity;
- views about the role that ethnicity plays;
- influence of religion/spirituality on the belief system, actions and behaviour;
- views and concerns about discrimination and institutional racism;
- importance and impact associated with physical characteristics;
- migration experience, if applicable;
- use of informal network and supportive institutions in the ethnic/cultural community;
- personal value systems;
- cultural health beliefs and practices;
- habits, customs, beliefs;
- current socioeconomic status;
- educational level and employment experiences;
- self-concept and self-esteem.

Purnell's model for cultural competence (Purnell and Paulanka, 2003)

The purpose of Purnell's model is to provide a framework for all health care providers in different disciplines and settings. Although the model was developed in America, it can be adapted for use in other countries by any care professional. It organises culture into different macro and micro elements that affect all people. Global society, community and the family are named as macro influences, and micro influences affecting the person are broken down into 12 domains as depicted below:

- heritage including country of origin, current residence and reasons for migration, economics, politics, educational attainment and employment choices;
- communication (verbal and non-verbal language skills);
- family roles and organisation (head of household and gender roles, role of elders and extended family members, acceptable alternative lifestyles such as single parenting, childless marriages, divorce, sexual orientation);
- work-related issues – for example, punctuality associated with culturally based attitudes, learning styles, autonomy and assertiveness;
- biocultural ecology including variations in skin colour and physical differences, genetic and hereditary diseases;
- high-risk behaviours including the use of tobacco, alcohol and recreational drugs, and high-risk sexual practices;
- nutrition including food choices, rituals and taboos, and how food and food substances are used during illness and for health promotion and wellness;
- pregnancy and childbearing practices including fertility practices, methods for birth control, views towards pregnancy and prescriptive, restrictive and taboo practices related to birthing and pregnancy;
- death rituals or culturally different ways of expressing grief and loss;
- spirituality including religious practices and the use of prayer, behaviours that give meaning to life and individual sources of strength;
- health care practice including traditional, magicoreligious and biomedical beliefs; individual responsibility for health; self-medicating practices; and beliefs about mental illness;
- health care practitioner concepts including the status, use and perceptions of traditional, magicoreligious and health care providers (Purnell and Paulanka, 2003).

Hodge: spiritual histories, life maps, ecomaps and ecograms (Hodge, 2001, 2005)

Also starting from an explicitly strengths-based perspective, Hodge (2001: 204) notes the need to capture the "subjective, often intangible nature of human existence" and offers both an 'initial narrative framework' and an 'interpretive anthropological framework' for assessing and understanding the personal subjective reality of spirituality in people's lives. He suggests that an individual's relationship with 'the ultimate' facilitates coping, promotes a sense of purpose, instils a sense of self-worth and provides hope for the future, while rituals serve to ease anxiety, promote a sense of security and establish a sense of being loved. In later work, Hodge (2005) advocates the use of spiritual histories and spiritual life maps to assess a person's spiritual journey and relationship with God (or transcendence) and the use of spiritual ecomaps and spiritual ecograms to focus on individuals' current spiritual relationships. Such techniques involve diagrams similar to those depicting family life, but have a spiritual overlay, which is used to help make people more aware of their spiritual worlds.

Furness/Gilligan Framework for assessing the significance of religion and belief

Despite policy rhetoric, there has, to date, been no particular model that ensures that issues arising from religion and belief are adequately addressed in social work and social care assessments or in interventions arising from them. We, therefore, offer a framework that is designed to be applied at all stages of practice (assessment, planning, intervention and evaluation) in the hope that it will fill this gap and be used as a matter of routine. It has been piloted with our social work students and others, and refined through feedback and application.

Underpinning principles

We start from nine interconnected key principles:

(1) Assessments need to be person-centred.
(2) Assessments need to be strengths-based.
(3) Practitioners need to be self-aware and reflexive about their own religious and spiritual beliefs, and their responses to the religious and spiritual beliefs of others.
(4) Practitioners need to adopt an approach to their practice that recognises the inevitable limits of their own knowledge and understanding of unique situations, and that is underpinned by openness and a willingness to review and revise their working hypotheses.
(5) Practitioners need to recognise service users' expertise about their own needs and beliefs, and to listen to what they say about these.
(6) Practitioners need to develop relationships with service users characterised by trust, respect and a willingness to facilitate.
(7) Practitioners need to actively seek out relevant information and advice regarding the religious and spiritual beliefs of those using their services.
(8) Service users need opportunities to discuss their religious and spiritual beliefs, and the strengths, difficulties and needs that arise from them.
(9) Practitioners need to be creative in their responses to these strengths, difficulties and needs.

Integration with existing assessment frameworks

In most settings it is, perhaps, unrealistic to expect practitioners to conduct a separate assessment of issues arising from religion and belief. Any *additional* assessments are also likely to be unwelcome to service users, many of whom tell researchers that they undergo too many already (see, for example, Dartington Social Research Unit, 2004), while it is desirable for many reasons to avoid assessments being duplicated or lacking coherence across services (see, for example, DH, 2001: 24). We have, therefore, endeavoured to produce a framework that can be integrated into the most frequently used existing frameworks for assessment – most notably, the Single Assessment Process (DH, 2002), the Framework for Assessment of Children in Need and their Families (DH, 2000) and the Common Assessment Framework (CAF) (DfES, 2006a) – and that is easily transferable to many others. In most of its aspects our framework builds on and extends elements already present in the existing frameworks, legislation and guidance (see Chapter Two), and seeks to make them both more relevant and more comprehensive, as regards religion and belief.

DH (2001: 23) promotes person-centred care in relation to services for older people and requires practitioners to "recognise individual differences and specific needs including cultural and religious differences" (see Chapter Two). In relation to assessments, it emphasises "the importance of people being fully involved" (p 20); the need to properly address the specific needs of people from diverse cultural groups (p 24); the need to assess older people's needs "in the round" (p 30); and the desirability of using proven assessment scales and tools (p 31). In relation to education and training, it recognises the "need to ensure that undergraduate and pre-registration programmes – across all professions – properly prepare staff for working with older people and with cultural and religious differences" (p 141).

With regard to older people from black and minority ethnic communities, it comments that:

> 2.31 Good assessment also requires that the needs and circumstances of older people ... are assessed in ways that are not culturally biased and by staff who are able to make proper sense of how race, culture, religion and needs may impact on each other. (p 31)

In relation to health promotion, it notes that:

> ... it would not be appropriate to advise a strict Muslim woman to take up a certain form of exercise which would mean that she would have to wear scant clothes for exercise or be in the same room as men. (p 108)

In the context of assessments of black children, Dutt and Phillips (2000: 48) place particular emphasis on the importance of assessing 'group identification', 'individual and personal identity', 'the development of a racial identity', 'ethnicity', 'cultural, religious and linguistic identity', 'culture', 'the acquisition of cultural identity' and 'religion' within the domain of children's developmental needs. They also place ethnicity, culture and religion at the centre of their model of identity (Dutt and Phillips, 2000: 45) along with issues such as language, class, gender, sexual identity and whether the individual is disabled or non-disabled.

They note that:

> 2.58 Whilst racial identity forms one important aspect of identity, individuals from the same racial group may have differences in terms of their cultural background, *religious observance* and linguistic identity. (Dutt and Phillips, 2000: 48, emphasis added)

They also advise that the religious and spiritual needs of black children and their families "require professionals to discuss the family's belief systems, religion, rites and traditions and record them routinely" (Dutt and Phillips, 2000: 51).

Dutt and Phillips (2000: 49) observe that:

> 2.69 Religion or spirituality is an issue for all families whether white or black. A family who do not practise a religion, or who are agnostic or atheists, may still have particular views about the spiritual upbringing and welfare of their children. For families where religion plays an important role in their lives, the significance of their religion will also be a vital part of their cultural traditions and beliefs.

In relation to assessments of disabled children, Marchant and Jones (2000) emphasise that:

> 3.124 Relationships with other families are an important part of life. Disabled children and their families may face barriers preventing them from taking part in social events or cultural or *religious celebrations* or holidays ... Supporting the social integration of disabled children often facilitates the integration of their parents, who gain opportunities to meet local parents at the school gate, *local members of their religious community*, workers in local services and so on. (Marchant and Jones, 2000: 101, emphasis added)

DfES (2006a: 28), meanwhile, suggests that practitioners undertaking a Common Assessment Framework (CAF) assessment will need, in assessing "Identity, including self-esteem, self-image and social presentation", to include consideration of "race, religion, age, gender, sexuality and disability".

In relation to section 47 enquiries and core assessments, DfES (2006b: 120) notes:

> 5.66 In accordance with the *Achieving Best Evidence* guidance (2002), all such joint interviews with children should be conducted by those with specialist training and experience in interviewing children ... Additional specialist help may be required if ... the interviewers do not have adequate knowledge and understanding of the child's racial, religious or cultural background.

It also emphasises that, in management reviews, 'analysis of involvement' should address the question, "Was practice sensitive to the racial, cultural, linguistic and religious identity of the child and family?" (DfES, 2006b: 176).

The Furness/Gilligan Framework

We suggest that, in undertaking assessments, interventions and evaluations, practitioners need to reflect explicitly on the following eight questions:

(1) Are you sufficiently self-aware and reflexive about your own religious and spiritual beliefs or the absence of them and your responses to others?

(2) Are you giving the individuals/groups involved sufficient opportunities to discuss their religious and spiritual beliefs and the strengths, difficulties and needs that arise from them?

(3) Are you listening to what they say about their beliefs and the strengths and needs that arise from them?

(4) Do you recognise individuals' expertise about their own beliefs and the strengths and needs that arise from them?

(5) Are you approaching this piece of practice with sufficient openness and willingness to review and revise your plans and assumptions?

(6) Are you building a relationship that is characterised by trust, respect and a willingness to facilitate?

(7) Are you being creative in your responses to individuals' beliefs and the strengths and needs that arise from them?

(8)   Have you sought out relevant information and advice regarding any religious and spiritual beliefs and practices that were previously unfamiliar to you?

As one social work manager told the authors:

> It is not about, "Is it religion? Is it not religion?" It's about what's going on for people. I'll say to my social workers, "Don't go in thinking it's going to be this and it's going to be that; just go in thinking 'I'm coming in to explore what's going on for you, what's happening in your life? And do you want us to help with that?' That's what we're employed to do. That's what our skills are."

A starting point?

Pargament (1997) identifies possible general questions to help counsellors (and others) to explore the relevance of religion to the situation by asking:

- Is the person religious or spiritual?
- Which religion or denomination does the person belong to?
- How often does he/she attend religious services or pray?
- Does the person believe in God?

He suggests that it is then important to move beyond simple descriptions of religion and to ask more pointed questions such as:

- In what ways is the person religious?
- What purpose does religion bring to the person's life?
- How is religion involved in the way he/she is coping with the problem?

Pargament (1997) warns that these types of questions can serve only to alert the worker to further exploration of religious matters and it is important to "look beyond *what* is said to *how* it is said" (Pargament, 1997: 377, emphasis in original).

Key questions

Answer the questions below in relation to your practice with a specific service user, family or group:

(1) Were you sufficiently self-aware and reflexive about your own religious and spiritual beliefs or the absence of them and your responses to those of this individual/group? (Give examples of how you reflected on these issues and the impact of this on your practice.)

(2) Did you give this individual/group sufficient opportunities to discuss their religious and spiritual beliefs and the strengths, difficulties and needs that arose from them? (Give examples of how you did this.)

(3) Did you listen to what they said about their beliefs and the strengths and needs that arose from them? (How?)

(4) Did you recognise their expertise about their own beliefs and the strengths and needs that arose from them? (How?)

(5) Did you approach this piece of practice with sufficient openness and willingness to review and revise your plans and assumptions? (Give examples of how you did this.)

(6) Did you build a relationship that was characterised by trust, respect and a willingness to facilitate? (How?)

(7) Were you creative in your responses to their beliefs and the strengths and needs that arose from them? (Give examples of how you did this.)

(8) Did you seek out relevant information and advice regarding any religious and spiritual beliefs and practices that were previously unfamiliar to you? (How?)

References

Campinha-Bacote, J. (1994) *The process of cultural competence in health care: A culturally competent model of care*, Wyoming, OH: Perfect Printing Press.

Campinha-Bacote, J. (1999) 'A model and instrument for addressing cultural competence in health care', *Journal of Nurse Education*, **38**(5), 203-7.

Canda, E.R. (1989) 'Religious content in social work education: a comparative approach', *Journal of Social Work Education*, **25**(1), 36-45.

Canda, E.R. and Furman, L.D. (1999) *Spiritual diversity in social work practice: The heart of helping*, New York: Free Press.

Clark, C.L. (2000) *Social work ethics politics, principles and practice*, Basingstoke: Palgrave.

Cox, J., Campbell, A.V. and Fulford, B. (eds) (2007) *Medicine of the person: Faith, science and values in health care provision*, London and Philadelphia, PA: Jessica Kingsley.

Crisp, B.R. (2008) 'Social work and spirituality in a secular society', *Journal of Social Work*, **8**(4), 363–75.

Dartington Social Research Unit (2004) *Refocusing children's services towards prevention: Lessons from the literature* (Research Report no 510), Nottingham: Department for Education and Skills (www.dcsf.gov.uk/research/data/uploadfiles/RR510.pdf).

DfES (Department for Education and Skills) (2006a) *The Common Assessment Framework for children and young people: Practitioners' guide* (www.everychildmatters.gov.uk/caf; or search www.teachernet.gov.uk/publications using the ref: 0337-2006BKT-EN).

DfES (2006b) *Working together to safeguard children. A guide to inter-agency working to safeguard and promote the welfare of children*, London: The Stationery Office (www.everychildmatters.gov.uk/_files/CCE39E361D6AD840F7EAC9DA47A3D2C8.pdf).

DH (Department of Health) (2000) *Assessing children in need and their families: Practice guidance*, London: HMSO (www.dh.gov.uk/en/Publicationsandstatistics/Publications/PublicationsPolicyAndGuidance/DH_4006576).

DH (2001) *National service framework for older people*, London: The Stationery Office (http://www.dh.gov.uk/en/Publicationsandstatistics/Publications/PublicationsPolicyAndGuidance/DH_4003066).

DH (2002) *The single assessment process: Guidance for local implementation* (www.dh.gov.uk/en/Publicationsandstatistics/Publications/PublicationsPolicyAndGuidance/DH_4008389).

Dominelli, L. (2002) *Anti-oppressive social work theory and practice*, Basingstoke: Palgrave Macmillan.

Dutt, R. and Phillips, M. (2000) 'Assessing black children in need and their families', in Department of Health, *Assessing children in need and their families: Practice guidance*, London: The Stationery Office, pp 37–72.

Fernando, S. (ed) (1995) *Mental health in a multi-ethnic society: A multi-disciplinary handbook*, London and New York: Routledge.

Furman, L.D., Benson, P.W., Grimwood, C. and Canda, E.R. (2004) 'Religion and spirituality in social work education and direct practice at the Millennium: a survey of UK social workers', *British Journal of Social Work*, **34**(6), 767–92.

Furness, S. (2003) 'Religion, belief and culturally competent practice', *Journal of Practice Teaching in Health and Social Care*, **15**(1), 61–74.

Furness, S. (2005) 'Shifting sands: developing cultural competence', *Practice*, **17**(4), 247-56.

Gerrish, K., Husband, C. and Mackenzie, J. (1996) *Nursing for a multi-ethnic society*, Buckingham and Philadelphia, PA: Open University Press.

Gilligan, P. (2005) '"It isn't discussed." Religion, belief and practice teaching: missing components of cultural competence in social work education', *Journal of Practice Teaching in Health and Social Care*, **5**(1), 75-95.

Gilligan, P. (2009) 'Considering religion and beliefs in child protection and safeguarding work: is any consensus emerging?', *Child Abuse Review*, early view online, doi: 10.1002/car.1059.

Gilligan, P. and Furness, S. (2006) 'The role of religion and spirituality in social work practice: views and experiences of social workers and students', *British Journal of Social Work*, **36**(4), 617-37.

Gray, M. (2008) 'Viewing spirituality in social work through the lens of contemporary social theory', *British Journal of Social Work*, **38**(1), 175-96.

Gray, M., Coates, J. and Yellow Bird, M. (eds) (2008) *Indigenous social work around the world: Towards culturally relevant education and practice*, Aldershot: Ashgate.

Green, J.A. (1999) *Cultural awareness in the human services: A multi-ethnic approach*, Needham Heights, MA: Allyn and Bacon.

Healy, K. (2005) *Social work theories in context: Creating frameworks for practice*, Basingstoke: Palgrave Macmillan.

Henley, A. and Schott, J. (1999) *Culture, religion and patient care in a multi-ethnic society*, London: Age Concern England.

Hodge, D.R. (2001) 'Spiritual assessment: a review of major qualitative methods and a new framework for assessing spirituality', *Social Work*, **46**(3), 203-14.

Hodge, D.R. (2005) 'Developing a spiritual assessment toolbox: a discussion of the strengths and limitations of five different assessment methods', *Health and Social Work*, **30**(4), 314-23.

Hogan-Garcia, M. (2003) *The four skills of cultural diversity competence* (2nd edn), London: Brooks Cole.

Howell, W.S. (1982) *The empathic communicator*, Minnesota, MN: Wadsworth Publishing Company.

Hugman, R. (1991) *Power in caring professions*, Basingstoke: Macmillan.

Husband, C. and Torry, B. (eds) (2004) *Transcultural Health Care Practice: An educational resource for nurses and health care practitioners*, London: RCN (www.rcn.org.uk/development/learning/transcultural_health/transcultural).

Isaacs, M.R. and Benjamin, M.P. (1991) *Towards a culturally competent system of care: Volume II*, Washington, DC: CASSP Technical Assistance Center, Georgetown University Child Development Center.

Laird, S.E. (2008) *Anti-oppressive social work: A guide for developing cultural competence*, London: Sage Publications.

Leininger, M. (1978) *Transcultural nursing: Concepts, theories and practice*, New York: Wiley.

Llewellyn, A., Agu, L. and Mercer, D. (2008) *Sociology for social workers*, Cambridge: Polity Press.

Loewenberg, F.M. (1988) *Religion and social work practice in contemporary American society*, New York: Columbia University Press.

Lyons, K., Manion, K. and Carlsen, M. (2006) *International perspectives on social work: Global conditions and local practice*, Basingstoke: Palgrave Macmillan.

Macionis, J.J. and Plummer, K. (2008) *Sociology: A global introduction* (4th edn), Harlow: Pearson Education.

MacKinlay, E. (2001) *The spiritual dimension of ageing*, London and Philadelphia, PA: Jessica Kingsley.

Marchant, R. and Jones, M. (2000) 'Assessing the needs of disabled children and their families', in Department of Health *Assessing children in need and their families: Practice guidance*, London: The Stationery Office, pp 73-112.

Mullaly, B. (2002) *Challenging oppression: A critical social work approach*, Toronto: Oxford University Press.

Papadopoulos, I. (ed) (2006) *Transcultural health and social care: A development of culturally competent practitioners*, Edinburgh: Churchill Livingstone.

Pargament, K.I. (1997) *The psychology of religion and coping: Theory, research, practice*, New York and London: The Guilford Press.

Payne, M. (2005) *The origins of social work: Continuity and change*, Basingstoke: Palgrave Macmillan.

Powell, F. (2001) *The politics of social work*, London: Sage Publications.

Purnell, L.D. and Paulanka, B.J. (2003) *Transcultural health care: A culturally competent approach* (2nd edn), Philadelphia: F.A. Davis.

Reamer, F.G. (2006) *Social work values and ethics* (3rd edn), New York: Columbia University Press.

Scales, T.L., Wolfer, T.A., Sherwood, D.A., Garland, D.R., Hugen, B. and Pittman, S.W. (eds) (2002) *Spirituality and religion in social work practice: Decision cases with teaching notes*, Washington, DC: Council on Social Work Education.

Singh, G. (1992) *Race and social work from 'black pathology' to 'black perspectives'*, Bradford: Race Relations Research Unit.

Stirling, B., Furman, L.D., Benson, P.W., Canda, E.R. and Grimwood, C. (2009) 'A comparative survey of Aotearoa New Zealand and UK social workers on the role of religion and spirituality in practice', *British Journal of Social Work*, advance access published 13 February, doi:10.1093/bjsw/bcp008.

Sue, D.W. (2006) *Multicultural social work practice*, Hoboken, NJ: John Wiley & Sons.

Religion, belief and social work with children and families

Parenting and family support practitioners would also be unwise to assume that religion is unimportant to a parent, child or young person just because they are not active within a faith community; or that it does not exert a significant influence on their values and overall approach to family life. The research showed that religion could be as important to those who just 'believed' as it was to those who both 'believed and belong'. (Horwath et al, 2008a: 3)

Introduction

Horwath et al (2008a, 2008b) report on the potential importance of faith to families holding a range of religious beliefs. They suggest that neither policy makers nor practitioners can afford to be complacent about the influence (positive and negative) of religion on family life. They recommend that more attention should be given to the influence of religious beliefs and practices on parenting, in both national and local guidance for practitioners, and conclude that:

> ... it is crucial that if people state they have a religious belief, when filling in the inevitable forms required to access services, professionals should, at the very least, enquire 'What does your faith mean to you?', 'How does it influence your life?' and, in the case of family members, 'How do your beliefs influence your family life?' (Horwath et al, 2008b: 54)

However, Crompton (1998: xv) found that, although "Children are legally entitled to spiritual and religious nurture, just as they are entitled to physical and cognitive care", attitudes towards religion among child and family social workers varied "from hostility to devotion, indifference to enthusiasm, rigidity to universalism". She argued then, as we would argue now, that the question of whether children have a chance to use the positive opportunities

their religion or a chance to explore and resolve the negative
~~of~~ the misuse of religion by others should not be dependent on the
~~values~~ of their social workers, but on their needs as assessed by competent
~~professionals~~ or perhaps through processes such as family group conferencing
~~(~~Ashley et al, 2006; Ashley and Nixon, 2007). The latter process may in
~~it~~self help to avoid difficulties that could arise as a result of practitioners'
~~u~~nresolved prejudices or lack of knowledge and provide an opportunity for
children, young people and their parents to involve members of their faith
community in agreeing and implementing an appropriate action plan.

Crompton (1996: sec 4, p 32) reminds us that practitioners may dislike
the beliefs and observances of the children with whom they work, but
they have a responsibility to respect the religion and beliefs of every child.
Moreover, in relation to looked after children, she suggests that shared
religious beliefs and observances between children and carers enhance a sense
of connectedness and that "Active encouragement to fulfil daily religious
duties helps to nurture children's sense of identity with birth family and
community, and sense of approval by the present carers" (Crompton, 1996:
sec 4, p 32). Smith (2000: 46), similarly, concludes that, for Jewish children in
the looked after system, "Jewish families play a key role in the transmission
and nurturing of Jewish identity".

Case examples: children in need

'Miriam'

The case of 'Miriam' (see Inset 1) demonstrates the importance of
understanding the potential significance of religion and belief to the ongoing
resilience of people in the face of adversity. Her social worker, speaking
of Muslim families in general, said, "They all somehow raise their faith as
something that is a strength for them. No matter what level they're at, it
always comes out as we go on with the assessment and the work. Their
faith comes to the fore."

> **Inset 1: 'Miriam'**
>
> 'Miriam' is a mother bringing up four children. As an adolescent, she was
> abused by her father and spent time 'in care'. She was subsequently abused
> by her husband, but eventually managed to escape him. Her youngest child
> was conceived as the result of 'marital rape'. Her social worker describes
> Miriam's life as "horrendous", but reports that Miriam attributes her survival

to her religious faith. She sees her youngest child and their needs as "a test for me", allowing her to demonstrate that she has the capacity to continue giving "despite what I've been through". A significantly younger man asked her to marry him and she was, initially, worried about whether it would be "fair on him" to accept his proposal. However, she was able to relate back to the story of the Prophet Mohammed marrying a wife who was 15 years older than him. Her social worker, who like Miriam is a practising Muslim, suggested that "there is symbolism in it, and the strength she derives from that is absolutely amazing".

The social worker spoke of Miriam being "open about her faith and where she wants to go, what she thinks it's done for her, how she coped using her faith, how she kind of mourns the loss of her faith at this current time in her life" and said, "it is very important for her to be able to express her views about her faith. It is ... definitely something she leans on ... because things are so hard for her". She felt that it had been very important in her work with Miriam that they had something in common.

'Paula'

'Paula's' case (see Inset 2) emphasises the importance of seeking out relevant information and advice regarding religious and spiritual beliefs and practices that are unfamiliar, and of giving people sufficient opportunities to discuss difficulties that arise from them.

Inset 2: 'Paula'

'Paula' is an eight-year-old, white, British child. She has multiple impairments and learning disabilities. Her parents and extended family are Jehovah's Witnesses. It is reported that the mother's attachment to Paula is "more or less nil", because she views her as "not accepted by God". It is reported that the family also see Paula as "unclean", as "different" and as "an outsider".

Concerns about her mother's attitudes resulted in a section 47 child protection investigation, including a thorough assessment. It emerged that, when Paula was younger, during one of her frequent medical emergencies, the doctors gave her a blood transfusion that neither of her parents would have consented to, if they had been asked. (The doctors acted to save and prolong Paula's life, but her family began to see her as "tarnished because of this blood that she was given".) This information helped the professionals involved to gain a better understanding of the issues, particularly in relation to concerns that the description of Paula as "unclean" may have been indicative of sexual abuse. However, the investigation and assessment did not, in itself, change the mother's behaviour or response.

A social worker with a strong religious faith (not a Jehovah's Witness) was, however, allocated to work in the case. She began by obtaining information about Jehovah's Witnesses via the Internet and checking this information with the family. It took this social worker several contacts to explore these issues and to begin to understand why Paula's mother thinks of her daughter as "unclean". However, it was only by doing this that the social worker felt confident that she could begin to assist this parent to respond more appropriately and/or to assess whether she was capable of providing Paula with good enough emotional care.

'Mary'

The case of 'Mary' (see Inset 3) illustrates not only the importance of giving people sufficient opportunities to discuss their religious and spiritual beliefs and the strengths, difficulties and needs that arise from them, but also some of the many challenges and dilemmas involved in practitioners being reflexive about their responses to the religious and spiritual beliefs of others and the impact of these on parents' care of their children.

Inset 3: 'Mary'

'Mary' is three years old. She has a very complex syndrome, missing internal organs and severe developmental delay. She has already had corrective surgery and in the doctors' view needs much other surgery and medical interventions. Mary also needs very practical support and nursing care, on a daily basis. Nurses visit the home to give feeds. Her parents have a strong Christian faith and view her condition as "God's will". They tend to initially resist suggestions of further medical interventions, such as a gastrostomy to allow tube feeding.

The social work manager involved described how the social work role has needed to be one of mediating between the family and the doctors. She reports the family as saying, "we don't want that [more intervention] because it's God's will and we want a more nurturing side". Of the family, she said, "I think that they're torn between their faith and what the doctors recommend, but also as parents they are saying 'I don't want to put my child through all of that stuff'". She comments that "We're floundering a bit ... we're trying to coax both sides really, to meet half way ... But the medics just have a list of things that need to be sorted and the family don't want." As regards the immediate issue of the gastrostomy, she reported that, to resolve the dispute, it was essential for the social worker to both acknowledge to the parents that they are "a loving, caring family" and to present the question in terms that were relevant to them, that is, "Would God want your little girl suffering through lack of food and nutrition?".

Looked after children

As detailed in Chapter Two, legislation and guidance and, most especially, the Children Act 1989 are very clear regarding the responsibilities of local authorities, and social workers acting as their agents, to give "due consideration ... to the child's religious persuasion, racial origin, cultural and linguistic background" (DH, 1989a: section 22(5)(c)), particularly as regards children in the looked after system. However, practitioners are given little guidance regarding matters such as what being brought up in a particular religious persuasion actually means. Seden (1995) notes that Assessment and Action Records (DH, 1995) ask 10- to 14-year-olds the following questions:

- Do you belong to a particular religion?
- If so, do you have enough opportunities to attend religious services?
- Do you have enough opportunities to follow the customs of your religion (for example, festivals, prayers, clothing, diet)?
- Who will help you take further action if needed?

She emphasises that simply asking adolescents these questions is unlikely to yield a meaningful assessment and that social workers need to develop specific skills and confidence to assess such matters. The case of 'Saleem' (Inset 4) illustrates the complexities involved and the need for social workers to adopt a framework such as that detailed in Chapter Three, which ensures that they: are reflexive about their own religious beliefs; give young people sufficient opportunities to discuss their religious and spiritual beliefs, including the ambiguities, ambivalence and contradictions such discussions might raise; listen to what young people say about their individual religious needs and beliefs, and how these might change over time; and, as always, build a relationship that is characterised by trust, respect and a willingness to facilitate. Regarding her own 'confidence' in doing such a piece of work, Saleem's social worker commented:

> I come from the same ethnic background, so when I got into the situation it was so much easier for me to tackle a lot of the issues compared to my colleague, who is very experienced, but felt that she couldn't say some of the things that I can say, because she thought she might be branded as being racist.

She recognises that workers from a variety of backgrounds may need to undertake such work, but acknowledged that it was much easier for her to establish the rapport needed because of factors such as ethnicity, having a Muslim name, sharing relevant languages, their ways of speaking to each other when first introduced and how she conducted herself around Saleem. She noted that, when he asked certain questions about religion, she did not need to say, "Oh I've got to check this". She was able to say, "Well this is what my interpretation is, but we can check this together". Workers will not always have these advantages and will, in many cases, need to consult relevant colleagues and literature for information and advice regarding religious and spiritual beliefs and practices that are unfamiliar to them.

Inset 4: 'Saleem'

'Saleem' is a looked after child who has been 'in care' for eight years. He was placed in a foster home with South Asian carers who were Muslims and appeared to meet his religious and cultural needs. This placement broke down and Saleem began living in a children's home. He initially complained that he was not able to pray. However, the manager already had connections with the local mosque and was able to arrange for Saleem to pray there. During Ramadam, Saleem was asked to participate in a fasting contract because, in the past, he had said, "I'm not able to fast here because the staff won't let me", despite evidence that the staff had been very supportive. They have undertaken cultural training and have contact with imams at the mosque. The social worker comments of the other young people in the children's home, "During Ramadam ... everyone was really supportive, really, really supportive of him, and there was a young girl who wasn't Muslim, but she said, "Oh I'll fast with you, just to see what it's like, I can lose a bit of weight". So he did feel supported.

While living at the children's home, Saleem started hanging out with a lot of friends who were of similar ethnicity and a similar age, and became increasingly interested in his culture and his religion. He also made it increasingly clear in review meetings that he wanted his case allocated to a social worker of South Asian origin. Once this had happened, his new social worker began doing direct

▶

work with him, looking at issues around his identity. She quickly established that Saleem wishes to move back home, where he feels he belongs.

The social worker has explored cultural and religious expectations with Saleem and with his father, who she reports as having "some quite intense views on … his culture … how boys develop into young adults … what they should do … how they should act, how they should behave at a certain age". He attends mosque and "likes to appear to be religious". In the worker's view, Saleem's father is, however, ignoring the fact that Saleem has been in care and has not had the advantages of living in a situation where views about culture and religion are consistent. In fact, Saleem has been living with a wide range of children, with females, with younger people, older people, people who have no religion and people who do not feel like they should have a religion. The social worker said that Saleem is concerned because he thinks he has got to fulfil certain expectations before he can move home. She has, therefore, needed to do some separate work with his parents, as well as working with them together.

She says of Saleem, "He's not religious … he's seen the negative sides of Islam, the extreme sides … I think it's been quite beneficial for him and for us to do some work together because we've looked at the basics." She comments that the issue of religion is complex in Saleem's life and that it interconnects with other aspects of 'identity'. She says, "When we talk about this young person and religion it's not religion as in it's something which is embraced with open arms, it's just an identity because he sees the young people around him who are Muslim … They're obviously going to the mosque and I think it's something which he's wanted to be a part of, because it's there and that's what everyone's doing, but at this moment in time he's just looking into it, but he appreciates the time and the support, there's no rush." She suggests that for Saleem his faith is now more attractive to him than it was in his foster home, partly because he has a choice and he can say, "It's a choice that I want to make and I want to believe and I want to follow because it's my choice". In contrast, at home, he thinks, "It's a must, I have to and I can't fit in" and this creates difficulties for him. Saleem has the opportunity to go to mosque and sees it as something that is expected of Muslim men. However, he does not go at present because he "doesn't feel like he fits in".

Regarding the impact of her own faith, Saleem's social worker said:

> I think for Saleem, one thing he likes, and he's commented on a couple of times, is the fact that I always say I don't see myself as particularly religious … So when I talk about being a Muslim, I'm not a devout

> practising Muslim, but ... it's something which has kind of grown on me because of different experiences in my life, and I think he liked that because I think in the past he said people said, "Oh if you're a Muslim ... you've got to do this and you've got to do that" and I said, "No, you've got a choice in what you have to do and it's a long process" ... One of the things I was quite worried about were his perceptions of ... what he sees on the news ... He said, "Everyone thinks if you're Muslim and you're a boy, you just want to become a suicide bomber ... it's like we're being judged" ... That was a really good opportunity to separate out what is religion, what are someone's beliefs, what is extreme, what is socially acceptable.

The same worker spoke of 'John' whose parents are devout Christians. Since he had come into the looked after system through choice, he did not want to practise Christianity. However, she commented, "He's very moral and we've had some very interesting conversations about the difference between being moral and being religious". The worker emphasised that this was underpinned by a holistic approach, which not only sees the child's needs (including needs arising from their religious and cultural background) as paramount, but which also respects their current views.

Adoption

Patel et al (2004: 6) note that: "The importance of the cultural identity of a child awaiting adoption, in terms of 'race', religion and ethnic background, is the subject of continuing debate and often controversial and heated discussion". They also report that Circular (98) 20 promotes the view that:

> Placement with a family of a similar ethnic origin and religion is very often most likely to meet the child's needs as fully as possible, safeguarding his welfare most effectively and preparing him for life in a multi-racial society. (DH, 1998: para 13)

However, at the same time it emphasises that it is "unacceptable for a child to be denied loving or adoptive parents solely on the grounds that the child and adopters do not share the same racial or cultural background" (DH, 1998: para 14).

Patel et al (2004: 10) note that, in their sample of 1,200 people, two thirds shared the law's view that, in principle, "the need for cultural matching", including religion, should be prioritised. However, in the context of a suitable placement not being found for a child after 12 months, they report that all groups of respondents gave cultural and religious matching increasingly lower priority as the length of time the child remained without an adoptive placement increased. It is nevertheless important to note that, although the rate at which views changed was generally similar between Christian, Sikh, Hindu and Jewish respondents, Muslim respondents maintained the view that a Muslim child should be placed with a Muslim couple in much greater numbers and for a longer period (Patel et al, 2004: 14). At the same time, the conversion of looked after children in foster care from one faith to another may both provoke serious public controversy and serve to illustrate contradictory thinking among the professionals involved. Cook (2009), for example, reports on a case where a local authority's fostering services team decided that no further children would be placed with a carer whose foster daughter had converted from Islam to Christianity, even though the carer said that she had spoken to social services about the girl's wish to become a Christian and that they had told the girl that she was free to convert if she wanted to.

Case law, in fact, recognises that religion may be more important than ethnicity, although, in relation to Jewish children, Smith (2000: 46) asserts that "professionals do not always place the same emphasis on the often invisible religious and cultural rights of children as they do on more explicit ethnic rights". Patel et al (2004) quote Bush J in *Re N (a minor) (adoption)* ([1990] 1 FLR 58): "a child brought up in a black Methodist household in Jamaica would have far more in common with a white Methodist English family than with a Nigerian Muslim family". The case of 'Aysha' (Inset 5) demonstrates the challenges involved for family placement social workers in balancing the religious and other needs of children, and in achieving pragmatic compromises that optimise children's welfare and development.

Inset 5: 'Aysha'

'Aysha' became a child looked after by the local authority when she was three years old, because of severe neglect. The adoption social worker described her role as being that of finding an adoptive family for Aysha. She first met Aysha when she was four years old. Aysha had both behavioural and psychological issues. Her birth parents were migrants from Bangladesh. They did not speak English and were described as "very, very traditional". The family attends mosque, fasts during Ramadan, and so on. The father was seriously ill and subsequently died.

Aysha was initially placed with her siblings in an Asian foster home, but was subsequently moved to an individual placement with white foster carers.

Work was begun to prepare her for 'moving on', but it took more than two years to find adopters. During this time, Aysha remained in direct contact with her siblings and her birth mother. The worker said that she was always clear that her objective was to find a placement that would reflect Aysha's cultural identity, including her religion, and that this was one of her top priorities. However, she reports that, "we tried extensively to get that and we didn't ... we weren't able to do that". During these attempts the authority considered three different couples. These included one whose partner was Asian (not Bangladeshi) and 'Muslim', but, in the event, this couple said that they would promote neither Aysha's Muslim faith nor her culture.

Initially, the birth mother did not want Aysha to go to white adopters, but, after being told of the unsuccessful efforts made to find adopters where at least one partner was Asian, she agreed to meet a white couple and accepted that they were the best option available. Although nominally 'Church of England', this couple do not practise a religion. The worker saw this as allowing them to be "very embracing of openness and accepting of whoever the person is". She also recognised potential problems for Aysha if, in the future, she wished to pursue her religion. She reports the couple as being apprehensive and anxious about whether they would be able to meet Aysha's needs, commenting, "[if] you're brought up in a religious faith, there are issues you know intrinsically that you could pass on to your children. If you're not brought up on that, if you're [operating] on a kind of academic basis or are slightly removed ... you haven't got the fluidity of it ... but ... they celebrate Eid; they make a fuss of it. They check out things with her. She has a Halal diet and ... [although] you could say, 'well, that doesn't make you Muslim ... she won't be brought up as a Muslim', she'll be brought up to promote [her religion] and have a cultural identity." However, she also noted that the adopters had some "mixed feelings" about Aysha eventually pursuing her religion and that, in contrast to what would be the likely attitude of many Muslim parents, the adopters emphasise that they are aiming to provide Aysha with the information which she will need in order to make an 'informed choice' about this. Aysha now speaks English and has almost no knowledge of Bangla or Urdu.

The adoption worker emphasised that, while the initial Asian foster carers were good at providing daily care and did their best to celebrate Eid and to provide a halal diet, they "weren't necessarily culturally sensitive" and were unenthusiastic about a religion they had chosen to leave. When Aysha was placed with "a white couple in a white area, in a very white authority", they were assessed as being well able to promote her welfare, but there were obvious doubts about their capacity to promote her cultural identity. The worker and the couple needed to undertake a lot of work around this issue.

The worker sought out relevant and age-appropriate books, while the couple contacted their nearest mosque to discuss what they were intending to do and to seek advice. (They were prepared to take the child to mosque if that was deemed necessary.) They also ensured that Aysha had direct contact with most of her siblings and 'letterbox' contact with her birth mother. The worker comments, "ultimately you are balancing permanency against [other things] and everything else is a bonus ... you have to break it down, into what is achievable". In her view, 'permanency', not 'religion', had to be the main priority. She agreed that there had been a pragmatic compromise, which had involved the local authority in abandoning the ideal of having a Muslim couple from Aysha's community. At the same time, she commented that, among Aysha's older sisters, there was "a very negative view of the Muslim faith", which challenged the local authority's view that a Muslim adopter should be found. They were, in fact, placed with Muslim carers and were attending mosque, but rejecting Islam, despite others' efforts to promote their cultural and religious identities.

The worker highlighted the fact that, despite outreach work with local mosques and some success in her authority in recruiting Asian and Muslim foster carers, they had had much more difficulty in recruiting adopters from Muslim communities, where she thought the concept, especially with regard to older children, was very unfamiliar and complicated by particular issues about boys' names and identities. She suggested that most looked after children who come from a Muslim faith background are being placed with Muslim carers. However, she also emphasised the potential complexities involved – for example, when a child with a Muslim mother and a non–Muslim father had been brought up to think of themselves as a Muslim, but, coincidentally, had also eaten foods such as bacon, which are forbidden (haram) in Islam.

Child protection and safeguarding

Please see Chapter Six.

Key questions

(1) What do you know about religious beliefs, traditions and observances (if any) of the children and young people you are working with?

(2) Are you able to distance yourself from your beliefs and attitudes in order to sufficiently respect and promote the religious beliefs and observances (if any) of the children and young people you are working with? (How?)

(3) Do you have any religious beliefs or observances that offer potential advantages in work with children and young people from particular religions or religious traditions? (What are they?)

(4) Do you think that children/young people have a right to actively participate in any religion that they choose?

(5) Are there limits to the extent to which biological parents and those with parental responsibility should be able to insist on children/young people engaging in particular religious observances?

(6) In what circumstances (if any) would you think it appropriate to prevent a child/young person having contact with a faith group or community?

References

Ashley, C. (ed) (2006) *The family group conference toolkit – a practical guide for setting up and running an FGC service*, London: Department for Education and Skills and Family Rights Group.

Ashley, C. and Nixon, P. (eds) (2007) *Family group conferences – where next?*, London: Family Rights Group.

Cook, B. (2009) 'Foster carer struck off for letting Muslim child convert', *Children & Young People Now*, 10 February (www.cypnow.co.uk/news/879756/Foster-carer-struck-off-letting-Muslim-child-convert/).

Crompton, M. (1996) *Children, spirituality and religion: A training pack*, London: CCETSW.

Crompton, M. (1998) *Children, spirituality, religion and social work*, Aldershot: Ashgate.

DH (Department of Health) (1989) *An introduction to the Children Act 1989*, London: HMSO.

DH (1995) *Looking after children*, London: HMSO.

DH (1998) *LAC (98) 20: Adoption: Achieving the right balance*, London: DH (www.dh.gov.uk/en/Publicationsandstatistics/Lettersandcirculars/LocalAuthorityCirculars/AllLocalAuthority/DH_4003577).

Horwath, J., Lees, J., Sidebotham, P., Higgins, J. and Imtiaz, A. (2008a) *Religion, beliefs and parenting practices. Findings informing change*, York: Joseph Rowntree Foundation (www.jrf.org.uk/sites/files/jrf/2264-faith-parenting-youth.pdf).

Horwath, J., Lees, J., Sidebotham, P., Higgins, J. and Imtiaz, A. (2008b) *Religion, beliefs and parenting practices. A descriptive study*, York: Joseph Rowntree Foundation (www.jrf.org.uk/bookshop/eBooks/2264-faith-parenting-youth.pdf).

Patel, T., Williams, C. and Marsh, P. (2004) 'Identity, race, religion and adoption: the public and legal view', *Adoption and Fostering*, **28**(1), 6-15.

Seden, J. (1995) 'Religious persuasion and the Children Act', *Adoption and Fostering*, **19**(2), 7-17.

Smith, G. (2000) 'Meeting the placement needs of Jewish children', *Adoption and Fostering*, **24**(1), 40-6.

Older people, religion and belief

The significance of a particular life event or transition will be influenced by its relationship to our values, priorities, and commitments. (Sugarman, 2001: 154)

Introduction

Every ten years the Office for National Statistics (ONS) conducts a population survey that is used to inform government policies and provides a good source of rich data about all areas of life in the UK (ONS, 2001). In 2005, there were 60.2 million people living in the UK; of these 16% were aged 65 years and over. There has been a change in the age composition of older people over the last 50 years. In particular, projections show a decrease of those aged 50-59 and increase of those aged 85 and over by 2031 (ONS, 2005). In terms of gender, older women outnumber older men, as death rates are higher among men than among women (ONS, 2005). Christian and Jewish communities have greater numbers of people aged over 65 years than those of other faiths (see Figure 5.1). Muslim, Hindu and Sikh communities have a younger age profile, reflecting later immigration and larger family sizes with more children (ONS, 2001). Muslims are the only religious group in which men outnumber women – 52% compared with 48%. This reflects the gender structure of Pakistani and Bangladeshi groups, in which men slightly outnumber women because of their migration history. Men also form the majority of the 'no religion' group, 56% (ONS, 2001).

Concerns about the increasing numbers of older people in developed countries and their perceived reliance on state support in later life have fuelled a debate on how best to care for this significant group (Estes et al, 2003; Vincent et al, 2006). Contemporary experiences of ageing have shifted from a traditional concern with problems to a focus on social and personal perceptions of ageing and experiences and how best to age well (Daatland and Biggs, 2006). Historically, old age has been associated with retirement from paid employment. However, current discussions about extending the retirement age to 70 years and beyond indicate that basing old age on a chronological time frame is inadequate. Traditionally, women

Figure 5.1: Age by religion

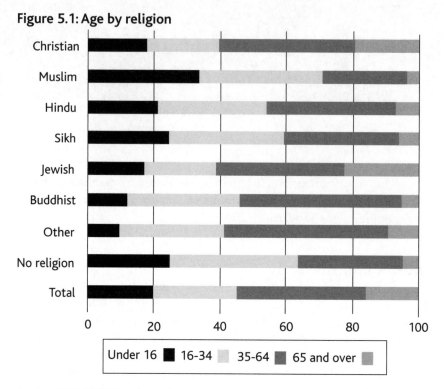

Source: ONS (2001)

of all religions/no religion may have stayed at home to perform domestic and childcare responsibilities, with considerable consequences on their pay, promotion and pension prospects (Sigle-Rushton and Perrons, 2006). Muslim women have the highest economic inactivity rate of all faith groups, at 68% compared with 28% for Christians and approximately 35% for both Hindus and Sikhs (Open Society Institute, 2005).

There is also a need to move away from ageist assumptions that cast older people as being in the final stage of life and stereotype all as being dependent and in poor health. Policy makers are starting to recognise the diverse needs and expectations of this broad age grouping where power, wealth and economic opportunity have impacted differently across time and generations (Vincent et al, 2006: 11).

The religious landscape and practices of the people living in the UK have changed remarkably over the past 60 years. There are emerging tensions and challenges facing the British government and within different religious hierarchies about the extent to which different belief systems can be accommodated, tolerated and accepted (Davie, 2007). In the UK, multiculturalism was, until recently, a favoured political initiative to address racism as it promotes both tolerance and acceptance of others' ways of life and views all cultural traditions as equally valid (Macionis and Plummer, 2008). However, critics argue that particular aspects of some cultural traditions are oppressive and discriminatory in nature and suggest that acceptance of some religious or cultural traditions may be a contradiction in terms within democratic and liberal societies (Barry, 2001).

In England, all local authority services for adults have been required to adopt a Single Assessment Process (SAP) in an attempt to standardise the collection and sharing of personal information that is used to inform an assessment of need (DH, 2002a, 2002b). Service users must give consent for the sharing of information and the assessment determines their eligibility for social care support under the Fair Access to Care criteria (DH, 2002c, 2003). Smale and Tuson (1993) identified three different types of assessment that are still valid and applicable today. Practitioners may use the procedural model to collect routine information that will be used to ascertain eligibility for a service; the questioning model may be used to inform the judgement of the practitioner about levels of risk and dependence; and the exchange model can be very helpful in allowing the practitioner to gain some awareness and understanding of the religious and cultural needs and wishes of the older person. Over the next two years, local authorities will be required to introduce personalised budgets (DH, 2008a). Each client will be allocated a personal budget to spend on meeting his or her care needs. The personalisation agenda will shape the relationship between the purchaser and the provider of services and the ways in which social workers interact and support older people to live more independently. The role of social workers will shift towards empowerment, advocacy and brokerage, rather than assessment and gatekeeping. It will be crucial that practitioners take into account a range of factors in order to work with people to ensure that appropriate services are contracted to meet the expressed needs of the older person.

Key Role One of the National Occupational Standards (NOS) requires training social workers to show that they can prepare for social work contact and involvement. Normally, the referral form will provide useful background information about the person including ethnic origin, religion and place of residence. This information should be located within knowledge of the profile of the local population. These statistics are freely available on local authority websites and are taken from census statistics. Clearly religious affiliation is going to be more significant in some localities than in others. Groups can also be clustered together within ethnic religious groupings such as Bangladeshi Muslims or Christian Pakistanis (Peach, 2006; Carling, 2008). A social worker who worked with a large Asian community, mainly made up of Muslims but also some Christians, commented that she quickly learned not to visit a Muslim family on a Friday afternoon because that was prayer time and equally not to park her car near a mosque in the town centre on a Friday afternoon because it had been 'blocked in' on previous occasions as people left the mosque.

The following sections will include demonstrations of how applying principles from the Furness/Gilligan Framework described in Chapter Three may help both inexperienced and experienced social workers to prepare for and work with those of different religions. The examples given suggest the particular importance in social work with older people of practitioners adopting a person–centred approach; recognising service users' expertise about their own needs and beliefs; actively seeking out relevant information and advice regarding the religious and spiritual beliefs of individuals; and providing opportunities for them to discuss their religious and spiritual beliefs and the strengths, difficulties and needs that arise from them.

Making transitions

An individual's sense of the meaning of life is continually shaped and redefined in response to life changes and transitions. Change is situational and it is how people adjust to the change that can make the transition easy or painful. Transitions may affect the individual or all of us; they may be predictable or unpredictable, voluntary or involuntary, but are part and parcel of life. Although individuals may respond to life events in different ways, responses can be broadly categorised within the following stages. An initial response may be of disbelief and immobilisation, followed by a reaction of elation or despair and then minimisation, self-doubt, accepting reality and letting go, testing and exploration, search for meaning and finally integration (Sugarman, 2001; Beckett, 2002). Some people make the transition successfully whereas others may get 'stuck' and need professional help to move on. Schlossberg et al (1995, cited in Sugarman, 2001: 150) identified situation factors that influenced capacity to cope with transitions:

- What set off the transition? (Trigger)
- How does the transition relate to other life events? (Timing)
- What aspects of the transition can the person control? (Control)
- Does the transition involve role changes? (Role change)
- Is the transition permanent or temporary? (Duration)
- Has the person had to deal with similar transitions? (Previous experience)
- Are there any other stresses facing the person? (Concurrent stress)
- Does the person view the transition positively or negatively? (Assessment)

Fiske and Chiriboga (1990, cited in Sugarman, 2001) developed a seven-category typology based on a longitudinal study into adulthood about what respondents valued in life:

- achievement and work (economic competence, rewards, success, social status);
- good personal relations (love and affection, happy relationship, friends);
- philosophy and religion (meaning of existence, adherence to an ethical code);
- social service (helping others, serving community);
- ease and contentment (security, relaxation);
- seeking enjoyment (recreation, exciting experiences);
- personal growth (self-improvement, being creative).

Social support is important within our private and public spheres of life but can have both positive and negative effects (Sugarman, 2001: 156). Tofler (1970, cited in Sugarman, 2001: 157) suggests that we can cope with changes, pressure, complexity and confusion provided that at least one area of life is stable. Support can come from a range of sources: from people who may be unfamiliar but offer a professional service or from long-lasting relationships; from deeply held religious beliefs or a strong personal and/or professional commitment to a philosophy, political ideology or cause; from places that provide confidence and familiar reassurance (home, street, neighbourhood or country); from favourite things and personal possessions that provide meaning and comfort (heirlooms, favourite clothes); from organisations such as the workplace, professional body and clubs that offer a sense of belonging, identification and stability. All of these areas may overlap and our support systems can include elements of place, people and things.

Exercise

- Can you identify your stability/comfort zones?
- How and when do you use these?
- What areas of your life would you like to change or retain?
- How can you nurture these areas?

Qualitative research has used narrative as a way of gathering individual views and opinions about wide-ranging topics. These accounts allow the individual to describe "their subjective experience and detail how they construct meaning to negotiate their understood world" (Nelson-Becker, 2004: 23). Narratives and story-telling have been found to help individuals to accept and come to terms with loss. Individuals may choose to share their stories of the loss using a factual and descriptive account, by providing an insight into their pain and sadness by sharing their feelings and emotions and/or by reflexive accounts that attempt to analyse, interpret and make sense of an event and reaction to it (Neimeyer and Anderson, 2002: 53). These different expressions can help practitioners to assess whether the person is coming to terms with the loss or not.

Forms of healing

All societies have developed culture-specific ways to deal with problems and distress. In the West, counselling and psychotherapy have become accepted psychological healing methods and "rely on sensory information defined by the physical plane of reality (western science)" while others have adopted more holistic approaches that "rely on the spiritual plane of existence in seeking a cure" (Sue, 2006: 211).

Western healing has tended to ignore or discredit alternative forms of healing. It is necessary at the very least to acknowledge these different help-giving networks as well as to question the use of some forms of 'healing' when the effects may be detrimental to the person's development and well-being.

Lee et al (1992) carried out a study of indigenous healing in 16 non-western countries and identified three common approaches. First, there was a reliance on the use of community, group or family to shelter the individual (Saudi Arabia), to solve problems as a group (Nigeria) and to reconnect them with family or significant others (Korea). Second, spiritual and religious beliefs and traditions of the community were used in the healing process. Examples included reading verses from the Koran and using religious houses or churches. The third approached involved the use of shamans, referring to people often called witches, witch doctors, wizards, medicine men or women, sorcerers and magic men or women. Shamans are also called *piris* and *fakirs* in Pakistan and Sudan and are perceived to be the keepers of wisdom. They are often respected elders of the community (Lee et al, 1992, cited in Sue, 2006: 211; Grey et al, 2008). People of all religions, as well as those of no religion, can turn to prayer and 'faith healing' in an attempt to deal with serious illness, injury or distress. 'Norah's' case (Inset 1) illustrates how belief (either our own or others') can shape and influence our thoughts.

Inset 1: 'Norah'

'Norah' had been married twice and had two sons and a daughter to her first husband. Her second husband died suddenly of leukaemia. Shortly after his death, she started to feel his presence, 'seeing' her husband in the house and dreaming of him every night. Norah started to worry and question what he wanted and why he kept coming back. Norah was a Christian but did not attend church but liked to watch *Songs of Praise* on television. She became distressed by these appearances and told her daughter Shirley about these apparitions. Shirley was a Pentecostal Christian and said that she wanted her mum to be at peace and would help her through prayer and healing. Norah had witnessed her daughter speaking in tongues at church but did not understand this. Her daughter explained, "It just comes to you, mum. I can't explain to you what I am saying but these just come to you." Norah agreed to let Shirley try to 'heal' her and they prayed together. Since then Norah has not been disturbed by visions of her late husband.

Pentecostals are so called because they practise the charisms, ie the 'gifts of the Spirit' listed by St Paul in chapter 12 of his first letter to the Corinthians. The name is derived from the Feast of Pentecost, when the Disciples were gathered in Jerusalem and were inspired by the Holy Spirit to speak in many languages, enabling them to preach the gospel to the nations. Speaking in tongues, along with prophecy, healing and leadership, are among the charisms practised in Pentecostal churches today. (Gledhill, 2006)

However, there have also been numerous reports of 'believers' who have been tricked and defrauded of money and possessions, have experienced threats to their physical health and psychological damage to their mental well-being by bogus confidence tricksters and have accepted leaders of cults taking advantage of others' vulnerabilities and exploiting their fears (Begum, 2004; Japantimesonline, 2005; BBC, 2007).

Dealing with death and dying

In terms of dealing with others' death and dying it is important to reflect on our own experiences or views; how have we been affected and how did we react? Rituals such as prayer and faith healing can provide solace and comfort for some. Even if practitioners do not believe these to be relevant social work interventions they need to be open to the possibility of facilitating them for others if this is meaningful and would bring comfort to that person. However, practitioners of faith also need to be extremely cautious not to impose their own beliefs on to others. A Christian nurse was suspended after offering to pray for a patient's recovery from illness (Staines, 2009). This would have been a very different matter if the service user had initiated the prayer or if the practitioner had prayed in private. The social worker needs to create opportunities that allow individuals to express any religious beliefs and any difficulties or fears they might have; they need to listen carefully and to be open-minded about any shared information. Sometimes this can be challenging and lead to the unexpected, as in the case of 'Barbara' (see Inset 2).

Inset 2: 'Barbara'

'Barbara' was a 68-year-old married woman who had been diagnosed with cancer and the social worker had visited to discuss 'end of life' care plans with her. Once all the practical arrangements had been agreed, the social worker asked Barbara if she needed any other help. Barbara responded by asking "what happens after?" This led the social worker to immediately struggle with how best to answer this question and possible discussions about God and a belief in an afterlife ran through her mind. However, after asking Barbara to clarify what she meant, it became clear that she was worried about who would look after her cat once she had died, as her husband did not like the cat! There was a very simple practical resolution of the matter by sharing her concerns with her husband.

Many studies have identified that people are drawn to train as social workers so that they can make a difference to the lives of others (Cree, 2003; Furness, 2007; DH, 2008b). In this chapter, the accounts of work carried out by social workers are very moving and clearly demonstrate that, by being responsive to people's religious and spiritual needs, the social workers have succeeded in helping to make the lives of their clients meaningful at critical periods of the person's life. Although death and dying can affect us at any time in the life course, the majority of those who die are aged over 65 years and die in hospital (Beckett, 2002; Holloway, 2007; ONS, 2008). Each year, more than half a million people die in England and Wales, with five deaths in every six involving people aged 65 and over and one in five of all deaths taking place in a care home (DH, 2006). It is vital that social work training programmes cover the theory and research relating to loss, transition and change, including issues arising from religion and belief, if students are to feel equipped to deal with matters of life and death.

Loss and grief

Loss and grief are socially defined and there are differences in how individuals and groups experience, respond and communicate their feelings both in public and private arenas. Loss can be temporary or final, symbolic or physical (Currer, 2007). There may be clear social expectations about how we express our feelings in situations of loss. This next section will concentrate on loss through death and how grief is expressed within different religious and cultural contexts.

Culture teaches people how to think, feel and act in the face of death and is expressed in shared rituals (Weinstein, 2002). The anglophone literature on death and dying tends to be Eurocentric and generally does not include discussion of how other cultures deal with such issues. Holloway (2007: 87) points out that "models of individual bereavement might not have universal currency in different social contexts". Therefore, it is vital to find out shared understandings of the rituals surrounding death. This can be discovered by seeking out relevant information regarding unfamiliar religious and spiritual beliefs and practices; being self-aware and reflexive about our own religious and spiritual beliefs and our responses to loss and bereavement; listening to others' views about their needs and beliefs; and being open to learning by engaging with others of different faiths. Despite the fact that the majority of people die in hospital and institutional settings, little attention had been paid to 'end of life' planning until the launch of the NHS End of Life Care (EoLC) programme in November 2004. This initiative is part of a wider strategy to give people greater choice in their place of death and care. Its website provides some useful resources for those caring or supporting those who are terminally ill (DH, 2006).

It is important to find out what constitutes a 'good' death for specific individuals. In some cultures and belief systems a 'good' death may require harmony, reconciliation and (re)union with family and a failure to gather all family members together either to be with the dying person or after death may result in guilt and anxiety (Holloway, 2007: 89). The following questions can aid the social worker to assist the person in making 'end of life' plans. Does the person want or have any control over what is happening and its effects? Who manages the affairs? Where do they turn for help and what do they expect from others? What is the place of belief systems to make sense and deal with death (Neimeyer and Anderson, 2002: 48; Currer, 2007)?

It can make a huge difference to people if they are given the opportunity to share their worries or other issues before they die. They may want to decide a type of funeral, where they want to die or, if they are in hospital, the appropriate clergy to visit them. Some people may wish to go into a care home run by a particular religious group because they want to end their days with people of the same faith. In the western world, a 'good' death is often seen in terms of a belief that the dying person should not die alone or in pain. It can be important that all family members are present at the death and certain rituals are performed to prepare the person for death. Often hospitals and hospices do not or cannot accommodate large numbers of people at the bedside and conflicts can occur between those who prefer peace and quiet to those families who wish to recite prayers and mourn collectively as is the case for Muslim Bengalis (Gardner, 2002: 199).

Inset 3: 'Esther'

'Esther' was a 67-year-old Jewish woman who survived the Holocaust. She had no relatives and came to live in this country after World War 2. She was still very mistrustful and suspicious of others and led a very quiet and secluded life. She lived in her own home and was terminally ill. After several visits, the hospice social worker had gradually been able to build a relationship and gain some trust. She found out that Esther had no contact with others from her religion and feared that her soul would not be saved if no one performed certain Jewish rituals that are necessary on and after death. There was a Jewish consultant working at the hospice and Esther agreed to meet him at her next visit. He was able to explain that on her death he would prepare her body for burial by washing (*rechitzah*), ritual purification (*taharah*) and dressing (*halbashah*). He also went through and explained the different blessings, prayers and readings from the Torah and other Jewish scriptures that he would recite to prepare her for the afterlife. Esther was able to die in peace comforted that the last of her rites of passage were carried out with care and attention following Jewish tradition (Ponn, 1998).

On many occasions, practitioners will need to seek out relevant information and advice about unfamiliar religious beliefs and practices. Often, service users are the best people to advise the practitioner on how best to meet their needs and it is vital that their expertise is acknowledged and sought. This willingness to engage and respond to service users' wishes will help to establish trust and mutual respect. Rather than rigidly imposing existing practices or ways of working it is crucial that practitioners can be creative in their approach and actively seek out alternatives that may best suit the needs of the individual, as in the case of 'Meena' (Inset 4).

Inset 4: 'Meena'

'Meena' was a widow and had no children. She had had periods of respite care provided by the local hospice and over that time the staff had built up a good relationship with her. She was admitted with only a few days left to live. Although she was not a practising Hindu, she expressed a wish to staff to have prayers read to her. As the staff were not familiar with any of the rituals associated with the Hindu faith and did not know of a practising Hindu who could perform these rites, they asked Meena how they could help. The staff team consisted of a Jewish student, a Jewish consultant, a Christian nurse and a Bahai social worker. They all gathered round her bed and read prayers so that she was able to die with her friends and hearing the word of God. A lamp was also lit near the bed as a sign that the soul could go to *svarga*, a place to rest after death (Pearson and Mackenzie, 1998).

There are significant variations in practices that mark the end of life. It is important that practitioners take time to respect any final wishes and practices as a last rite of passage. There are a number of useful resources that consider the various social and cultural processes and events that need to be taken into account in the preparation for and aftermath of death from different religious viewpoints (Johnson and McGee, 1998; Henley and Schott, 2001; Gardner, 2002; Gatrad and Sheikh, 2002a, 2002b; Woodward, 2005; Holloway, 2007; Crabtree et al, 2008). Most people are buried or cremated within three days of death and in accordance with religious and/or cultural traditions. Relatives and friends may also express their grief in different ways and again it is important to allow others to display their feelings without condemnation or judgement (Purnell and Paulanka, 2003).

Key questions

(1) What do you know about religious beliefs, traditions and observances (if any) of the older people you are working with?

(2) Are you able to distance yourself from your beliefs and attitudes in order to sufficiently respect and promote the religious beliefs and observances (if any) of the older people you are working with? (How?)

(3) Do you have any religious beliefs or observances that offer potential advantages in work with older people from particular religions or religious traditions? (What are they?)

(4) Can you identify previous cases where you could have been more proactive or aided the person to seek support, help or strength from their religious advisers? (What could you have done differently?)

(5) Have you experienced loss and bereavement? Were there any specific rituals that needed to be performed either prior to or after death? (If so, what were these and who carried these out?)

References

Barry, B. (2001) *Culture and equality*, Cambridge: Polity Press.

BBC (2007) 'Bogus spiritual healers', *Inside out* (www.bbc.co.uk/insideout/content/articles/2007/09/17/west_mid_spirit_healer_12_1_feature.shtml).

Beckett, C. (2002) *Human growth and development*, London: Sage Publications.

Begum, S. (2004) 'Exorcists condemned', *Asian News* (www.theasiannews.co.uk/news/s/491/491392_exorcists_condemned.html).

Carling, A. (2008) 'The curious case of the mis-claimed myth claims: ethnic segregation, polarization and the future of Bradford', *Urban Studies*, **45**(3), 553-89.

Crabtree, S.A., Husain, F. and Spalek, B. (2008) *Islam and social work: Debating values, transforming practice*, Bristol: The Policy Press.

Cree, V. (ed) (2003) *Becoming a social worker*, London and New York: Routledge.

Currer, C. (2007) *Loss and social work*, Exeter: Learning Matters.

Daatland, S.O. and Biggs, S. (2006) *Ageing and diversity: Multiple pathways and cultural migrations*, Bristol: The Policy Press.

Davie, G. (2007) *The sociology of religion*, London: Sage Publications.

DH (Department of Health) (2002a) *Guidance on the Single Assessment Process for older people* (HSC2002/001: LAC (2002)1), London: DH (www.dh.gov. uk/en/SocialCare/Chargingandassessment/SingleAssessmentProcess/ DH_079509#_5).

DH (2002b) *The Single Assessment Process: Guidance for local implementation*, London: DH.

DH (2002c) *Fair access to care services: Guidance on eligibility criteria for adult social care*, London: DH.

DH (2002d) *Fair access to care services: Policy guidance*, London: DH.

DH (2003) *Fair access to care services: Practice guidance – implementation questions and answers*, London: DH.

DH (2006) *Introductory guide to end of life care in care homes*, Leicester: DH (www.endoflifecareforadults.nhs.uk/eolc/files/F2024-EoLC_Guide_to_ EoLC_in_Care_Homes_V2_Apr2006.pdf).

DH (2008a) *LAC (2008) 1: Transforming adult social care*, London: DH (www.dh.gov.uk/en/Publicationsandstatistics/Lettersandcirculars/ LocalAuthorityCirculars/DH_081934).

DH (2008b) *Evaluation of the new social work degree qualification in England: Volume 1: Findings*, London: DH.

Estes, C.L., Biggs, S. and Phillipson, C. (2003) *Social theory, social policy and ageing: A critical introduction*, Maidenhead: Open University Press.

Furness, S. (2007) 'An enquiry into students' motivations to train as social workers in England', *Journal of Social Work*, **7**(2), 239-53.

Gardner, A. (2002) *Age, narrative and migration: The life course and histories of Bengali elders in London*, Oxford and New York: Berg.

Gatrad, A.R. and Sheikh, A. (2002a) 'Palliative care for Muslims and issues before death', *International Journal of Palliative Nursing*, **8**(11), 526-31.

Gatrad, A.R. and Sheikh, A. (2002b) 'Palliative care for Muslims and issues after death', *International Journal of Palliative Nursing*, **8**(12), 594-7.

Gledhill, R. (2006) '''Fringe' Church winning the believers'' (www. timesonline.co.uk/tol/new/uk/article757934.ece).

Henley, A. and Schott, J. (2001) *Culture, religion and patient care in a multi-ethnic society: A handbook for professionals*, London: Age Concern England.

Holloway, M. (2007) *Negotiating death in contemporary health and social care*, Bristol: The Policy Press.

Japantimesonline (2005) 'Honohana foot-cult guru gets 12 years for fraud' (http://search.japantimes.co.jp/cgi-bin/nn20050716a3.html).

Johnson, C.J. and McGee, M.G. (eds) (1998) *How different religions view death and afterlife* (2nd edn), Philadelphia, PA: The Charles Press.

Lee, C.C., Oh, M.Y. and Mountcastle, A.R. (1992) 'Indigenous models of helping in non-western countries: Implications for multicultural counselling', *Journal of Multicultural Counseling and Development*, **20**, 1-10.

Macionis, J.J. and Plummer, K. (2008) *Sociology: A global introduction* (4th edn), Harlow: Pearson Education.

Neimeyer, R.A. and Anderson, A. (2002) 'Meaning reconstruction theory', in N. Thompson (ed) *Loss and grief*, Basingstoke: Palgrave, pp 45–64.

Nelson-Becker, H.B. (2004) 'Spiritual, religious, nonspiritual, and nonreligious narratives in marginalized older adults: a typology of coping styles', in M. Brennan and D. Heiser (eds) *Spiritual assessment and intervention with older adults: Current directions and applications*, New York: The Haworth Pastoral Press, pp 21–38.

ONS (Office for National Statistics) (2001) *Census 2001*, London: ONS (www.statistics.gov.uk/cci/nugget.asp?id=955).

ONS (2005) *Focus on older people*, London: ONS (www.statistics.gov.uk/cci/nugget.asp?id=1263).

ONS (2008) *Mortality statistics: Deaths registered in 2006* (www.statistics.gov.uk/downloads/theme_health/DR-2006/DR_06Mort_Stats.pdf).

Open Society Institute (2005) *British Muslims in the labour market*, Budapest: Open Society Institute, EUMAP.

Peach, C. (2006) 'Islam, ethnicity and South Asian religions in the London 2001 Census', *Transactions of the Institute of British Geographers*, **31**(3), 353–71.

Pearson Mackenzie, A. (1998) 'Hinduism', in C.J. Johnson and M.G. McGee (eds) *How different religions view death and afterlife* (2nd edn), Philadelphia, PA: The Charles Press, pp 109–31.

Ponn, A.L. (1998) 'Judaism', in C.J. Johnson and M.G. McGee (eds) *How different religions view death and afterlife* (2nd edn), Philadelphia, PA: The Charles Press, pp 145–59.

Purnell, L.D. and Paulanka, B.J. (2003) *Transcultural health care: A culturally competent approach* (2nd edn), Philadelphia, PA: E.A. Davis Company.

Sigle-Rushton, W. and Perrons, D. (2006) *Employment transitions over the life cycle: A statistical analysis* (Transforming Work Working Paper Series no 36), Manchester: EOC.

Smale, G. and Tuson, G. with Biehal, N. and Marsh, P. (1993) *Empowerment, assessment, care management and the skilled worker*, London: NISW/HMSO.

Staines, R. (2009) 'Christian nurse suspended for offering to pray for patient returns to work', *Nursing Times*, 6 February (www.nursingtimes.net/primarycarenurses/breakingnews/2009/02/christian_nurse_suspended_for_offering_to_pray_for_patient_returns_to_work.html).

Sue, D.W. (2006) *Multicultural social work practice*, Hoboken, NJ: John Wiley & Sons.

Sugarman, L. (2001) *Life-span development frameworks, accounts and strategies* (2nd edn), Hove and New York: Psychology Press.

Tofler, A. (1970) *Future shock*, London: Pan.

Vincent, J.A., Phillipson, C. and Downs, M. (eds) (2006) *The futures of old age*, London: Sage Publications.

Weinstein, J. (2002) *Working with loss, death and bereavement: A guide for social workers*, Los Angeles and London: Sage Publications.

Woodward, J. (2005) *Befriending death*, London: SPCK.

6

Child abuse, adult abuse, religion and belief

Child abuse

> Children can be abused in any environment … It would be naïve to assume that child abuse could not happen within our faith. (Moules, 2006: 23)

There is no evidence that child abuse is any more prevalent in faith communities than elsewhere and some evidence that religion can provide reassurance to victims, many of whom report that they gain strength from their belief that God loves them unconditionally (Crompton, 1996, 1998; Doyle, 2001, 2006). Parkinson (1993), Seidman and Pedersen (2003) and Perkins and Jones (2004) all identify 'religiosity' as a positive factor in particular contexts, while Grotberg (1997) concludes that belief in "a power greater than seen" is a positive resilience factor for children and young people in the face of all adversity. In the context of sexual abuse, Kennedy (1995: 33-4) emphasises that "the child may gain great support, comfort and safety from his/her faith" and that "For a great many Christian children who have been abused, if they see God as loving, then the continuation of a Christian practice is essential for healing", even when this coincides with expressions of anger against God for not protecting them from the perpetrator.

There is no evidence that membership of any faith community provides protection from child abuse, or that it has ever done so (Farrell, 2004). There are, at the same time, indications that specific religious contexts may increase the likelihood of some types of abuse and change their impact.

Working together (DfES, 2006) emphasises that "All children, whatever their religious or cultural background, must receive the same care and safeguards with regard to abuse and neglect" (para 10.13) and, while emphasising that the assessment process should focus on the needs of the individual child, notes that:

- Assessment "should always include consideration of the way religious beliefs and cultural traditions in different racial, ethnic and cultural groups influence their values, attitudes and behaviour, and the way in which family and community life is structured and organised" (para 10.11).

- "Cultural and religious factors should not be regarded as acceptable explanations for child abuse or neglect, and are not acceptable grounds for inaction when a child is at risk of significant harm." (para 10.11)
- Professionals should:
  - "be aware of, and work with, the strengths and support systems available within families, ethnic groups and communities, which can be built on to help safeguard children and promote their welfare" (para 10.11);
  - "guard against myths and stereotypes – both positive and negative" (para 10.12).

In relation to interviewing children, it notes that: "Additional specialist help may be required if "the interviewers do not have adequate knowledge and understanding of the child's racial, religious or cultural background".

Others note the need for professionals to be alert to specific issues in particular contexts. Gilligan with Akhtar (2006), for example, in the context of work with Muslim women around the disclosure of child sexual abuse by members of Asian communities, highlight the significance of religious and cultural imperatives such as *izzat* (honour), *sharam* (shame) and *haya* (natural modesty) in influencing behaviour in response to child sexual abuse. They note not only the need for professionals to understand the significance of such imperatives as potential barriers to disclosure, but also the potential for religious conceptualisations of *izzat* to motivate members of Muslim communities towards entirely appropriate responses to child sexual abuse.

Three very specific types of issues are dealt with below. However, it needs to be emphasised that, while these serve to illustrate the breadth and significance of the ways in which religion, belief and child abuse interact, they can, in the space available, provide only illustrations rather than a fully comprehensive picture. Moreover, there is dispute within and between professionals and within academic writing around which issues are relevant to discussions of religion and child abuse. For example, there are contrasting opinions regarding whether circumcision of male infants for religious purposes constitutes child abuse (BMA, 2006; Hinchley and Patrick, 2007; Baker, 2008) and suggestions that issues such as female genital mutilation and 'forced marriages' are more appropriately explored as 'cultural' rather than 'religious' phenomena (see, for example, Macey, 1999; Rahman and Toubia, 2000; Samad and Eade, 2002).

It should also be noted that victims and survivors of child abuse that occurs in contexts that have no religious elements might find the support they need for recovery in the context of faith communities and faith-based agencies. Edwards (2007) provides a brief overview of factors relating to faith, religion and safeguarding children, which includes an appendix of useful contacts for particular faiths.

'Amy'

In the case of 'Amy' (Inset 1), the social workers had to recognise that the parents' beliefs were resulting in life-threatening neglect of their baby who, if not removed from their care, would die. They had to apply general safeguarding principles, regardless of the origins and motivations of the parents' behaviour, while, at the same time, ensuring that they and the foster carer respected the parents' beliefs, in so far as this was consistent with Amy's welfare. The child's welfare and safety remained paramount and was given appropriate priority, but, in order to ensure that she could ultimately be returned to her parents' care, the practitioners involved again needed to be self-aware and reflexive; to listen respectfully to expositions of unfamiliar beliefs; and to offer creative responses to these while ensuring Amy's nutrition and development.

Inset 1: 'Amy'

'Amy' is the youngest child of a family who live as part of a self-contained, very private community in a relatively remote rural area. All the children are home educated and their parents refuse inoculations and provide their own medical care. The group's beliefs centre on variants of Buddhist teaching, with a strong emphasis on following a strict vegan diet. When Amy was eight months old, a woman living nearby alerted the statutory agencies to the fact that she had seen a baby who was very pale and very small for her age. The health visitor went to the house and was refused access, but, eventually, children's services obtained access with police support. They assessed Amy as being very close to death and she was, subsequently, found to be suffering major organ failure through starvation. In fact, the mother's milk had dried up and Amy was being fed only on puréed fruit. Amy's parents refused to allow the professionals either to remove or to feed her. They said that their religion allowed no milk other than a mother's breast milk and no solid foods other than fruit. The mother had previously said "no" to any medical intervention in her pregnancy or at Amy's birth. The social worker commented, "We respected that right, because that's her right, but then we found out that this baby was in a dreadful state (she was eight months old and weighed only about 6lbs) ... we had to remove her, through a court order".

Of the mother, the social worker commented, "She was genuinely distressed by what we were doing. She loved the baby and loved her other children. There was no sense of neglect in the way that we see neglect on a daily basis in social work. There was a lot of love, a lot of attachment but, at the same time, there was an attitude of 'if this baby isn't meant to survive, she won't survive'."

Amy recovered in hospital and, after a contested court hearing, she and her mother went to live with a foster carer. While she was in this placement, Amy was fed on specialist organic and vegetarian baby foods. However, her mother was, initially, very unhappy with this and said that the foster carer and the professionals were committing "sacrilege" by doing this to the child and that, as a result, Amy would not be accepted in the family in the way that the other children were.

Ultimately, the foster carer established a good relationship with Amy's mother and they used the Internet to find information about acceptable foods and supplements. The social worker reports that, "nothing was totally acceptable to the mother but she knew that she had to compromise, if she was ever going to get the baby back and return to her community". The rest of that community, including Amy's father, remained very angry. They wrote lengthy letters to the local paper and to children's services, quoting from their religious teachings. They took the view that the statutory agencies had intruded on their human rights, in terms of freedom to practise their religion and to have a family life.

Once an acceptable feeding regime had been established, Amy was returned to her parents' care and her name removed from the child protection register.

'Clerical' abuse and safeguarding systems within faith communities

Many Christian faith communities have, during the past decade, established internal child protection procedures and systems for cooperation with relevant statutory services (www.ccpas.co.uk; Nolan, 2001; Gamble, 2002; Methodist Church Connexional Team, 2003; Church of England, 2004; COPCA, 2006; Kennison, 2008). They have done so, in part, in the context of a growing recognition of the issues and, in part, in response to public pressure following a series of well-publicised 'scandals', particularly in relation to how the Roman Catholic and Anglican hierarchies have responded to the sexual abuse of children and young people by individual priests, such as Father Thomas Doherty in the Diocese of Salford (Binns, 1998) and Father Michael Hill in the Diocese of Arundel and Brighton (Studd et al, 2002). (See also Plante, 2004; BBC, 2007a.)

There are also several local initiatives within Muslim communities to promote child protection in mosques and madrasas – for example, in Lancashire, West Yorkshire and South Wales. The Muslim Parliament of Great Britain (2006) offers guidance on developing child protection procedures in these contexts, while the Blackburn with Darwen Area and Lancashire Area Child Protection Committees have joined with the Lancashire and Blackburn Councils of Mosques to produce relevant guidance (available online at www.blackburn.gov.uk/server.php?show=ConWebDoc.1076&s etPaginate=No).

Such developments have resulted in at least a greater awareness of the issues within many faith communities. However, at the same time, serious concerns are still expressed regarding the ability of faith organisations to deal appropriately with child abuse, especially when the alleged or proven perpetrator is in a position of authority (see, for example, MACSAS, 2006; Gilligan, 2009). At least one Roman Catholic bishop suggests that clerical sexual abuse has occurred in "an *unhealthy* church atmosphere", which has helped build "a *climate of abuse*" (Robinson, 2007: 16, emphasis added), while Siddiqui (2006: 1) suggests that "The Muslim community is at present in a state of denial – denial of the fact that child abuse takes place in places of worship including in mosques, *madrasas* (mosque schools) and families".

Cumberlege (2007) reports generally positive progress in the Catholic Church in England and Wales. However, five years after the Bishops' Council announced its commitment to fully implement the recommendations of Nolan (2001) (*Independent Catholic News*, 2001), Cumberlege (2007: 22) notes concern that "Bishops and Congregational Leaders may be minimising the distressing consequences, the harmful impact and the anguish that follows in the wake of child abuse" and that "This ... has impeded the delivery of consistently good – let alone excellent – safeguarding arrangements" (2.21). The report also notes that:

> The '*paramountcy principle*' which places the child's welfare as the paramount consideration, is well established in family law but is not unequivocally accepted within the Church. There is dispute and perceived inconsistencies in its implementation particularly when it comes to the Church's response to allegations of abuse against priests. (Cumberlege, 2007: 4, emphasis in original)

At the same time, there is a noticeable discrepancy between the total number of Catholic priests known to have been convicted of criminal offences against children and sentenced to serve a term of imprisonment of 12 months or more and the number reported by the Catholic Office for the Protection of Children and Vulnerable Adults (COPCA) and its successors as laicised, in line with Recommendation 78 of Nolan (2001). Two laicisations were reported in both 2003 and 2004, but none in 2002, 2005 or 2006 (see COPCA annual reports 2002-07 available via 'Documents' at www. csas.uk.net/), while Cumberlege (2007) makes no mention of 'laicisation'. Controversy, also, continues around the financial support that some dioceses have provided to clergy convicted of offences against children (BBC, 2002), the provision of accommodation for such perpetrators in property owned by a diocese and the failure of some dioceses to inform the public about the ongoing canonical status of perpetrators.

There is evidence to suggest that abuse within the context of faith communities often has additional or specific impacts on victims. Those involved in work with survivors report that, although churches and other religious groups may offer help and assistance in their recovery, particular aspects of Christian teaching may be extremely unhelpful to victims (Milgrom and Schoener, 1987; Armstrong, 1991; Kennedy, 1995; Crompton, 1996, 1998; Flynn, 2008; Farrell, 2009). Farrell (2009: 39) reports that a majority of research participants considered that 'God' had been "integral within the abuse". Kennedy (2000, 2003), following Carlson Brown and Parker (1989) and Redmond in Manlowe (1995), argues that victims' beliefs may cause them to see suffering as redemptive and encourage acceptance of abuse. She notes that: "There is a strong Christian message that the adult is not to be questioned" (Kennedy, 2003: 3) and that God is male. She also suggests that there is an undercurrent of belief that males are more God-like and that, for some, the experience of abuse, especially by clergy, is experienced not only as betrayal by trusted authority figures, but also as abuse by God. On the basis of her work with mainly female Christian survivors, Kennedy (2003: 4) concludes that:

> Victims of abuse find it incredibly difficult to understand why it is that God/Jesus did not protect them. They blame God/Jesus for their abuse. It's quite something to feel betrayed by your human family, but really huge to feel betrayed by an all-powerful deity.

In cases of abuse by clergy, there is an often-repeated pattern of victims not disclosing abuse until they are mature adults – sometimes waiting until their parents have died or until separate and public disclosures have been made by others. Victims and survivors speak of both their difficulties in making disclosures and the immediacy of the impact of perpetrators' abuse of them, even 30 years after the event. Asked about his decision to come forward to the police, one victim said:

> It's something I had to do. It's not been easy. I'll never know the true effect it's had because it has stolen my childhood. It has stolen

my education. I don't know what I would have gone on to be. It's like it was just yesterday. (BBC, 2008)

Victims' delay in making disclosures is also indicative of the extreme powerlessness they have felt. However, cases of so-called 'historical' abuse by clergy continue to result in convictions, as in the cases of Rev David Smith in the Anglican Diocese of Bath and Wells and Father William Green in the Catholic Diocese of Salford. Smith was convicted in May 2007 of 12 offences, including ten of indecent assault, committed between 1983 and 2001 against children then aged less than 16 years (BBC, 2007b). Green was convicted in August 2008 of 27 offences of indecent assault and indecency committed between 1968 and 1987 against children then aged between eight and 15 years (*Manchester Evening News*, 2008). Those abused were giving evidence as adults in their 30s, 40s and 50s.

Child abuse linked to beliefs in spirit possession

Beliefs in spirit possession and accusations of witchcraft, especially in the context of Pentecostal Christian churches, have played a role in a small number of high-profile cases of physical and emotional abuse of children (Stobart, 2006; Loweth, 2007, 2008; Gilligan, 2008). They have led to calls for legislation to make it an offence for anyone to make such accusations or to carry out any form of ritual or rite connected with them (AFRUCA, 2006, 2007). Moreover, in the case of Victoria Climbié, it is apparent from Laming (2003) that such beliefs played a significant role in the life and perceptions of her aunt and some role in Victoria's death. The media has also reported extensively on cases such as those of 'Child B' who was cut, beaten, kicked, starved and whipped and had chilli peppers rubbed in her eyes, in the context of being accused of being a witch (Dodd, 2005), and of a father jailed for five years after branding his son with a steam iron and forcing chilli powder into his mouth "to drive the devil out" (Davies, 2006).

In the context of migrants to Britain, Africans Unite Against Child Abuse (AFRUCA) (2007: 12) stresses that the majority of churches and mosques are "decent places of worship providing their congregation with spiritual support and assistance in settling into their new lives in the UK", but also points to a minority of faith organisations "with ulterior motives" who will "not engage in anyway or form with statutory agencies" and are:

> ... promoting negative practices towards children, including scapegoating as witches and carrying out extreme exorcism rites on victims or asking them to be sent home to be killed or to die.

Stobart (2006) provides the only systematic analysis of relevant cases, to date. She analysed 38 cases, involving 47 children. She noted that boys and girls are equally at risk and that the majority of the children involved are aged between eight and 11 years. Twenty cases involved 'Christian' households and five 'Muslim' households. Churches had some involvement in 16 cases and mosques in three cases. Stobart (2006) notes that this involvement was usually characterised by matters such as carers' requests for exorcism or fasting, or a religious leader 'diagnosing' the child. (Five children alleged being beaten in a place of worship.) Her research highlights the fact that children "with a difference", and especially disabled children, are particularly vulnerable to accusations and abuse and that in only three of 25 possible cases was a sibling also abused. She comments that:

> When family troubles begin or are exacerbated, a child displaying behaviour the family views as problematic (establishing individuality through to disobedience) or the disabled child, is more vulnerable to being accused. (Stobart, 2006: 20)

AFRUCA (2007: 7) emphasises the need to take account of the variety of abuse to which a child 'diagnosed' as a witch or as possessed by the devil is inevitably exposed, especially "Psychological and emotional abuse: in the form of verbal abuse, curses, and the knowledge that one is hated by everyone because one is a witch". At the same time, although in the cases analysed by Stobart (2006) all but one of the families are first- or second-generation migrants, beliefs in spirit possession are not confined to African or other minority ethnic communities in Britain. They are found among almost all ethnic groups and communities. Hinduism, Judaism, Roman Catholicism, Islam and Anglicanism all have rites of exorcism (Sikhism and Jainism are, in fact, the only major religious faiths that do not allow for the possibility of spirit possession). Moreover, despite campaigning by AFRUCA and others, the official view in Britain is that beliefs in spirit possession do not necessarily result in child abuse. Hence, although DfES (2007) asserts that safeguarding professionals need to be able to identify any links between individual cases of abuse and individual faith leaders as well as any relevant wider belief, faith or community practices, Stobart (2006), with the support of the then Minister for Children, recommended providing places of worship with information about 'good practice' in "praying for", "delivering" or "exorcising" children.

'Tariq'

In the case of 'Tariq' (see Inset 2), the social worker recognised that she needed to overcome her initial fears and prejudices in order both to understand what had happened and to assess the risks effectively. As envisaged in the framework suggested in Chapter Three, she needed, in particular, to be self-aware and reflexive about her responses to unfamiliar beliefs and practices; to give Tariq's family opportunities to discuss their beliefs; to listen respectfully to these; to recognise her own lack of knowledge; to seek relevant knowledge about beliefs in 'jinns' and exorcisms in Muslim communities (Philips, 1997, 2006; Dein et al, 2008); and to revise her plans and assumptions about Tariq's presenting behaviour in accordance with the knowledge and understanding she had gained.

Inset 2: 'Tariq'

'Tariq' is 14 years old. He appears to be autistic, but has never had a formal diagnosis. Tariq's family has lived in Britain for about 22 years. However, until five years ago, his mother did not leave her home and her mother-in-law did all the shopping. Tariq's mother was responsible for the housework and the cooking, but Tariq's grandmother was responsible for most of the day-to-day care of the children. Tariq's mother comes from a very small village in rural Pakistan. She has had no formal education and cannot read or write. Tariq's father spends long periods of time abroad. Members of the family describe themselves as being from a very strict sect of Islam, but, unlike other male members of the family, Tariq does not attend mosque. The social worker said, "The family feel that he has no awareness of himself in terms of being a Muslim. They feel that he doesn't really understand about religion."

Two years ago, Tariq and his parents visited Pakistan for four months. When Tariq returned to school in Britain, staff reported his behaviour as "unmanageable" and he was educated in isolation. (He was withdrawing himself and lying down in a back room.) When teachers tried to encourage him to join in activities, he responded with very difficult behaviour and, for the first time ever, went towards someone to hit them. The school felt that it could not contain him. This was the point at which Tariq's case had been allocated to the current social worker.

During the social worker's assessment it emerged that, while in Pakistan, Tariq and his mother had stayed in the mother's village where she had taken him to a 'holy man' who told her that Tariq was possessed by two spirits; one was

▶

an 'evil jinn', the other was a 'good jinn'. One was telling him to love his family and be good to his family and the other one was telling him to be nasty and horrible to them. The holy man said that they would need to perform a ritual to try and purge Tariq of the evil spirit. The social worker said, "Now as far as I'm aware, it was something about getting him up in the middle of the night ... and then lots of people standing around and chanting or singing, standing around him and I think there was some sort of ceremonial breaking of something; whether it was a stick or a glass jar I'm really not sure. The result of this was that Tariq's behaviour really went through the roof and that reinforced mum's belief because she felt that it was the evil jinn fighting to stay in his body." The social worker describes the mother as having "utter faith" in the holy man, who also performed a ritual on her to deal with her chronic illness. (At the end of this ritual he said, "You don't have [chronic illness] any more, you don't have to have your tablets", so she stopped taking her medication for about three months and became ill.)

Adult abuse

Some of the issues presented in relation to children and young people can also affect adults:

> Each case of elder abuse is different and occurs for many reasons, and is potentially influenced by the abuser's individual personality, family of origin, social class, race or ethnicity, religion or religiosity, age and gender. Elder abuse takes place within different sub-cultural contexts which influences attitudes and values with regards to the elderly as well as the definition of acts of commission and omission as right and wrong. (Kosberg et al, 2003: 84)

There have been long-standing debates about how best to define adult abuse (Eastman, 1984, 1994; Fulmer and O'Malley, 1987; Royal College of Nursing, 1991; Bennett et al, 1997; Mowlam et al, 2007). Although *No secrets*, the guidance for local authorities that sets out the policies and procedures for the protection of vulnerable adults from abuse (DH, 2000), *does* provide key definitions of the terms 'abuse' and 'vulnerable adult', current government thinking suggests that revisions may take place following the consultation to review *No secrets* (DH, 2008).

The definition states:

> Abuse may consist of a single act or repeated acts. It may be physical, verbal or psychological, it may be an act of neglect or an omission

to act, or it may occur when a vulnerable person is persuaded to enter into a financial or sexual transaction to which he or she has not consented, or cannot consent. Abuse can occur in any relationship and may result in significant harm to, or exploitation of, the person subjected to it. (DH, 2000: 9)

A vulnerable adult is defined as a person aged 18 or over:

... who is or who may be in need of community care services by reason of mental or other disability, age or illness; and who is or who may be unable to take care of him or herself, or unable to protect him or herself against significant harm or exploitation. (Lord Chancellor's Department, 1997: para 87)

In its annual report 2007–08, the Commission for Social Care Inspection (CSCI, 2008) reported an increase in the percentage of abuse cases, from 13.9% in 2004–05 to 23.1% in 2007–08. As well as there being an actual rise in incidents, this increase may, in part, be attributed to a growing awareness and higher profile of the issue, while some poor practice issues may have been wrongly categorised and referred as *potential* abuse cases (CSCI, 2008: 27).

The complex nature of adult abuse has meant that it is likely that few victims ever report the abuse and, therefore, it has been difficult to ascertain an accurate picture of the scale and prevalence of adult abuse in England (this is comparable to other western countries). A recent report identified that the circumstances and personal characteristics of the individual were important and that having strong religious and spiritual beliefs was a major source of support and could help to protect them from enduring harmful effects (Mowlam et al, 2007: 10).

In researching for this section of the chapter, the authors found it difficult to find cases for inclusion that related directly to religion. Factors that may prevent such cases coming to the attention of social workers or adult safeguarding officers may include the hidden and sensitive nature of the topic, an acceptance by members of that religious community that certain cultural practices and customs are acceptable and, therefore, are not 'abusive' or that the types of mistreatment (listed below) do not occur. In Chapter Seven we discuss the case of 'Javid', who is a practising Sufi who presents with some alarming and worrying symptoms that result in his family carrying out a 'spiritual cleansing' against his will. Clearly, his family believe that this ritual will help to alleviate his symptoms and drive out any bad spirits. In his case, matters of capacity and consent do not feature for the family and they genuinely believe that they are acting in the best interests of Javid. The social worker has a duty to protect Javid and needs to work with the family to persuade them to appreciate that the 'spiritual cleansing' is likely to exacerbate his symptoms and that they could be endangering themselves and Javid by their actions. There may be several cases of this type occurring within a number of religious traditions but, up until now, this does not appear to have come to the attention of local safeguarding boards.

What is 'adult abuse'?

No secrets (DH, 2000) identifies the following different forms of abuse:

- **physical abuse,** including hitting, slapping, pushing, kicking, misuse of medication, restraint, or inappropriate sanctions;
- **sexual abuse,** including rape and sexual assault or sexual acts to which the vulnerable adult has not consented, or could not consent, or was pressured into consenting to;
- **psychological abuse,** including emotional abuse, threats of harm or abandonment, deprivation of contact, humiliation, blaming, controlling, intimidation, coercion, harassment, verbal abuse, isolation or withdrawal from services or supportive networks;
- **financial or material abuse,** including theft, fraud, exploitation, pressure in connection with wills, property or inheritance or financial transactions, or the misuse or misappropriation of property, possessions or benefits;
- **neglect and acts of omission,** including ignoring medical or physical care needs, failure to provide access to appropriate health, social care or educational services, the withholding of the necessities of life, such as medication, adequate nutrition and heating;
- **discriminatory abuse,** including racist, sexist, that based on a person's disability, and other forms of harassment, slurs or similar treatment (DH, 2000: 9).

The guidance states that any allegation should be treated with an open mind and, in order to justify intervention, the degree of seriousness of the abuse must be considered, the vulnerability of the individual, the nature and extent of the abuse, the length of time it has been occurring, the impact on the individual and the risk of repeated or increasingly serious acts on this individual or others.

Financial abuse

The Centre for Policy on Ageing carried out a literature review on the financial abuse of older people on behalf of Help the Aged (Crosby et al, 2007). It is difficult to identify the extent of financial abuse but O'Keefe et al (2007) found between 227,000 and 342,000 people aged 66 or over living at home in the UK (0.66% of older people) reported experiencing financial abuse by a close friend, relative or care worker in the past year. Over 50% of financial abuse cases were perpetrated by a son or daughter and nearly 70% by a family member. A number of studies suggest that financial abuse is one of the most prevalent types of abuse (Fitzgerald, 2004; O'Keefe et al, 2007). 'Gladys' (Inset 3) is one such case.

Inset 3: 'Gladys'

'Gladys' was 78 years old and had found it difficult to manage the stairs following a hip replacement. She decided to sell her house and went to live with her daughter in her bungalow. Her daughter worked full time and was not able to care for Gladys during the day so she contacted the local authority adult services office to find out what help could be offered. The daughter spoke to the duty social worker and confided that she was very worried about her mother's mental state, as she believed she was talking to the 'spirits'. The social worker visited Gladys but found her to be perfectly rational. The daughter indicated that she could no longer care for her mother while she was in this state of mind. The social worker tried to keep an open mind and to assess Gladys on that basis. In order to determine the veracity of the daughter's claim, the social worker arranged for Gladys to stay in short-term care for two weeks in order for her to be assessed by staff. Over this period, none of the staff observed any unusual behaviour. However, Gladys told staff that she had given the money from the sale of her home to her daughter to look after her. The finance department was asked to investigate Gladys's financial affairs and, after she decided that she wanted to stay in permanent residential care, they were able to recoup her money in order for her to pay for her care.

The relevance of Gladys's case for inclusion in this book is more to do with the attempt by her daughter to 'cloud' the issue by exploiting her mother's religious beliefs and the practitioner's potential prejudices about these. The receptivity and open-mindedness of the social worker to the claim allowed her to be accepting of different explanations. She was able to arrange for care home staff to determine the truth behind the allegation and this led to challenging the daughter's account and uncovering financial misappropriation of her mother's assets.

Inset 4: 'Anne'

'Anne' had been caring for her husband who had dementia for a number of years. She was worried about her financial situation, as she had to contribute to the care home fees whenever her husband stayed for respite care. Over the past three years she had been enticed to send money to claim winnings on overseas lotteries and for different charms promising good luck and fortune. She was receiving over 20 letters each day and sent off four or five cheques for small amounts of money each week. Anne's sister found out and tried to get her to redirect her mail. Anne refused to take notice and continued with her payments. Anne fell and broke her leg and this meant that she could not care for her husband. Her husband's social worker visited her during her rehabilitation and she confided her financial worries and that she had paid over £5,000 to claim different prizes and for the lucky charms. She agreed that she would allow her mail to be redirected to her nephew's home and allow him to vet her mail. Anne returned home and, although she was not able to recoup any of her money, her family were able to protect her from further scams.

In Anne's case, the social worker was able to gain her confidence by being sympathetic to her situation and by encouraging her to talk about her financial worries. He did not dismiss her belief in good luck charms but tried to be realistic and alert her to the dangers of sending money to confidence tricksters who took advantage of people in her situation. He was accepting of her belief system but, on the other hand, identified that she was at risk of financial exploitation. As an outsider, he was able to work with Anne and together they identified ways that her family could offer her some support and protection.

Speaking out

A recent study carried out on behalf of Age Concern Scotland (Bowes et al, 2008) reported that 46 (81%) older people from black and minority ethnic (BME) backgrounds who were interviewed said they would do nothing if they were being mistreated. The issues involved in not reporting mistreatment need to be looked at in culturally sensitive ways. All voluntary sector and advocacy groups and religious organisations could play an important part in educating others about abuse and encouraging those affected to speak out and be offered better protection.

It is not only those living in domestic settings who do not report or alert others to an abusive relationship or situation. Furness (2006, 2009) interviewed 19 care home managers and 19 residents to find out their views about inspection and regulation, and their understanding of abuse and ways to better protect older people. Recommendations included the need for care homes to develop ways of encouraging resident comment about their experiences of living in care homes and also for staff to listen, value and respond to feedback. Managers can underestimate the effects and impact of abusive practices and consequently these can be overlooked and perpetuated in daily routines. Furness developed a framework to aid managers to deal with allegations of abuse to be used alongside local authority procedures (see Figure 6.1). The assessment of the situation needs to be informed by cultural and ethnic perspectives. Anetzberger et al (1996, cited in Kosberg et al, 2003) reported that the perception of the existence and severity of elder abuse differed between those of different cultural backgrounds in the US and identified some of the difficulties and challenges in conducting cross-cultural and cross-national research on elder abuse. Furness (2006, 2008) reported that managers rated different types of abuse as more serious than others and residents identified some practices as abusive whereas managers did not. Although 78% of the residents indicated that they would report concerns to the manager, only 50% believed that their concerns would be taken seriously. Clearly, it is important for the manager or any other person investigating an allegation of abuse to find out the victim's feelings, views and level of distress. A Canadian small-scale study found that, if nurses perceived hurt to the patient, they would class it as abuse (Hirst, 2002). These two small-scale studies provide an insight into the dangers of making assumptions about the nature and extent of abuse based on subjective opinions that will not help to prevent or deal with deliberate or unintentional acts of abuse.

The role of faith leaders in confronting and dealing with elder abuse has received little attention in Britain. A pilot study in Canada found out that although religious leaders were well placed to help older people suffering abuse, there were a number of barriers that prevented them from acting and speaking out. If abuse had been disclosed by either abusers or victims in confession, clergy felt duty-bound to maintain confidentiality rather than seek out other possible interventions such as alerting family, friends and outside agencies. Community protectiveness was perceived as a barrier that prevented disclosure. This included public perceptions of the faith leader and of the faith community itself. The authors advocated for religious leaders of all faiths to play a proactive role in preventing elder abuse and offering support to those affected by abuse (Podnieks and Wilson, 2003, 2004).

Figure 6.1

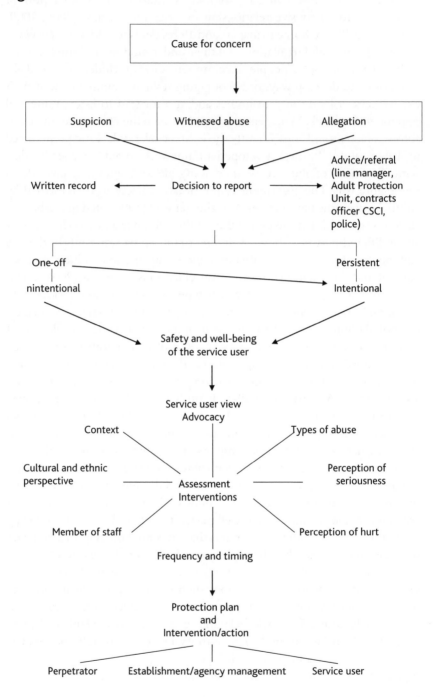

Key questions

(1) Do you have the knowledge you need to respond to abuse within a religious context?

(2) Do you expect there to be relatively more or less abuse in faith communities than elsewhere?

(3) How can religious or other beliefs help someone who has been abused?

(4) How would you respond if someone told you that they blamed God for their being abused by others?

(5) Should there be legislation to make it an offence for anyone to make accusations that someone is 'possessed' or to carry out any form of ritual or rite connected with such accusations?

References

ADSS (Association of Directors of Social Services) (2005) *Safeguarding adults: A national framework of standards for good practice and outcomes in adult protection work*, London: ADSS.

AFRUCA (Africans Unite Against Child Abuse) (2006) *Afruca proposal for a UK law against diagnosing children as witches* (www.bnlf.org.uk/Documents/Afruca_Econsultation_feb07.pdf).

AFRUCA (2007) *Response to the government's consultation on the draft guidance – safeguarding children from abuse linked to a belief in spirit possession* (www.afruca.org/documents/AFRUCA%20spirit%20possession%20consultation%20response.pdf).

Annetzberger, G., Korbin, J.E. and Tomota, S.K. (1996) 'Defining elder mistreatment in four ethnic groups across two generations', *Journal of Cross-Cultural Gerontology*, **11**(2), 187-212.

Armstrong, H. (1991). *Taking care: A church response to children, adults and abuse*. London: National Children's Bureau.

Baker, D. (2008) 'Circumcision "the unkindest cut of all"', *The Times*, 24 March (www.timesonline.co.uk/tol/life_and_style/health/article3598023.ece).

BBC (2002) 'Child abuse priest housed by Church', *BBC News Online*, 9 February (http://news.bbc.co.uk/1/low/uk/1810527.stm).

BBC (2007a) 'Archbishop promises abuse review', *BBC News Channel*, 25 May (http://news.bbc.co.uk/1/hi/uk/6690273.stm).

BBC (2007b) 'Vicar jailed for child sex abuse', *BBC News Channel*, 3 May (http://news.bbc.co.uk/1/hi/england/bristol/6620445.stm).

BBC (2008) 'Priest "'stole victim's childhood"', *BBC News Channel*, 1 October (http://news.bbc.co.uk/1/hi/england/manchester/7647318. stm).

Bennett, G., Kingston, P. and Penhale, B. (1997) *The dimensions of elder abuse: Perspectives for practitioners*, Basingstoke: Macmillan.

Binns, A. (1998) 'Investigation call', *Todmorden News*, 27 February (http:// caads.blogspot.com/).

BMA (British Medical Association) (2006) *The law and ethics of male circumcision – guidance for doctors*, London: British Medical Association (www. bma.org.uk/ap.nsf/AttachmentsByTitle/PDFmalecircumcision2006/ $FILE/Circumcision.pdf).

Bowes, A., Avan, G. and Macintosh, S. (2008) *They put up with it – what else can they do? Mistreatment of black and minority ethnic older people and the service response*, Edinburgh: Age Concern Scotland (www. ageconcernandhelptheagedscotland.org.uk/documents/115).

Carlson Brown, J. and Parker, R. (1989) 'For God so loved the world', in R. Carlson, J. Brown and C.R. Bohn (eds) *Christianity, patriarchy, and abuse: A feminist critique*, Cleveland, OH: The Pilgrim Press.

Centre for Policy on Ageing (2008) *The financial abuse of older people*, London: Centre for Policy on Ageing.

Church of England (2004) *Protecting all God's children. The child protection policy for the Church of England* (3rd edn), London: Church House Publishing (http://cofe.anglican.org/info/papers/protectingchildren.pdf).

COPCA (Catholic Office for the Protection of Children and Vulnerable Adults) (2006) *Annual Report 2006*, Birmingham: COPCA (www.copca. org.uk/csas/publicdocuments/COPCAAnnualReportfinal2006.pdf).

Crompton, M. (1996) *Children, spirituality and religion: A training pack*, London: CCETSW.

Crompton, M. (1998) *Children, spirituality, religion and social work*, Aldershot: Ashgate.

Crosby, G., Clark, A., Hayes, R., Jones, K. and Lievesley, N. (2007) *The financial abuse of older people: A review from the literature*, London: Help the Aged (http://policy.helptheaged.org.uk/NR/rdonlyres/F548A288-161D-4BC7-84EF-CF03069CE146/0/financialabuse240408.pdf).

CSCI (2008) *Annual report and accounts 2007–08*, London: The Stationery Office (www.cqc.org.uk/_db/_documents/7738-CSCI-AR-1bm.pdf).

Cumberlege Commission Report (2007) *Safeguarding with confidence – keeping children and vulnerable adults safe in the Catholic Church*, London: Incorporated Catholic Truth Society (www.cathcom.org/mysharedaccounts/ cumberlege/report/Foreword.asp?FontSize=13).

Dalley, G. (2008) *Briefing note on the new Health and Social Care Bill*, London: Relatives and Residents Association (www.relres.org/pdf/policy/BRIEFING_NOTE_ON_THE_HEALTH_AND_SOCIAL_CARE_BILL.pdf).

Davies, C. (2006*)* 'Pastor is arrested after inquiry into claims of cruelty to "child witches"', Telegraph.co.uk, 14 January (www.telegraph.co.uk/news/main.jhtml?xml=/news/2006/01/13/nwitch13.xml&sSheet=/news/2006/01/13/ixhome.html).

Dein, S., Alexander, M. and Napier, D. (2008) '*Jinn*, psychiatry and contested notions of misfortune among East London Bangladeshis', *Transcultural Psychiatry*, **45**(1), 31–55.

DfES (Department for Education and Skills) (2006) *Working together to safeguard children: A guide to inter-agency working to safeguard and promote the welfare of children*, London: The Stationery Office (www.everychildmatters.gov.uk/_files/AE53C8F9D7AEB1B23E403514A6C1B17D.pdf).

DfES (2007) *Safeguarding children from abuse linked to a belief in spirit possession*, Nottingham: DfES Publications (www.everychildmatters.gov.uk/_files/02469E1FF4089D7030FBD0E11815C511.pdf).

DH (Department of Health) (2000) *No secrets: Guidance on developing and implementing multi-agency policies and procedures to protect vulnerable adults from abuse*, London: The Stationery Office (www.dh.gov.uk/en/Publicationsandstatistics/Publications/PublicationsPolicyAndGuidance/DH_4008486).

DH (2008) *Safeguarding adults: A consultation on the review of the 'No secrets' guidance*, London: DH (www.dh.gov.uk/en/Consultations/Liveconsultations/DH_089098).

Dodd, V. (2005) 'Police investigate religious links after witchcraft abuse of child, 8', *The Guardian*, 4 June (www.guardian.co.uk/uk/2005/jun/04/ukcrime.children).

Doyle, C. (2001) 'Surviving and coping with emotional abuse in childhood', *Clinical Psychology and Psychiatry*, **6**(3), 387–402.

Doyle, C. (2006) *Working with abused children: From theory to practice* (3rd edn), Basingstoke: Palgrave Macmillan.

Eastman, M. (1984) *Old age abuse*, London: Age Concern England.

Eastman, M. (1994) *Old age abuse*, London: Age Concern England/Chapman and Hall.

Edwards, H. (2007) *Faith, religion and safeguarding*, NSPCC Internal Briefing Paper (www.nspcc.org.uk/inform/trainingandconsultancy/consultancy/helpandadvice/faithreligionandsafeguarding_wdf47840.pdf).

Farrell, D. (2004) 'An historical viewpoint of sexual abuse perpetrated by clergy and religious', *Journal of Religion and Abuse*, **6**(2), 41–80.

Farrell, D. (2009) 'Sexual abuse perpetrated by Roman Catholic priests and religious', *Mental Health, Religion and Culture*, **12**(1), 39-53.

Fitzgerald, G. (2004) *Hidden voices: Older people's experience of abuse – an analysis of calls to the Action on Elder Abuse helpline*, London: Action on Elder Abuse/Help the Aged.

Flynn, K.A. (2008) 'In their own voices: women who were sexually abused by members of the clergy', *Journal of Child Sexual Abuse*, **17**(3), 216-37.

Fulmer, T. and O'Malley, T. (1987) *Inadequate care of the elderly: A health care perspective on abuse and neglect*, New York: Springer.

Furness, S. (2006) 'Recognising and addressing elder abuse in care homes: views from residents and managers', *Journal of Adult Protection*, **8**(1), 33-49.

Furness, S. (2009) 'A hindrance or a help? The contribution of inspection to the quality of care in homes for older people', *British Journal of Social Work*, **29**(3), 488-505.

Gamble, D. (2002) *Time for action: Sexual abuse, the churches and a new dawn for survivors*, London: Churches Together in Britain and Ireland.

Gilligan, P. with Akhtar, S. (2006) 'Cultural barriers to the disclosure of child sexual abuse in Asian communities: listening to what women say', *British Journal of Social Work*, **36**(8), 1361-77.

Gilligan, P. (2008) 'Child abuse and spirit possession: not just an issue for African migrants', *childRIGHT*, **245**(April), 28-31.

Gilligan, P. (forthcoming, December 2009) 'Faith-based approaches', in M. Gray and S. Webb (eds) *Ethics and value perspectives in social work*, London: Palgrave MacMillan.

Grotberg, E. (1997) 'The international resilience project', in M. John (ed) *A charge against society: The child's right to protection*, London: Jessica Kingsley, pp 19-32.

Hinchley, G. and Patrick, K. (2007) 'Is infant male circumcision an abuse of the rights of the child? Yes/no', *British Medical Journal*, **335**(1180), 8 December, doi:10.1136/bmj.39406.520498.AD (www.bmj.com/cgi/content/full/335/7631/1180).

Hirst, S.P. (2002) 'Defining resident abuse within the culture of long-term care institutions', *Clinical Nursing Research*, **11**(3), 267-84.

Independent Catholic News (2001) 'Bishops pledge to fully implement child protection report', 16 November (www.indcatholicnews.com/news.php?viewStory=13606).

Kennedy, M. (1995) *Submission to the National Commission of Inquiry into the Prevention of Child Abuse*, London: Christian Survivors of Sexual Abuse.

Kennedy, M. (2000) 'Christianity and child sexual abuse – the survivors' voice leading to change', *Child Abuse Review*, **9**(1), 124-41.

Kennedy, M. (2003) 'Christianity and child sexual abuse – survivors informing the care of children following abuse', paper presented to Royal College of Psychiatrists (www.rcpsych.ac.uk/pdf/Margaret%20Kennedy %201.11.03%20Christianity%20and%20Child%20Sexual%20Abuse%20- %20Survivors%20informing%20the%20care%20of%20children%20follow ing%20abuse.pdf).

Kennison, P. (2008) 'Child abuse in a religious context: the abuse of trust', in P. Kennison and A. Goodman (eds) *Children as victims*, Exeter: Learning Matters, pp 61-77.

Kosberg, J.L., Lowenstein, A., Garcia, G. and Biggs, S. (2003) 'Study of elder abuse within diverse cultures', in E. Podnieks, J.L. Kosberg and A. Lowenstein (eds) *Elder abuse: Selected papers from the Prague World Congress on Family Violence*, New York: The Haworth Press, pp 71-89.

Laming, Lord (2003) *The Victoria Climbié Inquiry: Report of an inquiry*, London: HMSO (www.victoria-climbie-inquiry.org.uk/finreport/finreport. htm).

Lord Chancellor's Department (1997) *Who decides? Making decisions on behalf of mentally incapacitated adults*, London: Department for Constitutional Affairs, HMSO (www.dca.gov.uk/menincap/meninfr.htm).

Loweth, J. (2007) '"Preacher" tortured his sons', *Bradford Telegraph and Argus*, 14 November (www.thetelegraphandargus.co.uk/search/display. var.1831039.0.preacher_tortured_his_sons.php).

Loweth, J. (2008) '"Tyrant" dad may never be freed', *Bradford Telegraph and Argus*, 24 January (www.thetelegraphandargus.co.uk/search/display. var.1989831.0.tyrant_dad_may_never_be_freed.php).

Macey, M. (1999) 'Religion, male violence and the control of women: Pakistani Muslim men in Bradford', *Gender and Development*, **7**(1), 48-55.

Manchester Evening News (2008) 'Pervert priest jailed', 1 October (www. manchestereveningnews.co.uk/news/s/1069987_pervert_priest_jailed).

Manlowe J. (1995) *Faith born of seduction: Sexual trauma, body image, and religion*, New York: University Press.

Methodist Church Connexional Team (2003) *Safeguarding – a policy for good practice in the care of children and young people 2003*, London: Methodist Publishing House.

Milgrom, J.H. and Schoener, G.R. (1987) 'Responding to clients who have been sexually exploited by counselors, therapists, and clergy', in M.D. Pellauer, B. Chester and J.A. Boyajian (eds) *Sexual assault and abuse: A handbook for clergy and religious professionals*, San Francisco, CA: Harper and Row, pp 209-18.

MACSAS (Minister and Clergy Sexual Abuse Survivors) (2006) '*Time to hear*': *Submission to Cumberlege Commission* (www.macsas.org.uk/PDFs/ Resources/Time%20to%20Hear.pdf).

Moules, S. (2006) 'The Catholic churches' response to allegations of child abuse', in Muslim Parliament of Great Britain, *Child protection in faith-based environments: A guideline report*, London: Muslim Parliament of Great Britain.

Mowlam, A., Tennant, R., Dixon, J. and McCreadie, C. (2007) *UK study of abuse and neglect of older people: Qualitative findings*, London: Comic Relief and the Department of Health (http://assets.comicrelief.com/cr09/docs/older_people_abuse_report.pdf).

Muslim Parliament of Great Britain (2006) *Child protection in faith-based environments: A guideline report*, London: Muslim Parliament of Great Britain (www.muslimparliament.org.uk/Documentation/ChildProtectionReport.pdf).

Nolan, Lord (2001) *A programme for action. Final report of the independent review on child protection in the Catholic Church in England and Wales*, London: Catholic Bishops' Conference of England and Wales (www.bishop-accountability.org/resources/resource-files/reports/NolanReport.pdf).

O'Keeffe, M., Hills, A., Doyle, M., McCreadie, C., Scholes, S., Constantine, R., Tinker, A., Manthorpe, J., Biggs, S. and Erens, B. (2007) *UK study of abuse and neglect of older people: Prevalence survey report*, London: National Centre for Social Research.

Parkinson, F. (1993) *Post traumatic stress,* London: Sheldon.

Perkins, D.F. and Jones, D.R. (2004) 'Risk behaviours and resiliency within physically abused children', *Child Abuse and Neglect*, **28**(5), 547-63.

Philips, A.A.B. (1997) *The exorcist tradition in Islam*, Sharjah, United Arab Emirates: Dar Al Fatah Printing.

Philips, A.A.B. (translator and annotator) (2006) *Ibn Taymeeyah's essay on the jinn* (2nd edn), Raleigh, NC: International Islamic Publishing House (http://islamicbookstore.com/b3163.html).

Plante, T.G. (ed) (2004) *Sin against the innocents: Sexual abuse by priests and the role of the Catholic Church*, Westport, CT: Praeger (www.questia.com/read/113147050?title=Preface).

Podnieks, E. and Wilson, S. (2003) 'Elder abuse awareness in faith communities: findings from a Canadian pilot study', in E. Podnieks, J.L. Kosberg and A. Lowenstein (eds) *Elder abuse: Selected papers from the Prague World Congress on Family Violence*, New York: The Haworth Press, pp 121-35.

Podnieks, E. and Wilson, S. (2004) 'Raising awareness of abuse of older persons: an issue for faith communities', in M. Brennan and D. Heiser (eds) *Spiritual assessment and intervention with older adults: Current directions and applications*, New York: The Haworth Pastoral Press, pp 55-86.

Rahman, A. and Toubia, N. (eds) (2000) *Female genital mutilation: A guide to laws and policies worldwide*, London: Zed Books.

Robinson, G. (2007) *Confronting power and sex in the Catholic Church Reclaiming the spirit of Jesus*, Melbourne: John Garratt Publishing.

Royal College of Nursing (1991) *Guidelines for nurses: Abuse and older people*, London: Royal College of Nursing.

Samad, Y. and Eade, J. (2002) *Community perceptions of forced marriage*, London: Community Liaison Unit, Foreign and Commonwealth Office (www.fco. gov.uk/resources/en/pdf/pdf1/fco_forcedmarriagereport121102).

Seidman, E. and Pedersen, S. (2003) 'Holistic contextual perspectives on risk, protection and competence among low-income urban adolescents', in S.S. Luthar (ed) *Resilience and vulnerability*, Cambridge: Cambridge University Press, pp 318-42.

Siddiqui, G. (2006) 'Breaking the taboo of child abuse', in Muslim Parliament of Great Britain, *Child protection in faith-based environments: A guideline report*, London: Muslim Parliament of Great Britain, pp 1-3.

Stobart, E. (2006) *Child abuse linked to accusations of 'possession' and 'witchcraft'*, London: DfES (www.dfes.gov.uk/research/data/uploadfiles/RR750. pdf).

Studd, H., Gledhill, R. and McDonald, C. (2002) 'Child abuse "hotspots" uncovered in five Catholic dioceses', *The Times*, 21 November (www. timesonline.co.uk/tol/news/uk/article833730.ece).

7

Mental health, religion and belief

> ... across all the major religions there seemed to be an acceptance that much of what we would describe as mental illness is, in fact, the result of spiritual activity and therefore the only effective way of dealing with such activity is to adopt supernatural means. (Copsey, 1997: 15)

Introduction

The starting point of this chapter is the notion that good health and mental well-being are vital ingredients that make up everyone's quality of life. Most of us will experience or be affected by some form of mental illness or distress over our lifetime. Our mental health can deteriorate rapidly in response to a range of life events including illness, genetic and personality dispositions, crisis and traumatic experiences, and can be relatively short-term or of an enduring nature. We all need to develop a sense of our own coping mechanisms in order to stand a better chance of dealing with life's challenges and stresses.

It is important to recognise, in this as in other fields, that many unusual beliefs concern power and those in positions of power. These can include religious beliefs about God or powerful agencies such as the FBI or governments. Referrals for professional help will also tend to stem from the presenting problem. Remaining person-centred, self-aware and reflexive about their own beliefs and those of others will help the worker to be receptive to other perspectives. Religious issues might emerge by asking open-ended questions and the worker needs to be mindful of not making assumptions or missing cues that will allow further probing (see Chapter Three). In terms of identifying coping strategies, it is important to find out to what degree religion is part of the problem (if at all) and to what degree it is or could be part of the solution (Pargament, 1997: 372). People might not be religious prior to hearing voices or exhibiting other unusual behaviour that is connected to religion, but they will try to make sense of their experience within their existing cultural reference points. Psychiatrists may have difficulty distinguishing between mystical and contemplative states, ecstatic and near-death or out-of-body experiences, and people who experience these states may fear being diagnosed or labelled as mad if they disclose these events to others (Loewenthal, 1995: 148). A recovery model approach is favoured by health and social work intervention teams where they work with people's own belief systems to support them to build a sense of resilience (Mental Health Foundation, 2007; Campbell et al, 2008). This means recognising and not negating people's experiences, using narratives as a way of asking the service user to explain their experiences and finding out the views of family members in order to determine how best to understand and support the individual.

'Omar's' case (Inset 1) illustrates the importance of finding out who has the appropriate knowledge and influence (if any) to effect change and how they can be co-opted to assist in the recovery process.

Inset 1: 'Omar'

'Omar' is 32 years old and married with four children. He has had a number of jobs and as a practising Muslim attends Friday prayers each week. About two years ago, his family started to become worried as he slept with a knife under his pillow and described seeing visions (the Prophet on a white horse) and hearing angels who instructed him to crash his car. At around the same time, his cousin who was a Sufi had spoken to Omar about his beliefs and Omar had become a Sufi. The social worker encouraged Omar to speak to his Sufi leader and to find out whether what he was describing was normal in a spiritual sense or whether he shared any worries about Omar's behaviour. It became clear that his behaviour was viewed as unusual and his sheikh agreed to help by talking to Omar about his visions so that the social worker could concentrate on Omar's recovery, his interactions with his children and his role in the household. (Omar's wife was doing all the household chores with help from Omar's father who used to take the children to school in the morning.) Omar's day revolved around prayer and reading the scriptures. The social worker encouraged Omar to speak to his sheikh about his role in his family, as the sheikh was also married with children. The family and the sheikh also encouraged Omar to take his medication. The medication did alleviate Omar's symptoms; however, he missed his spiritual experiences and kept stopping his medication to recreate the visions.

In 2000, the Mental Health Foundation published findings from a user-led study that identified people's strategies for living with mental distress. The most helpful strategies and supports reported were: relationships with others;

medication; physical exercise; religious and spiritual beliefs; money; personal strategies; and other activities such as hobbies, home and creative expression. Clearly, religion has the potential to support people through distressing times. Sharing experiences and finding and making connections through belonging to different types of self-help and support groups such as 'survivor'-led groups and the 'Hearing Voices' network have been instrumental in helping those with mental illness to cope and gain strength from others facing similar problems (Barker and Buchanan-Barker, 2008: 67).

The social worker dealing with 'Peter's' case needed to connect with people who saw the relevant issues from Peter's perspective and to make certain that he was aware of them as a potential source of support to him. To ensure that he helped Peter to remain safe within a supportive network, the worker also needed to recognise Peter's expertise about his own beliefs and to approach his professional responsibilities with an openness that accepted the importance of Peter's experiences, regardless of whether or not they appeared 'real' or 'rational'.

Inset 2: 'Peter'

'Peter' was aged 22 years when he was referred to the mental health team. His parents had divorced when he was 12 and he had an older sister and a younger brother. His family had not been particularly religious but he started to hear the voice of Jehovah instructing him to do penance. This could range from self-harm to a refusal to eat and drink. On one occasion he collapsed from hunger and had to be taken to hospital as he was dangerously dehydrated. The social worker engaged with Peter by talking about the scriptures and his interpretation of them, using this as a way to talk about harm and protection. Eventually, Peter and his family agreed to have some contact with the local Jehovah's Witness congregation. The social worker got in touch with them and they visited Peter at home. Gradually, he agreed to attend the services at Kingdom Hall. The congregation have been accepting and supportive towards Peter.

Chapter Two has already identified key legislation to orientate the reader to relevant law and policy relating to mental health. This chapter will not differentiate in detail between different mental health conditions, as there are numerous resources to help readers find out this information (Kumar and Clark, 2002; BBC Health, 2008; Mental Health Foundation, 2008; Archambeault, 2009). Instead, we will concentrate on the role of religion in aiding recovery (or not) and findings from relevant research in this area will be discussed with a view to opening up new and alternative ways of understanding and offering support. There are a number of useful websites listed at the end of this chapter that will help the reader to appreciate the importance of developing culturally sensitive approaches and services that will better meet the needs of their diverse service users.

Research findings

The relevance of religion and spirituality and their association with positive mental health outcomes has gained considerable interest and support (Loewentahl, 1995, 2006; Koenig et al, 2001; Swinton, 2001; Weaver et al, 2003; Merchant et al, 2008). The literature suggests that there has been considerably more interest among practitioners and researchers to explore the role of religion and spirituality in relation to mental health than in other areas of work, apart from perhaps in the field of loss and bereavement. There are a number of possible reasons for this. Fernando (2002: 41) argues that, although western psychiatry has been developed within a Christian culture, its secular approach with a separation between science and religion has dominated and has largely ignored the relationship between religion and spiritual concerns and mental illness/mental health. Fernando (1995, 2002) makes the distinction between western and eastern approaches to understanding mental distress and the dangers of western psychiatrists interpreting symptoms based on western models of madness rather than attempting to frame them within cultural models. Rack (1982: 99) wrote that "cultural differences in the manifestation of distress and the way such manifestations are interpreted represent diagnostic pitfalls for the practitioner". As a psychiatrist working in Bradford, Rack came into contact with people of diverse backgrounds and identified that different cultures held varying views about the causes of mental illness, its symptoms and treatment. It is therefore crucial to find ways of acknowledging and incorporating cross-cultural approaches in order to benefit all those using and working within mental health services.

Concerns about the over-representation of certain groups diagnosed with a mental illness have led to a number of research projects and publications aimed at identifying the possible reasons for this phenomenon, presenting ways of tackling any inequalities and discrimination and developing culturally appropriate services (Nazroo, 1997; Bugra, 1999; Bugra and Bahl, 1999; Fernando, 2002; Sproston and Nazroo, 2002; NIMHE, 2003; Rogers and Pilgrim, 2003; DH, 2005; Mental Health Act Commission, 2006). Aspinall and Jackson (2004: 7) highlighted some problems with research studies that did not provide a true picture of mental illness in the wider community and identified some worrying statistics that need further investigation. Data from the Ethnic Minority Psychiatric Illness Rates in the Community (EMPIRIC) study revealed that there were no marked differences in common mental disorder (depression, anxiety, mixed anxiety and depression disorder, phobia, obsessive-compulsive disorder and panic disorder) between ethnic groups (Sproston and Nazroo, 2002). This representative population-based survey found that black Caribbeans did not have significantly higher rates of psychotic illness than other ethnic groups but rates were twice as high as the white population. Suicide rates among young Asian women were more than twice as high as those of young white women. There were higher rates of in-patient admission among black patients. The authors recommend a systematic collection and repository of research that will add to the knowledge base and promote good practice in the delivery of mental health services.

The National Institute for Mental Health in England (NIMHE), now superseded by the National Mental Health Development Unit (NMHDU; see www.nmhdu.org.uk), was established with a remit to champion good practice in the field of mental health. Its values statement makes explicit the recognition of values in all aspects of mental health policy and practice, and their impact on mental health practice, and calls for respect for the diversity of values of individual service users and their communities (Fulford and Woodbridge, 2007). It recommends that practice is user-centred and that the values of individual users are placed at the centre of policy and practice. Practitioners need to recognise that there are many diverse routes to recovery, and recovery plans should build on the personal strengths and resiliencies of individual users. Their support can come from and between service users, their family members, friends, communities and providers, between different provider disciplines (such as nursing, psychology, psychiatry, medicine, social work) and between different organisations (including health, social care, local authority housing, voluntary organisations, community groups and faith communities).

Many people seek out alternative help when faced with health problems. Muslims may consult *hakims*, who are practitioners of the Islamic *Umani* (or *Umani-Tibb*) that is developed from Arab traditional medicine (Rack, 1982; Fernando, 2002). *Vaids* are practitioners of Ayurvedic medicine, the traditional medicine of India, derived from Hindu beliefs, who believe that there are three natural elements: wind, water and fire. These are represented by three humours: breath, phlegm and bile. Illness is characterised by a deficit or excess of one or other. Rack (1982) reported that, in 1979, Aslam conducted a survey of 250 Pakistanis and Indians living in the UK. His findings were of interest in that 202 (81%) of the sample still consulted *hakims*. Although this study was carried out in 1979, it is likely that the findings are still relevant today. Alternative treatments (homeopathy, herbalism, osteopathy and chiropractice, spiritualism and hypnotherapy) continue to be popular in western countries. New arrivals import their own culture-specific ways of dealing with medical matters that often exist alongside western-style medicine (Rack, 1982: 174).

Buddhism, Hinduism, Islam, Judaism and Christianity all have traditions that can help the individual to adjust and create meaning and hope after suffering severe loss and trauma (Boehnlein, 2006: 637). Religious faith can enhance the ability of some to cope with negative life events or may result in increased religious faith (Connor et al, 2003). The overall finding for the Judaeo-Christian tradition is that higher levels of religious involvement are modestly associated with better health (Koenig, 1998; McCullough and Larson, 1999; Koenig et al, 2001). It appears that "the very fact of belonging to, participating in and feeling part of a religious community can be beneficial in terms of reducing psychological distress and preventing mental health problems" (Swinton, 2001, 2007). Beit–Hallahmi and Argyle (1997) draw on several studies to show that members of religious congregations are more satisfied with their lives as a whole compared to non-members. They cite a study by Shams and Jackson (1993) who found that mosque membership and social support by the community were key factors in assisting individuals under stress to cope better with their situation. However, those same faith groups, while enhancing community cohesion and social support for their members, can also result in a separation and isolation from those of other faiths and ethnicities (Beit-Hallahmi and Argyle, 1997: 229). A long-term study by Coleman et al (2004) of the religious experiences of 342 mainly Christian older people also found that religion could have both negative and positive effects on mental health.

Leavey et al (2007) identified that religious pastors – priests, rabbis or imams – may not be, or may not feel themselves to be, adequately equipped to support those with mental health issues who present themselves for pastoral care. In 2003, the Church of England General Synod endorsed the development of a resource to help churches and their members have a greater understanding of mental health issues and suggested ways to offer pastoral and spiritual care. This resource can be adapted for use by other faith communities (reference listed at the end of this chapter). People, of all faiths, can believe that mental illness is caused by spirit or demon possession. In Arabic the word for madness is *jinoon*, which is derived from the word *jinn* meaning spirits (El-Hadi, 2000: 101). Many Islamic scholars accept that *jinn* can possess people, and passages in the Koran and Hadith affirm the belief that *jinn* can cause erratic behaviour in words, deeds and movements (Dein et al, 2008: 37). Dein et al (2008) carried out ethnographic interviews with 40 Bangladeshis living in East London about their perceptions of misfortune with respect to the role of *jinn* spirits. Respondents typically categorised illness into physical factors (*shordi bemar*), psychological illness (*sintha bemar, fagol bemar*) and spiritual illness (*jinn bemar* and *Allah bemar, uffri bemar, batash* – evil wind). They described problems relating to *jinn* possession as low mood, speaking rubbish, withdrawal, a failure to observe Islamic practices and behaviours such as stealing and adultery in marriage. Exorcism was generally accepted as a healing tool and traditional explanations of misfortune were seen to help people to cope with unexplained physical symptoms, distress and psychological disturbance (Dein et al, 2008: 49).

Given the sensitive and controversial nature of the topic, it is not surprising that there have been few studies that have explored the effects of exorcism on individuals. One study indicated the dangers and actual harm that was caused by carrying out exorcisms or 'spiritual cleansing', particularly with those who have a diagnosed or undiagnosed mental illness (Fraser, 1993) and more worrying has been the reported increase and impact of carrying out exorcisms (Malia, 2001; Dein et al, 2008; Gilligan, 2008). Copsey (1997: 15) explored the role of faith communities in the community mental health programme in one borough of London. He recommended the development of mental health services that were sensitive to the family, culture and faith. These could be developed by bringing members of faith groups together to foster greater care by the community. He suggests that some people belonging to all the major religions believe that much of what is conventionally described as 'mental illness' is, in fact, the result of spiritual activity and that the only effective way of dealing with it is "to adopt supernatural means". Father Joseph Mahoney, a Catholic chaplain in Detroit who works with people suffering from multiple personality disorder, states: "A popular culture has developed in which some Catholics, if confronted by phenomena that confuse or frighten them, will immediately diagnose the phenomena as demonic and begin a process of ordering an evil entity to leave the person. I believe it to be spiritually dangerous, psychologically dangerous and abusive, and scandalous" (*National Catholic Reporter*, 2001). There is a clear need for a more open dialogue at national and local levels to explore and expose these different belief systems. It is vital that mental health professionals can be alert to the potential harm and distress that can be inflicted on the individual by family members and faith leaders who genuinely believe that the person is possessed and carry out certain rituals against the will of the individual. If the individual has the mental capacity to agree to participate in the ritual then this is a very different matter to forcing the person to undergo the ritual cleansing or exorcism.

The 'real' cases of 'Michael' (Inset 3) and 'Javid' (Inset 4) illustrate the potential use and abuse of exorcisms.

Inset 3: 'Michael'

'Michael' is a white, single, British man who is in his 30s. He had no history of mental health problems but was convinced that his motorbike was possessed. He described to the social worker how different people rang him up and told him not to ride his bike that day, as he was likely to have an accident or some other misfortune when riding his bike. These predictions had come true and confirmed his fears that his bike was possessed. The social worker was open-minded and prepared to listen to Michael. Although she was sceptical, she supported him in contacting the local vicar to ask if he would carry out an exorcism. The vicar agreed to exorcise the motorbike and Michael had no further problems. In this case, there was no need for any medical intervention and Michael's belief in the exorcism worked to rid him of his distress.

Inset 4: 'Javid'

'Javid' is 18 years old and lives with his extended family, all of whom are practising Sufis. Javid had been addicted to heroin and had a conviction for assault. His behaviour started to concern his family when he began to hoard his own and his family's faeces by not allowing them to flush the toilet and he then smeared faeces on the Koran. This was an extremely serious matter. Muslims believe that any intentional desecration of the holy book is blasphemous and such an offence carries a sentence of life imprisonment in Pakistan. Javid could not understand or speak Arabic, but used to watch Arabic television all day. He also became aggressive when people turned their backs to him. Child protection services had to be called in when he kicked his brothers after they had turned their backs to him. He was removed to a psychiatric hospital for an assessment as he was putting both his and others' lives at risk. He recovered enough to be discharged, as there did not appear to be any apparent reason for his behaviour. The social worker subsequently found out that his family had been forcing him to undergo an exorcism or a 'spiritual kind of cleansing' by restraining him against his will and forcefully pouring water down his throat. He responded with violence, as he believed that his family were draining the spiritual energy running through his body by these exorcisms. The conflict centred on the fact that, although his family were trying to help him, Javid saw this as interference. The brother told the social worker that he was considering burning his brother for desecrating the Koran. He also said that, if fellow Muslims attending the mosque were aware of his actions, then they might kill him.

The dilemma facing the social worker was how best to protect Javid? His family had been supportive but their actions were aggravating his condition and there were real dangers of further harm either by him towards them or by them or others towards Javid. When some of his behaviour reoccurred he was readmitted to hospital for further assessment. Although Javid agreed to move to alternative accommodation, it had been impossible to find suitable housing and he had no option but to return home. At this time, Javid was taking methadone and his family would not allow him to go out alone for fear that he would start using non-prescription drugs again. The social worker felt in an impossible situation. The family genuinely believed that Javid was possessed and the social worker had to try to convince them that Javid had mental health problems and potentially they were putting themselves and Javid at greater risk if they continued with the exorcisms.

Javid's case clearly illustrates that carrying out an exorcism without the person's consent is abusive and can potentially exacerbate any mental health symptoms. This case also raises issues about adult protection and whether Javid should have been reported to the local adult safeguarding board (see Chapter Six).

Dealing with depression

Depression is the most common and treatable of all mental health problems (Koenig et al, 2001; Mental Health Foundation, 2006). Its symptoms may include: feelings of sadness or misery; unexplained tiredness and fatigue; a lack of motivation; a loss of appetite for food, sex or company; excessive worry; feeling like a failure; unjustified feelings of guilt; feelings of worthlessness or hopelessness; sleep problems; and physical symptoms such as back pain or stomach cramps (Cornah, 2007: 10). Studies have shown a positive association between church attendance and lower levels of depression among adults, children and young people (Olszewski, 1994).

Koenig et al's (2001: 135) review of relevant research concerned with religion and depression supported the following conclusions:

■ Jews and people who are not affiliated with any religion are at an elevated risk for depressive disorder and depressive symptoms.
■ Some aspects of religious involvement are associated with less depression.
■ Religious involvement can help people to cope with stressful life events.

- Religious or spiritual activities may lead to a reduction in depressive symptoms.

Loewenthal and Cinnirella (1999) carried out semi-structured interviews with 59 women from five cultural-religious groups in Britain (black Christian, Hindu, Jewish and Muslim) on the efficacy of different forms of help for depression and schizophrenia. Participants identified that religious forms of help, particularly prayer, could be more helpful than medication or psychotherapy for depression. Hussain and Cochrane (2003) interviewed ten women (three Hindus, six Muslims and one Sikh) and three carers living in Birmingham to find out their coping strategies to deal with depression. For some, maintaining gender roles was a motivating factor that helped them to fulfil their obligations to others. Affiliation and social support were also helpful to some but not to others, who were wary of breaches of confidentiality. Some coped by placing their trust in God, seeking comfort in religion or religious behaviour. Several reasons were given for the low take-up of services, including an acceptance of one's karma or fate, learning to accommodate depression, a lack of language skills and a lack of knowledge of, or contact with, services. Although religion can be a source of great support, it can also serve to make people more passive and powerless to change. Fazil and Cochrane (1998, cited in Hussain and Cochrane, 2003), identified six predictive factors that the Pakistani women in their sample associated with their depression. Culturally specific factors were social isolation, living with extended family, an unhappy marriage and intergenerational conflicts. Two other predisposing factors were loss of mother and low intimacy. Their findings, along with Beliappa (1991), suggest that migration and resettlement, along with historical and local experiences, influenced mental health.

There may be several reasons that prohibit people from accessing appropriate mental health services. Service users may not have a good enough grasp of English to adequately describe their symptoms; certain words in their first language may not translate into English and vice versa; their perception of the role of doctor may be only to treat physical illnesses; mental illness may be related to madness and therefore unacceptable; and individuals may seek help from family or non-medical help with emotional disorders. Causes of mental illness among Pakistanis, Indians and Bangladeshis may be based on magical and supernatural explanations and blamed on an unbalanced diet, climate, immoral behaviour and deliberate poisoning by an enemy. Religious belief can shape the way people express their mental distress. The experiences of Mariyam Maule send a powerful message about how nursing staff's attitudes, ignorance and lack of understanding served to confirm and reinforce her negative thoughts and beliefs in devil possession and the presence of evil *jinn*:

... attitudes of acceptance and a fundamental belief in there being a meaning behind people's expressions of distress would have enabled staff to hear, acknowledge and validate Mariyam rather than judge, ignore and pathologize her. (Maule et al, 2007: 91)

These studies suggest that religious affiliation in itself is not a barrier to accessing mental health services, but that there is a need to develop, first, 'mental health literacy' within minority ethnic cultures (including religious cultures) and, second, cultural and religious literacy among mental health professionals. Racism within psychiatry has often been cited as the sole cause of the disproportionate presence of BME patients in mental health institutions. However, some doubts are now being expressed about the validity of such generalised conclusions, as researchers identify alternative (or additional) reasons for the variations in the mental health experience of different ethnic groups (Singh and Burns, 2006; Tummey and Turner, 2008).

Key questions

(1) Can you identify any cases where religion was a key factor in the life of the service user? (In what ways?)
(2) Was their faith helpful to their recovery? (How?)
(3) Was their faith unhelpful to their recovery? (How?)
(4) What was your role in assisting the person to make sense of their experiences? (In what way/s could you have done anything differently?)

Resources

- NMHDU
  www.mentalhealthequalities.org.uk/our-work/later-life/
  mental-health-and-well-being-of-black-and-minority-ethnic-
  elders
- The Church of England Archbishops' Council/Mentality/
  NIMHE (2004) *Promoting mental health: A resource for
  pastoral and spiritual care*
  www.cofe.anglican.org/info/socialpublic/homeaffairs/
  mentalhealth/parishresource.pdf
- Department of Health website relating to mental health
  www.dh.gov.uk/en/Healthcare?NationalServiceFrameworks/
  Mentalhealth/index.htm

- Directgov provides information about public services and your rights as a citizen
  www.direct.gov.uk/en/DisabledPeople/HealthAndSupport/MentalHealth/index.htm
- Jehovah's Witnesses official website
  www.watchtower.org
- Mental Health Foundation (2007) *Keeping the faith: Spirituality and recovery from mental health problems*, London: Mental Health Foundation
  www.lbc.org.uk/MHF%20Keeping%20the%20Faith.pdf
- The King's Fund website provides links to published reports and papers relating to mental health
  www.kingsfund.org.uk/applications/research/index.rm?filter=publications
- The Royal College of Psychiatrists
  www.rcpsych.ac.uk/publications.aspx
- The Sainsbury Centre for Mental Health
  www.scmh.org.uk/

References

Archambeault, J. (2009) *Social work and mental health*, Exeter: Learning Matters.

Aslam, M. (1979) 'The practice of Asian medicine in the United Kingdom', unpublished PhD thesis, Department of Pharmacy, University of Nottingham.

Aspinall, P. and Jackson, B. (2004) *Ethnic disparities in health and health care: A focused review and selected examples of good practice*, 'Executive summary', London: DH/London Health Observatory (www.lho.org.uk/Download/Public/8832/1/Ethnic_Disparities_Exec_Summary_4.pdf).

Barker, P. and Buchanan-Barker, P. (2008) 'Spirituality', in R. Tummey and T. Turner (eds) *Critical issues in mental health*, Basingstoke: Palgrave Macmillan, pp 58-71.

BBC Health (2008) 'Mental health' (www.bbc.co.uk/health/conditions/mental_health).

Beit-Hallahmi, B. and Argyle, M. (1997) *The psychology of religious behaviour, belief and experience*, London and New York: Routledge.

Beliappa, J. (1991) *Illness or distress? Alternative models of mental health*, London: Confederation of Indian Organisations.

Boehnlein, J.K. (2006) 'Religion and spirituality in psychiatric care: looking back, looking ahead', *Transcultural Psychiatry*, **43**(4), 634-51.

Bugra, D. (1999) *Mental health of ethnic minorities: An annotated bibliography*, London: Gaskell.

Bugra, D. and Bahl, V. (eds) (1999) *Ethnicity: An agenda for mental health*, London: Gaskell.

Campbell, J., Stickley, T. and Bonney, S. (2008) 'Recovery as a framework for care planning', in A. Hall, S.D. Kirby and M. Wren (eds) *Care planning in mental health: Promoting recovery*, London: Blackwell Publishing, pp 111–35.

Coleman, P.G., Ivani-Chalian, C. and Robinson, M. (2004) 'Religious attitudes among British older people: stability and change in a 20-year longitudinal study', *Ageing and Society*, **24**(2), 167–88.

Connor, K.M., Davidson, J.R.T. and Lee, L.C. (2003) 'Spirituality, resilience and anger in survivors of violent trauma: a community survey', *Journal of Traumatic Stress*, **16**(5), 487–94.

Copsey, N. (1997) *Keeping faith: The provision of mental health community services within a multi-faith context*, London: Sainsbury Centre for Mental Health (www.scmh.org.uk/pdfs/keeping+faith.pdf).

Cornah, D. on behalf of the Mental Health Foundation (2007) *The impact of spirituality on mental health: A review of the literature*, London: Mental Health Foundation (www.mentalhealth.org.uk/publications/?entryid5=38708&q=0%c2%acfaith%c2%ac).

Dein, S., Alexander, M. and Napier, A.D. (2008) 'Jinn, psychiatry and contested notions of misfortune among East London Bangladeshis', *Transcultural Psychiatry*, **45**(1), 31–55.

DH (Department of Health) (2005) *Delivering race equality in mental health care: An action plan for reform inside and outside services and the Government's response to the independent inquiry into the death of David Bennett*, London: DH (http://213.121.207.229/upload/DRE%20ACtion%20Plan.pdf).

El-Hadi, A. (2000) 'The Muslim community: beliefs and practices', in A. Lau (ed) *South Asian children and adolescents in Britain*, London and Philadelphia, PA: Whurr Publishers, pp 83–105.

Fazil, Q. and Cochrane, R. (1998) 'The cultural dimension in a causal model of depression', Fourteenth International Congress of Cross Cultural Psychology, Bellingham, WA.

Fernando, S. (ed) (1995) *Mental health in a multi-ethnic society: A multi-disciplinary handbook*, London and New York: Routledge.

Fernando, S. (2002) *Mental health, race and culture* (2nd edn), Basingstoke: Palgrave.

Fraser, G.A. (1993) 'Exorcism rituals: effects on multiple personality disorder', *Disassociation*, **6**(4), 239–44.

Fulford, K. W. M. and Woodbridge, K. (2007) 'Values-based practice: help and healing within a shared theology of diversity', in M.E. Coyte, P. Gilbert and N. Nicholls (eds) *Spirituality, values and mental health: Jewels for the journey*, London and Philadelphia, PA: Jessica Kingsley, pp 45-57.

Gilligan, P. (2008) 'Child abuse and spirit possession: not just an issue for African migrants', *childRIGHT*, **245**(4 April), 28-31.

Hussain, F. and Cochrane, R. (2003) 'Living with depression: coping strategies used by South Asian women living in the UK suffering from depression', *Mental Health, Religion & Culture*, **6**(1), 21-44.

Koenig, H.G. (1998) *Handbook of religion and mental health*, San Diego, CA: Academic Press.

Koenig, H.G., McCullough, M.E. and Larson, D.E. (eds) (2001) *Handbook of religion and health*, Oxford: Oxford University Press.

Kumar, P. and Clark, M. (eds) *Clinical medicine* (5th edn), Edinburgh: W.B. Saunders.

Leavey, G., Loewenthal, K. and King, M. (2007) 'Challenges to sanctuary: the clergy as a resource for mental health care in the community', *Social Science and Medicine*, **65**(3), 548-59.

Loewenthal, K. (1995) *Mental health and religion*, London: Chapman & Hall.

Loewenthal, K. (2006) *Religion and mental health*, Cambridge: Cambridge University Press.

Loewenthal, K.M. and Cinnirella, M. (1999) 'Beliefs about the efficacy of religious, medical and psychotherapeutic interventions for depression and schizophrenia among women from different cultural-religious groups in Great Britain', *Transcultural Psychiatry*, **36**(4), 491-504.

Malia, L. (2001) 'A fresh look at a remarkable document: exorcism: the report convened by the Bishop of Exeter', *Anglican Theological Review*, winter (http://findarticles.com/p/articles/mi_qa3818/is_/ai_n8942546 ?tag=artBody;col1).

McCullough, M.E. and Larson, D.B. (1999) 'Religion and depression: a review of the literature', *Twin Research*, **2**(2), 126-36.

Maule, M., Trivedi, P., Wilson, A. and Dewan, V. (2007) 'A journey – with faith: complex travels through the mental health system', in M.E. Coyte, P. Gilbert and N. Nicholls (eds) *Spirituality, values and mental health: Jewels for the journey*, London and Philadelphia, PA: Jessica Kingsley, pp 89-101.

Mental Health Foundation (2000) *Strategies for living: Report of user-led research into people's strategies for living with mental distress*, London: Mental Health Foundation (www.mentalhealth.org.uk/publications/ ?EntryId5=43591).

Mental Health Foundation (2006) *Fundamental facts*, London: Mental Health Foundation.

Mental Health Foundation (2007) *Recovery* (www.mentalhealth.org.uk/information/mental-health-a-z/recovery/).

Mental Health Foundation (2008) *Mental health A-Z* (www.mentalhealth.org.uk/information/mental-health-a-z/).

Mental Health Act Commission (2006) *Count me in: The National Mental Heath and Ethnicity Census: 2005 Service User Survey*, London: MHAC.

Merchant, R., Gilbert, P. and Moss, B. (2008) *Spirituality, religion and mental health: A brief evidence resource* (www.rcpsych.ac.uk/pdf/Gilbert%20Evidence%20Resource%20Doc.x.pdf).

National Catholic Reporter (2000) 'Exorcism and mental illness', 1 September (http://findarticles.com/p/articles/mi_m1141/is_38_36/ai_65344587/?tag=content;col1).

Nazroo, J. (1997) *Ethnicity and mental health*, London: Policy Studies Institute.

NIMHE (National Institute for Mental Health in England) (2003) *Inside outside: Improving mental health services for black and ethnic communities in England*, Leeds: NIMHE.

Olszewski, M.E. (1994) *The effect of religious coping on depression and anxiety in adolescents*, Corvallis, OR: Valley Library.

Pargament, K.I. (1997) *The psychology of religion and coping: Theory, research, practice*, New York and London: The Guilford Press.

Rack, P. (1982) *Race, culture and mental disorder*, London and New York: Routledge.

Rogers, A. and Pilgrim, D. (2003) *Mental health and inequality*, Basingstoke: Palgrave.

Shams, M. and Jackson, P.R. (1993) 'Religiosity as a predicator of well-being and moderator of the psychological impact of unemployment', *British Journal of Medical Psychology*, **66**(4), 342-52.

Singh, S.P. and Burns, T. (2006) 'Race and mental health: there is more to race than racism', *British Medical Journal*, **333**(7569), 648-51.

Sproston, K. and Nazroo, J. (eds) (2002) *Ethnic minority psychiatric illness rates in the community* (EMPIRIC), London: The Stationery Office.

Swinton, J. (2001) *Spirituality and mental health: Rediscovering a 'forgotten' dimension*, London and Philadelphia, PA: Jessica Kingsley.

Swinton, J. (2007) 'Researching spirituality and mental health – a perspective from the research', in M.E. Coyte, P. Gilbert and N. Nicholls (eds) *Spirituality, values and mental health: Jewels for the journey*, London and Philadelphia, PA: Jessica Kingsley, pp 292-305.

Tummey, R. and Turner, T. (eds) (2008) *Critical issues in mental health*, Basingstoke: Palgrave Macmillan.

Weaver, A.J., Flannelly, L.T., Garbarino, J., Figley, C.R. and Flannelly, K.J. (2003) 'A systematic review of research on religion and spirituality in the *Journal of Traumatic Stress*: 1990–1999', *Mental Health, Religion & Culture*, **6**(3), 215–28.

8

Learning disabilities, religion and belief

… people with learning disabilities can have strong religious affiliations and interests. Forms of religious expression include but are not confined to involvement with faith agencies, but full religious expression requires support for the person's religious needs to be fulfilled. (Hatton et al, 2004a: 24)

Introduction

A learning disability may be caused by any condition that impairs the development of the brain before, during or after birth. The main causes relate to genetic conditions, chromosomal deviations, cranial malfunctions such as hydrocephalus, congenital factors such as maternal factors and substance exposure and the environment (Thomas and Woods, 2003: 24). The person's capacity to learn is affected and they may not learn things as quickly as others. People usually have a learning disability from birth or sometimes from early childhood. Although these are usually permanent conditions, the richness and quality of individuals' development is often dependent on the quality of their environment and the sensitivity and skills of those caring for them. Religion can be important to people with a learning disability and they may have particular needs and strengths arising from their beliefs. This element of their lives can often be overlooked. This chapter aims to recognise that individuals should be able to participate in religious practices and worship along with other members of their faith. We consider ways of supporting people who wish to participate more fully in their religious practices and how to respect their rights and wishes regarding marriage.

Learning disabilities are often categorised as 'mild', 'moderate' or 'severe'. People described as having a learning disability vary a great deal in their capacity to live independently and in the help they need from others. Some people require help with basic needs such as washing and dressing or with matters such as reading religious texts. Many, however, will live independently with much less support and may have literacy skills. A minority present behaviour that is sometimes challenging and have additional sight or hearing impairments, autism, mental health problems or a variety of other health-related issues.

In 2004, Emerson and Hatton were commissioned by the Department of Health to identify current and future numbers of people with learning disabilities in England. They estimated that around 985,000 people have a learning disability; this is around 2% of the population (Emerson and Hatton, 2008). They acknowledged the difficulty of both determining an accurate number as well as predicting demographic trends but indicated that there is likely to be a modest increase of people with learning disabilities based on the following factors:

- increased life expectancy, especially among people with Down's syndrome;
- growing numbers of children and young people with complex and multiple disabilities who now survive into adulthood;
- a sharp rise in the reported numbers of school-age children with autistic spectrum disorders, some of whom will have learning disabilities;
- greater prevalence among some minority ethnic populations of South Asian origin (DH, 2001: 16).

About 60% of adults with learning disabilities live with their families (DH, 2001) and receive most care and support from them (Fitzpatrick and Wood, 2007). About 39,500 people with learning disabilities live in care homes and hospitals. Around 34,000 people with learning disabilities are receiving help from support workers paid for by the Supporting People programme. Most of these people live in hostels or shared housing (DH, 2005a).

Social workers are, often, involved with families of disabled children at the point of initial diagnosis and at times of transition and crisis (Gilligan and Taylor, 2008). O'Hara (2003: 167-8) reports that research on the attitudes of white middle-class parents within a Judaeo-Christian faith suggests that the birth of a child with learning disabilities either stimulates a greater faith or results in a complete loss of faith, with some parents believing that they were being punished for their sins. Fatimilehin and Nadirshaw (1994) found that variations in attitudes between Asian and white British families were related to cultural and religious differences rather than to any descriptive characteristics of the parent or their child. For example, Asian British families had more contact with a 'holy' person. They tended to believe in a spiritual explanation/cause for their child's learning disability, that religion had something particular to say about learning disability and that their faith helped them to cope but offered little social or practical support. They also wanted care to be provided by a relative when they were no longer able to provide it themselves. In contrast, white British families did not offer a spiritual explanation for their child's disability, religion/faith offered them social support and generally they wanted their child to be cared for in a community home provided by statutory/voluntary services.

O'Hara (2003: 168) notes that the Hindu belief in the concept of karma – that is, the cycle of reward and punishment for deeds and thoughts as the immortal spirit is reborn into another body – "may provide an understanding for what has happened and lead to a sense of resignation or acceptance". She also notes that Middle Eastern cultures may regard disability as punishment from heaven, as emanating from spirits or as caused by an 'evil eye' (Aminidav and Weller, 1995), while many Chinese people use prayers to ancestors and seeking supernatural power as coping strategies to aid forbearance (Cheng and Tang, 1995). Shah (1992) suggests that Asian parents do not have a positive or encouraging attitude towards disability, because of their religious or superstitious beliefs, although McGrother et al (2002) argue that South Asian cultures are generally more accommodating of people with disabilities than their white counterparts. These differing and sometimes opposing viewpoints serve to remind us that we need to ascertain the belief systems of each family and not to assume that family beliefs are predictable and applicable to all. An understanding of religious beliefs can offer an insight into the attitudes and views of the family about the disability.

Stienstra (2002) reviewed current literature in relation to the intersection of disability and religion. She reports several studies (Idler and Kasl, 1992, 1997a, 1997b; Bennett et al, 1995; Haworth et al, 1996; Chang et al, 1998; Rogers-Dulan, 1998; O'Connor et al, 1999; Nosek, 2001) that suggest that religious participation is a positive factor in the lives of people with a range of disabilities and their carers, and that religion can provide a personal coping resource throughout the lifecycle. She also reports literature that illustrates and argues that the religious experiences of people with disabilities are, too often, ones of exclusion and marginalisation (Stiteler, 1992; Elshout, 1994; Nash, 1997; King, 1998).

Acquiring religious beliefs

> To most believers religion appears as a total ideology with a sense of the 'natural' and the 'real' without which it is impossible to conceive the world they inhabit. (Beit-Hallahmi and Argyle, 1997: 97)

Most children will adopt the religion practised by their parents or other adults who are significant in their lives. They will join them in celebrating religious festivals; taking part in prayers; reading scriptures; or following religious customs, rituals and traditions in and outside of the home. A study by Grewal et al (2004), for example, found that an important role of Muslim grandparents and elders was to teach the younger generation about their religion as a means of transmitting cultural and ethnic values. Parents pass on family values and shape their child's moral development by modelling and showing approval or disapproval of certain kinds of behaviour so that children learn to act appropriately within their social and cultural world. This also involves reflecting "on the consequences of their actions and whether they will lead to the sort of outcomes they wish to achieve" (Eaude, 2008: 29). Children need to internalise their motivation for action by appreciating and realising that the action is worthwhile in itself and is not reliant on extrinsic rewards or punishments. Rules provide a framework to help children to locate boundaries and parental and societal expectations of them.

Studies involving children and young people with sensory and physical impairments may provide some useful pointers to consider in relation to the religious development of children with learning disabilities. Atkin et al (2002) carried out a study with young deaf people and their families. They identified the problem of teaching deaf young people about their religion, as mosques and temples made no provision for British Sign Language (BSL) nor showed any deaf awareness. Hussain's (2005) study explored the views of 29 Muslim and Sikh disabled young people, their parents and siblings. She found that young disabled people did not have the same opportunities for religious and cultural socialisation as their siblings. In a similar way, it is very unlikely that many religious institutions accommodate people with learning disabilities. Parents may struggle to impart cultural and religious values to their children or have low expectations of their child's ability to participate and identify with their faith. Work is needed with faith organisations and communities, as elsewhere, to make places of worship accessible and to ensure that congregations and faith leaders are sufficiently aware, understanding and responsive to the needs of people with learning disabilities or other impairments.

'Margaret's' case (Inset 1) illustrates the importance of adopting the principles discussed in Chapter Three (the Furness/Gilligan Framework), listening to what people say about their beliefs and religious needs and being creative in responses to them. It also highlights the risk that professionals may not always recognise these as mainstream and significant matters or may not expect agencies to recognise them as such. In this case, appropriate and significant action was taken, but not recorded in the case notes for subsequent practitioners. At the same time, it is also relevant to note that Horwath et al (2008: 1) report that "Parents with disabled children had mixed views on the support received from their faith communities. Some said they had not received adequate help or been welcome with their child at places of worship."

Inset 1: 'Margaret'

'Margaret' is eight years old and has been diagnosed with autism. She has limited cognition and mobility and limited communication and motor skills. When the team manager discussed the assessment with the social worker who had completed it, she noted that the written report explored many issues and that the family's religion was entered on the form as "Christian". However, the fact that Margaret and her family are Roman Catholics emerged only when the team were talking about cases for possible discussion with the authors of this book. More importantly, it also emerged in the subsequent debate, but not from the report, that their religious faith is very important to the family. In the team discussions, the social worker disclosed that she had in fact not only talked about what was, for them, the pressing issue of Margaret's inability to access the local church to attend mass, but also undertaken significant work to resolve these difficulties, without making relevant recordings of her actions!

The family had felt that there was support within the church that Margaret could benefit from and they wanted her to attend services and other events. Margaret, herself, felt that she was missing out and was asking, "Why aren't I going?" She was excluded from something that involved the rest of her family and was important to them. The worker contacted the parish priest and encouraged the family to speak with him and resolve their anxieties about how others would react to some of Margaret's likely behaviours during mass. The priest had agreed to change a number of things in the service and to explore what could be done about some of the physical barriers, so that it would be easier for Margaret's family to attend with her. The social worker's intervention allowed the priest to explain to the rest of the congregation how Margaret might behave (for example shouting out during the service) and to encourage them to accept this.

As a result, the family feel much more comfortable in taking her to church and in allowing her to run up and down while the service is going on. They needed the social worker's help to say, "We'd love to bring our little girl. We think she'd benefit from it but we're not sure what people will think if she starts acting out." The social worker's intervention opened up the discussion and, as a result, very positive support networks have become available to Margaret and her parents.

Regarding the original assessment form, the manager remarked that, when she had read this, it had not occurred to her that religion was an issue in Margaret's case. Asked to speculate why it had been omitted, she commented, "I think that's because it's been a culture of not writing about religion in a form unless it's a Muslim family and even when it is a Muslim family it'll be four lines". In fact, the social worker could easily have included the issues in the section of the form recording family and environmental factors. While actually recognising the issues and taking effective action, she had in the meantime and in the words of her manager "put down the bog standard family and environmental factors – the standard information". As this manager remarked, written assessments need to give an accurate picture. Thus, for example, if family members go to church, mosque or temple on a regular basis, this needs to be recorded. If a particular child does not accompany them and a grandparent cares for the child, all the pertinent facts need to be recorded and not just that "grandma babysits twice a week".

Many faith organisations do, of course, appreciate that people with learning disabilities have a fundamental human right of freedom of religious expression (Swinton, 1997, 2001; Hatton et al, 2004a). Hatton et al (2004a: 8) carried out an action research project with 42 adults who had learning disabilities, their family members and service representatives at five different sites over two years. They found that, although most of the participants said that they belonged to a religious group, only a minority attended a place of worship on a regular basis. Most of the Muslim service users reported not attending the mosque as children, with only a minority attending Arabic school at a mosque. They also reported that religious beliefs helped parents to make sense of the experience of having a child with a disability as well as helping the person with the learning disability to achieve a positive and valued social role and lifestyle. Faith communities can provide new sources of friendship and support.

An initiative in Leeds, called Faith Can, brought together Sikh and Christian parents of children who had learning disabilities and their respective faith communities so that their children were able to attend the gurdwara and church for worship and participate in other social activities. Clearly, this is an area of great potential that could be developed across the country and across different faiths (Hatton et al, 2004b).

Relationships and marriage

People with learning disabilities and their advocates have fought for them to have the right to sexual relationships of their choice. However, issues of consent, capacity and vulnerability can cause concern to parents, carers and support workers.

The Mental Capacity Act 2005 (MCA) came into full effect on 1 October 2007 (DH, 2005b). The MCA applies to anyone (with some exceptions) who is aged 16 years or over in England and Wales. The following five principles should be applied to all situations where mental capacity is an issue:

- Every adult has the right to make his or her own decisions and must be assumed to have capacity to do so unless it is proved otherwise.
- People must be supported as much as possible to make a decision before anyone concludes that they cannot make their own decision.
- People have the right to make what others might regard as an unwise or eccentric decision.
- Anything done for, or on behalf of, a person who lacks mental capacity must be done in their best interests.
- Anything done for, or on behalf of, people without capacity should be the least restrictive of their basic rights and freedoms.

The first two principles make it clear that the person should be presumed to have capacity and support given to help them to make the decision before it is decided that they lack capacity (Myron et al, 2008: 6). A capacity test is carried out on the balance of probabilities that it is more likely than not that the person lacks capacity. Strategies and safeguards need to be in place to protect the rights of people who have a learning disability. There have been some cases where overprotective parents have not allowed their young offspring to have sexual relationships or to marry, while others have arranged marriages without the full understanding of the different parties involved.

In most South Asian communities, all adults are usually expected to marry, as a right and as a religious and social duty. The Universal Islamic Declaration of Human Rights (Islamic Council, 1981), for example, states that: "Every person is entitled to marry, to found a family and to bring up children in conformity with his religion, traditions and culture" (Article XIX-a). In Islam, marriage is a universally recognised right, and the Declaration also states that: "*No person may be married against his or her will*" (Article XIX-I, emphasis added) (see also Rude-Antoine, 2005). Moreover, in Bangladesh, both Hindu and Muslim parents may follow the idea of *kanya dan*, meaning that "parents have the religious duty to marry their daughters before or soon after puberty" (Blanchet, 2003: 22; O'Hara and Martin, 2003).

In the UK, the report from the working group on forced marriage in England and Wales defines forced marriage as "a marriage conducted without the valid consent of both parties, where duress is a factor" (Home Office, 2000: 4). Khanum (2008) conducted a study in Luton and reported that coerced or forced marriage had historically been practised in many different communities. Her findings informed the House of Commons (2008) report and concluded that "due to the relative size within the UK population, forced marriage was now most common in the UK among South Asian communities" (House of Commons, 2008: 14). Khanum emphasised that this was a 'cultural', rather than a 'religious', problem.

Currently, forced marriage is not a criminal offence. The government's Forced Marriage Unit deals with over 5,000 enquiries and around 300 cases each year (Buckley, 2008; House of Commons/Home Affairs Committee, 2008). This is likely to be an underestimation as many cases go unreported. The Forced Marriage (Civil Protection) Act 2007 came into operation in autumn 2008 and allows those affected to seek an injunction to prevent a forced marriage. This will, however, provide little protection for the individual who has learning disabilities or for those not living in England or Wales and without the same rights of protection. In debates prior to the passing of this legislation, arguments were made for and against the criminalisation of forced marriages. Those arguing against suggested that, although criminalisation might send a message to all communities that forced marriage is unacceptable, it could, at the same time, dissuade people from coming forward and make the practice more covert. Families that decide not to involve full consent and choice may do so for a variety of reasons. *Izzat* is a South Asian concept of family and personal honour that usually puts the collective (for example, the extended family) before the rights and feelings of the individual. Adults with learning disabilities have been forced into marriage in an effort by their family members to avoid shame being brought on the family and community. Not marrying and having a relationship with someone of whom their family disapproves are other examples of actions that a family might perceive as endangering their *izzat*. Adults with learning disabilities have been forced into marriage as a means of obtaining financial security for their families. A family may also view arranging their daughter's marriage to a man with learning disabilities as a good option if they are unable to pay a dowry. Adults with learning disabilities may be deserted or divorced by their spouses once their spouses' immigration status is secure. Other possible factors that motivate families to coerce a young person with a learning disability to marry against their will include: honouring long-standing family commitments; maintaining ties with the homeland; ensuring land, property and wealth remain within the family; responding to peer group and family pressure; power and control over unwanted behaviour and sexuality; preventing 'unsuitable' relationships; gaining a carer and ensuring long-term support for a son or daughter with learning disabilities; beliefs that marriage may 'cure' the disability and allow the person to lead a 'normal' life (Samad and Eade, 2003; Foreign and Commonwealth Office, 2004: 4; VoiceUK et al, 2007). Valios (2008) reports that the Forced Marriage Unit is starting to collect data about the numbers of people involved who have either learning disabilities or mental health issues, because of concerns about the numbers of young people who cannot give consent and are being married against their will. 'Abul's' case (Inset 2) illustrates some of the relevant issues.

Inset 2: 'Abul'

'Abul' is a 22-year-old man born in Britain who is of Pakistani Muslim origin. He has moderate learning disabilities and relies on his family to help him with dressing and other personal care tasks. His family arranged for him to marry his 18-year-old cousin who lives in Pakistan. She is not aware of his learning disability. The family wish to arrange a marriage for Abul so that he can be cared for by his wife and to maintain ties with their relatives in the homeland. Abul told his social worker that he was getting married shortly but did not want to go to Pakistan. She spent time talking to him about his wishes and ascertained that he did not want to get married. He agreed that the social worker could speak to his parents about this. When the social worker tried to broach the subject with Abul's parents, she was told firmly that it was none of her business and was a 'religious' matter. She persisted and advocated on Abul's behalf by stating that he did not consent to this arrangement. The family agreed reluctantly to postpone the wedding.

Voice UK, Respond and the Ann Craft Trust (2007) wrote a detailed response to the Joint Committee on Human Rights relating to forced marriages of adults with learning disabilities. Their main points included:

- Forcing an adult with learning disabilities into a marriage is a violation of human rights.
- In contrast to an arranged marriage that involves an adult with learning disabilities being given a choice and freely consenting to the marriage, a forced marriage is not an accepted religious or cultural practice. Indeed, within Islam, the consent of both partners is explicitly required (Islamic Council, 1981: section XIX). Like all consensual marriages, an arranged marriage can help adults with learning disabilities to lead full and positive lives. An arranged marriage can provide an adult with learning disabilities with such things as a full-time carer, sexual relations, children, contact with an extended family network, contact with friends, financial security, improved immigration status and love.
- The central issues in both forced and arranged marriages involving adults with learning disabilities are consent and choice. Adults with learning disabilities need support to understand the nature of marriage and all it entails so that they are able to make informed decisions and engage in mutually supportive relationships.

■ Both parties to the marriage must give consent and understand the nature of the person's learning disability. In both forced and arranged marriages, a person's learning disability is sometimes kept secret for fear of jeopardising the marriage and of damaging family honour.

■ The susceptibility of many adults with learning disabilities makes them vulnerable to this form of exploitation.

It is vital that there is an increased awareness among those working with adults with learning disabilities about forced marriage. Social workers and other practitioners may need to be challenged regarding simplistic notions of cultural relativism and helped to overcome their fear of being accused of racism, so that they will challenge and report such forced marriages appropriately. Practice guidance has been published to aid social workers to deal with young people and vulnerable adults facing forced marriage in a respectful way and from an informed perspective (Foreign and Commonwealth Office, 2004). The Secretary of State for the Home Department (2008) has acknowledged the need to change attitudes within local communities and to condemn forced marriages. A number of specific proposals include increasing the age of those who can sponsor or be sponsored as a spouse from 18 to 21 years and to improve systems for investigating allegations of abusive marriage practices.

Key questions

(1) Do you have faith-based views about people with learning disabilities?

(2) Do you consider the religious beliefs of people with learning disabilities and the needs that arise from them?

(3) How do you demonstrate your respect for the beliefs of people with learning disabilities?

(4) Are the groups and communities to which you belong accessible to people with learning disabilities?

(5) Are you sufficiently aware of the rights and risks for people with disabilities in relation to forced marriages?

References

Aminidav, C. and Weller, L. (1995) 'Effects of country of origin, sex, religiosity and social class on breadth of knowledge of mental retardation', *British Journal of Developmental Disabilities*, **41**(1), 48–56.

Atkin, K., Ahmad, W.I.U. and Jones, L. (2002) 'Young South Asian deaf people and their families: negotiating relationships and identities', *Sociology of Health & Illness*, **24**(1), 21–45.

Beit-Hallahmi, B. and Argyle, M. (1997) *The psychology of religious behaviour, belief and experience*, London and New York: Routledge.

Bennett, T., Deluca, D.A. and Allen, R.W. (1995) 'Religion and children with disabilities', *Journal of Religion and Health*, **34**(4), 301–11.

Blanchet, T. with Zaman, A., Biswas, H., Dabu, H.M. and Lucky, M.A. (2003) *Bangladeshi girls sold as wives in North India*, Dhaka: Drishti Research Centre (www.childtrafficking.com/Docs/blanchet_2003_final_report_up_marriage_4.pdf).

Buckley, H. (2008) *Presentation to the Home Affairs Committee Seminar*, London: Foreign and Commonwealth Office Forced Marriage Unit.

Chang, B., Noonan, A.E. and Tennstedt, S.L. (1998) 'The role of religion/spirituality in coping with caregiving for disabled elders', *The Gerontologist*, **38**(4), 463–70.

Cheng, P. and Tang, C.S. (1995) 'Coping and psychological distress of Chinese parents of children with Down's Syndrome', *Mental Retardation*, **33**(1), 10–20.

DH (Department of Health) (2001) *Valuing people: A new strategy for learning disability for the 21st century* (Cm 5086), London: The Stationery Office (www.archive.official-documents.co.uk/document/cm50/5086/5086.pdf).

DH (2005a) *Valuing people: What do the numbers tell us?*, London: HMSO.

DH (2005b) *The Mental Capacity Act*, London: HMSO (www.dca.gov.uk/legal-policy/mental-capacity/mca-summary.pdf).

Eaude, T. (2008) *Children's spiritual, moral, social and cultural development: Primary and early years* (2nd edn), Exeter: Learning Matters.

Elshout, E. (1994) 'Women with disabilities: a challenge to feminist theology', *Journal of Feminist Studies in Religion*, **10**(2), 99–134.

Emerson, E. and Hatton, C. (2004) *Estimating future need/demand for supports for adults with learning disabilities in England*, Lancaster: Institute for Health Research, Lancaster University (www.lancs.ac.uk/fass/ihr/research/learning/download/estimatingfutureneed.pdf).

Emerson, E. and Hatton, C. (2008) *People with learning disabilities in England, CeDR research report*, Lancaster: Institute of Health Research, Lancaster University (www.lancs.ac.uk/cedr/publications/CeDR%202008-1%20People%20with%20Learning%20Disabilities%20in%20England.pdf).

Fatimilehin, I.A. and Nadirshaw, Z. (1994) 'A cross-cultural study of parental attitudes and beliefs about learning disability (mental handicap)', *Mental Handicap Research*, **7**, 202-27.

Fitzpatrick, J. and Wood, A. (2007) *Short breaks: Supporting family carers and people with learning disabilities to have short breaks that work for them*, Boulder, CO: Paradigm/Valuing People Support Team.

(The) Foreign and Commonwealth Office (2004) *Young people and vulnerable adults facing forced marriage: Practice guidance for social workers*, London: The Foreign and Commonwealth Office (www.minheder.nu/social_workers_guidance_doc.pdf).

Gilligan, P. and Taylor, J. (2008) 'Social services and social work support for disabled children, children with complex care needs, and their families', in J. Teare (ed) *Caring for children with complex needs in community settings*, Oxford, Blackwell Publishing, pp 149-166.

Grewal, I., Nazroo, J., Bajekal, M., Blane, D. and Lewis, J. (2004) 'Influences on quality of life: a qualitative investigation of ethnic differences among older people in England', *Journal of Ethnic and Migration Studies*, **30**(4), 737-61.

Hatton, C., Turner, S., Shah, R., Rahim, N. and Stansfield, J. (2004a) *Religious expression, a fundamental human right: The report on an action research project on meeting the religious needs of people with learning disabilities*, London: The Mental Health Foundation.

Hatton, C., Turner, S. and Shah, R. with Rahim, N. and Stansfield, J. (2004b) *What about faith? A good practice guide for services on meeting the religious needs of people with learning disabilities*, London: The Mental Health Foundation.

Haworth, A.M., Hill, A.E. and Glidden, L.M. (1996) 'Measuring religiousness of parents of children with developmental disabilities', *Mental Retardation*, **34**(5), 271-9.

Home Office (2000) *A choice by right: The report of a working group on forced marriage*, London: Home Office Communications Directorate (www.fco.gov.uk/resources/en/pdf/a-choice-by-right).

Horwath, J., Lees, J., Sidebotham, P., Higgins, J. and Imtiaz, A. (2008a) *Religion, beliefs and parenting practices. Findings informing change*, York: Joseph Rowntree Foundation (http://www.jrf.org.uk/sites/files/jrf/2264-faith-parenting-youth.pdf).

House of Commons/Home Affairs Committee (2008) *Domestic violence, forced marriage and 'honour'-based violence: Sixth report of session 2007-08: Volume 1*, London: The Stationery Office (www.publications.parliament.uk/pa/cm200708/cmselect/cmhaff/263/263i.pdf).

Hussain, Y. (2005) 'South Asian disabled women: negotiating identities', *The Sociological Review*, **53**(3), 522-38.

Idler, E.L. and Kasl, V.S. (1992) 'Religion, disability, depression, and the timing of death', *American Journal of Sociology*, **97**(4), 1052-79.

Idler, E.L. and Kasl, V.S. (1997a) 'Religion among disabled and nondisabled persons I: cross-sectional patterns in health practices, social activities, and well-being', *The Journals of Gerontology – Psychological Sciences and Social Sciences*, Series B, 52B, **6**, S294–S305.

Idler, E.L. and Kasl, V.S. (1997b) 'Religion among disabled and nondisabled persons II: attendance at religious services as a predictor of the course of disability', *The Journals of Gerontology – Psychological Sciences and Social Sciences*, Series B, 52B, **6**, S306–S316.

Islamic Council (1981) *Universal Islamic Declaration of Human Rights*, London: Islamic Council (www.alhewar.com/ISLAMDECL.html).

Khanum, N. (2008) *Forced marriage, family cohesion and community engagement: National learning through a case study of Luton*, Luton: Equality in Diversity (www.luton.gov.uk/Media%20Library/Pdf/Chief%20executives/ Equalities/Forced%20Marriage%20Report%20-%20Final%20Version. pdf).

King, S.V. (1998) 'The beam in thine own eye: disability and the black church', *Western Journal of Black Studies*, **22**(1), 37–48.

McGrother, C.W., Bhaumik, S., Thorpe, C.F., Watson, J.M. and Taub, N.A. (2002) 'Prevalence, morbidity and service need among South Asian and white adults with intellectual disability in Leicestershire, UK', *Journal of Intellectual Disability Research*, **46**(4), 299–309.

Myron, R., Gillespie, S., Swift, P. and Williamson, T. (2008) *Whose decision? Preparation for and implementation of the Mental Capacity Act in statutory and non-statutory services in England and Wales*, London: The Mental Health Foundation.

Nash, M.C. (1997) 'Disability, religion, and ritual: experiences of people who have learning difficulties in a "treetop community" in Scotland', *Scottish Journal of Religious Studies*, **18**(2), 181–97.

Nosek, M.A. (2001) 'Psychospiritual aspects of sense of self in women with physical disabilities', *Journal of Rehabilitation*, **67**(1), 20–6.

O'Connor, T., Rao, V., Meakes, E. and Van de Laar, T. (1999) 'Horse of a different color: ethnography of faith and disability', *The Journal of Pastoral Care*, **53**(3), 255–68.

O'Hara, J. (2003) 'Learning disabilities and ethnicity: achieving cultural competence', *Advances in Psychiatric Treatment*, **9**(3), 166–76 (http://apt. rcpsych.org/cgi/reprint/9/3/166?ck=nck).

O'Hara, J. and Martin, H. (2003) 'Parents with learning disabilities: a study of gender and cultural perspectives from East London', *British Journal of Learning Disabilities*, **31**(1), 18–24.

Rogers-Dulan, J. (1998) 'Religious connectedness among urban African American families who have a child with disabilities', *Mental Retardation*, **36**(2), 91–103.

Rude-Antoine, E. (2005) *Forced marriages in Council of Europe member states: A comparative study of legislation and political initiatives*, Strasbourg: Directorate General of Human Rights (www.coe.int/T/E/Human_Rights/Equality/PDF_CDEG(2005)1_E.pdf).

Samad, Y. and Eade, J. (2003) *Community perceptions of forced marriages*, London: Community Liaison Unit, Foreign and Commonwealth Office (www.fco.gov.uk/resources/en/pdf/pdf1/fco_forcedmarriagereport121102).

Secretary of State for the Home Department (2008) *Domestic violence, forced marriage and 'honour'-based violence: The government reply to the sixth report from the Home Affairs Committee Session 2007-08 HC263* (Cm 7450), London: The Stationery Office (www.official-documents.gov.uk/document/cm74/7450/7450.pdf).

Shah, R. (1992) *The silent minority: Children with disabilities in Asian families*, London: National Children's Bureau.

Stienstra, D. (2002) *The intersection of DISABILITY and race/ethnicity/official language/religion*, Winnipeg: Canadian Centre on Disability Studies (www.disabilitystudies.ca/Documents/Resaerch/Completed%20research/Intersection%20of%20disability/Intersection%20of%20disability.pdf).

Stiteler, V.C.J. (1992) 'Singing without a voice: using disability images in the language of public worship', *Liturgical Ministry*, **1**, 140-2.

Swinton, J. (1997) 'Restoring the image: spirituality, faith, and cognitive disability', *Journal of Religion and Health*, **36**(1), 21-7.

Swinton, J. (2001) *A space to listen: Meeting the spiritual needs for people with learning disabilities*, London: The Mental Health Foundation.

Thomas, D. and Woods, H. (2003) *Working with people with learning disabilities*, London and New York: Jessica Kingsley.

Valios, N. (2008) 'Forced marriage of people with learning disabilities', *Community Care*, 28 August (www.communitycare.co.uk/Articles/2008/08/22/109193/forced-marriage-of-people-with-learning-disabilities.html).

VOICE UK, Respond and the Ann Craft Trust (2007) *Forced marriages of adults with learning disabilities* (extract from submission to the Joint Committee on Human Rights Inquiry into the Human Rights of Adults with Learning Disabilities) (www.respond.org.uk/campaigns/Forced_Marriageof_People_with_Learning_Disabilities.html).

Religion, belief, migrants, refugees and asylum seekers[1]

9

Religion has historically played a key role for various migrant groups, providing a vital social space and helping to maintain an ethnic memory. (Burrell and Panayi, 2006, cited in Herbert et al, 2006: 15)

Context

Britain is often described accurately as a country of migrants and, for many, the only useful definition of so-called 'Britishness' lies in the nation's long-running capacity to welcome and incorporate a rich diversity of people from many cultures and locations. The reasons for migration, the geographical origins of migrants, the nature of settlement patterns and particular characteristics change over time and between different individuals and communities. To give some examples from the three centuries prior to 1970:

- In 1656, the Protectorate allowed 300 Jews to settle in Britain, ending a period of nearly 400 years, during which they had been forbidden either to reside or to practise their religion.
- In 1685, the first of over 20,000 Huguenot refugees took sanctuary in England after the government of France declared Protestantism illegal. (They formed approximately 5 per cent of London's population.)
- By 1770, it is estimated that 14,000 Africans were living in Britain.
- Between 1845 and 1850, an estimated 200,000 Irish people fled to Britain in the aftermath of the Famine, greatly increasing the numbers of Roman Catholics in many industrial cities.
- Between 1880 and 1914, an estimated 250,000 Jews moved to Britain to escape pogroms and persecution in Russia and Eastern Europe.
- In 1945, 100,000 Polish refugees and 15,700 German and 1,000 Italian former prisoners of war decided to stay in Britain.

- Between 1946 and 1950, 85,000 Ukrainians, Yugoslavs, Estonians, Latvians and Lithuanians came to Britain.
- By the end of the 1960s, in the wake of active recruitment of overseas labour by employers, about one million people, largely from the Indian subcontinent and the West Indies, together with 900,000 Irish-born people, had settled in Britain. (For further details see Council for Racial Equality [2007].)

Over several centuries, such migrants, and especially those seeking asylum, have frequently shared experiences of (often faith-based) persecution, violence and poverty. They have often also been met with suspicion, prejudice and oppression on arrival and, in some cases, continue to be on the receiving end of both personal and institutional racism. Moreover, the Institute for Public Policy Research (2007: 21) reports that, in determining whether indigenous white communities showed hostile attitudes to new migrants, "the role of race, religion and ethnicity emerged as influential ... with cultural difference being closely associated with non-white communities and Muslim communities", adding that indigenous white participants in the study "felt that white migrants had far fewer cultural differences than non-white or non-Christian communities, and it was therefore easier for them to integrate".

Clearly, all newly arrived migrants are vulnerable to some degree, while a refugee is, by definition, someone who:

> ... owing to a well-founded fear of being persecuted for reasons of race, religion, nationality, membership of a particular social group or political opinion, is outside the country of his nationality and unable or, owing to such fear, is unwilling to avail himself of the protection of that country; or who, not having a nationality and being outside the country of his former habitual residence ... is unable or, owing to such fear, is unwilling to return to it. (UNHCR, 2007: 16)

The comments of a manager working in an agency serving refugees (Inset 1) provides the examples of Sikhs fleeing Afghanistan and Christians fleeing Iran.

Inset 1: Fear of being persecuted for reasons of religion

We have a large number of people from Iran who have converted into Christianity ... they have not been able to practise openly in Iran. We had a large influx of Sikhs from Afghanistan, when the Taliban regime came into

> force. We found that there was a large number of Sikh people coming and claiming asylum because the Sikh temples were being burnt down and, as you know, the Taliban regime wanted everything their own way and no other way was acceptable; so, in terms of the religious side of things, there was a lot of people coming over who then weren't able to practise any religion within those countries (Manager, refugee agency).

Many refugees and asylum seekers have physical and psychological health needs arising from severe trauma experienced in their country of origin or extreme hardships en route to Britain (Gorst-Unsworth and Goldenberg, 1998; Burnett and Peel, 2001; MRCF, 2002; Nazer and Lewis, 2003; Keitetsi, 2004; Misra et al, 2006; Various, 2007; Beah, 2008). On arrival they are faced with what the Refugee Council (see www.refugeecouncil.org.uk/) describes as a "very tough" system involving a "long" and "complex" application process, which leaves many forbidden to work, dependent on vouchers for food and either homeless or with no control over where they live. Refugees and asylum seekers are a relatively small group within the general population, but one in which almost all individuals are likely to be in need of services, at least in the short term. For example, Whittaker et al (2005: 178) report that: "Psychiatric disorder is twice the level in refugee children than in their indigenous peers, even without exposure to war (Tousignant et al, 1999)". We share Humphries' (2004) view that UK immigration laws are unacceptably oppressive and suggest that involvement in their implementation presents major dilemmas to social workers in terms of both professional and personal values, including those that arise from religious beliefs. We note Briskman and Cemlyn's (2005: 416) stark conclusion that, in both Australia and the UK, the approach to immigration and asylum seeking is often characterised by "xenophobia and racism", which has been heightened by events such as 11 September 2001 and the 2002 Bali bombing, and which results in "increased demonising of Muslims" – a phenomenon also highlighted by writers such as Modood (2006), Parekh (2006) and Valtonen (2008).

Fekete (2005) notes that the so-called 'war on terror' across Europe is having a major impact on all Muslims and on those perceived to be Muslims, whether they are new migrants or already living in settled communities. They are frequently cast, in the media and elsewhere, as the 'enemy within'. Fekete (2005: 3) argues that in "the process, the parameters of xeno-racism, which targets impoverished asylum seekers, have been extended to Muslim communities" and that moves are being made to "promote monocultural homogeneity through assimilation". Moreover, commentators such as Modood (2005) and Hubbard (2005) suggest that, in Britain and elsewhere, 'colour racism' is being replaced by 'cultural racism', which seeks to reinforce cultural privilege while relying on generalisations about a group's uniform and static way of life – notably its religion and religious practices.

The United Nations High Commissioner for Refugees (UNHCR) (2006: 17) reports that there were 20.8 million refugees and 'people of concern' worldwide, including 3.7 million (18%) in Europe, while 175,000 refugees had settled in the UK in 2005; 40% of whom were under 18 years. According to the Home Office (2008a), including dependants, there were 28,300 applications for asylum in the UK in 2007. Most applicants were Afghan, Iranian, Chinese, Iraqi or Eritrean. However, the number and origin of asylum applications have varied considerably over time and are dependent on the location of political, military, ethnic and religious crises. There were just over 4,000 applications in 1987 and 32,500 in 1997, while Patel and Kelley (2006) report that applications reached a peak of 84,130 in 2002. Between 1993 and 1997, the main countries producing refugees who came to the UK were India, Somalia, Pakistan, Sri Lanka, Turkey and the former Yugoslavia (MRCF and CUS Consultants, 2002).

Overall, 6,540 (28%) of the applications in 2007 resulted in grants of asylum (14%), humanitarian protection/discretionary leave (8%) or allowed appeals (5%), while 6,800 applications were awaiting an initial decision at the end of 2007. Of the 14,935 appeals determined by immigration judges in 2007, 23% were also allowed (Home Office, 2008a).

Since 2000, asylum seekers have been compulsorily dispersed throughout the country – a system that Anna Reisenberger, Acting Chief Executive of the Refugee Council, describes as leaving them "vulnerable to racism and extreme isolation" (Morris, 2007) and which, in Plymouth, for example, Butler (2005: 148) says is characterised by "A failure of strategic planning", which "has led to a lack of clustering, making it difficult to develop a cultural or ethnic community to support newcomers". However, the majority of refugees and asylum seekers remain in London and the South East of England.

Recognised refugees are entitled to the same social and economic rights as UK citizens, but, since 2005, people recognised as refugees have been given permission to remain in the UK for a maximum of five years. This increases their difficulties in rebuilding shattered lives and putting down new roots. During the period in which their asylum claims are being considered, the National Asylum Support Service (NASS) assesses their need for financial support and arranges longer-term accommodation for them. According to the Home Office (2008b): "Accommodation is normally provided on a no choice basis in one of the designated cluster areas" and "Asylum seekers in receipt of the full support package … are able to access the full range of council services available to any other council tax payer. This includes services such as healthcare, education and social work." When an asylum seeker comes to the end of the asylum process, having been refused asylum

and having exhausted all appeals, they have no rights t
or support. Thus, they are often left destitute without
financial support and are required to move, therefore c
with the mosques, churches and temples that they h
However, section 4 of the Immigration and Asylum
the provision of some support to former asylum se
accommodation and vouchers only and is predominate.,
with no children. (Asylum seekers with children continue to be
as asylum seekers for support purposes until they leave the UK.) Such
individuals, again, have no control over where they are accommodated
or who they share accommodation with, while vouchers are valid only at
specified supermarkets, which do not necessarily carry a range of foodstuffs,
such as halal meat, which will meet religious requirements. Where they do,
these are likely to be relatively highly priced.

Social work with asylum seekers and refugees in Britain and elsewhere
sometimes provides vivid examples of how faith-based practice extends the
range of interventions available, and challenges and ameliorates the impact
of bureaucratic services provided by statutory agencies, offering sanctuary
to those whom state authorities might seek to detain, exclude and deport
(Cemlyn and Briskman, 2003; Hayes and Humphries, 2004). Coton (2007:
3) comments that:

> Asylum seekers are in danger of becoming some of the most
> vulnerable, alienated and demonized members of society. Focus
> needs to be regained on this as a humanitarian issue which requires
> a great deal of sensitivity. Christians believe that refugees should be
> treated as people, with compassion, understanding and respect.

Pohl (2006: 83), also, notes that:

> Christians have made significant contributions to the articulation
> of concerns about human dignity, protecting individual rights, and
> caring for the most vulnerable. Part of that capacity has emerged
> from understandings and practices of offering hospitality to
> strangers, and from reflections on the needs of strangers.

It is, perhaps, also important to recognise that refugees and asylum seekers
have not been the largest group of new arrivals in the UK during the early
years of the 21st century. Migrants continue to arrive from countries such
as Australia, India and Pakistan and, since 2004, have come – initially in
increasing, but later in reducing – numbers from new European Union
(EU) states in Eastern Europe, most notably from Poland. These migrants
have frequently, but not always, come as temporary workers. As measured

y grants of national insurance numbers, a total of 713,000 foreign workers came to work in Britain in 2005, of whom 223,000 were Poles, 49,000 were Indians, 29,000 were Slovakians, 25,000 were Pakistanis and 24,000 were Australians. In 2007, there were an estimated two million foreign nationals working in the UK compared to 0.9 million in 1997 (Statistics Commission, 2007).

The remainder of this chapter focuses primarily on issues with regard to religion, refugees and asylum seekers. However, it is relevant to note that, where other migrants seek services, practitioners will need to be aware of issues that may arise from their religious and spiritual background, and of factors such as the differences between Eastern Orthodox and Roman Catholic traditions or the different traditions of Polish and Maltese Roman Catholicism. Davis et al (2007: 42) describe new migrants in London as "a section of the Catholic community facing tough living conditions, harsh working conditions and constant economic and personal uncertainty" and conclude that: "This faithful, vulnerable and energetic group take their Catholicism seriously and have high hopes of the Church and her Bishops when it comes to assistance in their days of need".

Lessons from earlier migrants and particular communities

The 'Connecting histories' project led by Birmingham City Archives (BCA), which ran between February 2005 and July 2007, reports that:

> Religion was a crucial aspect of the heritage and cultural practice that migrants brought with them to Britain. As they settled, their lives were infused with religion: celebrations, dress, food, relationships, architecture, education and charity often had their basis in religious tradition. Religion was an important source of spiritual and social support to people in diasporic communities who were uprooted from a familiar world into one that was strange and unknown. Gathering with fellow worshippers on a regular basis could give people the sense of belonging to a family when their families might have been very distant from them back in their countries of origin. The institutions that developed enabled traditional practices to continue yet the change of environment also served to challenge them. Through rituals, celebrations and architecture religion provided migrants with the spiritual strength, group identity and visible presence to overcome both isolation and alienation. (BCA, 2007)

However, Christian migrants from the Caribbean usually encountered a religious landscape that was not only strange to them in terms of the atmosphere and style of worship and levels of attendance, but also one where they found that they were not welcome because of racial prejudice. BCA (2007) quotes one respondent, who recalled his first experience of attending a church in Birmingham, saying: "we put on our best suits and went to the church. But after the service the vicar told us not to come again. His congregation wouldn't like it, he said" (Birmingham ILT Services, 1987: 71). Such experiences led most contemporary black Christian migrants, like their Hindu, Sikh and Muslim counterparts, to set about establishing distinct spaces for themselves to cater for the spiritual needs of their community.

BCA (2007) emphasises that churches, mosques, gurdwaras and temples, as well as being places of worship, housed welfare services and supplementary schools, and provided a meeting place where religious and cultural identities were reaffirmed. It cites studies which report that the black churches in Birmingham often provided a range of important social services such as lunch clubs, advocacy and mediation (Small, 1994) and, during the 1970s, helped many people to overcome the alienation they felt (Gerloff, 1992).

The Irish Studies Centre (2005) similarly notes the important role of religion in the lives of Irish migrants – for example, the particular effort put into building Catholic schools during the 19th and early 20th centuries, and the fact that, for the 80% of Irish migrants from a Catholic background, and perhaps regardless of patterns of mass attendance, Catholicism has been as significant as a cultural identity as it has a religious belief. Between 1951 and 1961, over 500,000 Irish migrants came to Britain at a time when "they were leaving a culture where attending Sunday mass was almost universal. As a result new churches and schools were built to cater for them in Britain and attendances at mass increased dramatically" (Irish Studies Centre, 2005). More recently, similar patterns in mass attendance have been noted as the result of Polish migration since 2004 (Bates, 2006), while Davis et al (2007: 31) report that recent Catholic migrants regard the church as "a refuge" and "a harbour of hope".

Herbert et al (2006) also found that, for many Ghanaian migrants, religion was central to their emotional resilience and psychological survival, particularly in the face of adverse situations. They report that many articulated their belief in the temporary nature of their adversity in terms of a religious narrative, and cite Burrell and Panayi (2006) in support of the view that religion has played a key role for a variety of migrant groups by providing a social space and helping to maintain ethnic memory. Herbert et al (2006: 15) also present evidence that membership of churches has helped to counter people's feelings of frustration and exclusion. Respondents often described churches as "a respite and sanctuary from their work", as "like a small family" and as "inclusive and caring".

Whittaker et al (2005: 183) note that religion is a strong force in the lives of young Somali refugees, "promoting psychological well-being and providing guidance in difficult periods", while "The *Qur'an* was a source of guidance in how to react, understand, and cope with loss and difficulties".

The refugee and asylum manager who was interviewed noted that Sikh families from Afghanistan have been welcomed into Sikh temples throughout the country. At the same time, he noted that, for Christians from Iran who are unlikely to share a common language with indigenous church congregations, integration might be more difficult. However, they appear to be welcomed by relevant churches, and his agency helps service users to make contact with them. He remarked:

> We're talking about people who are fleeing horrendous situations, and one of the things that makes them come through, through hell really, is their belief in their God, their religious beliefs, their faith. We always think "everything else has gone against you, but you've got your faith in God". It's a survival mechanism. We do have clients who have openly said, "If there was a God why would we have to go through this?" They've stopped practising their faith, whereas the others have actually clutched onto it even tighter.

How does the state respond to 'religion' in the context of asylum seekers?

A variety of official procedures and guidance exist that clearly acknowledge the potential significance of religion to refugees and asylum seekers, and to the reasons for their need to seek asylum (see Chapter Two). However, reports from those directly involved suggest that these are given little priority in day-to-day practice. The asylum and refugee manager reported that many people will request to be accommodated "near a church, near a mosque, near a Sikh temple", but that they are often accommodated so far away that "they can't actually get to the place of worship". He suggested that, although the requirement to give consideration to religion is clearly stated in the dispersal policy, "the reality is, yes, it's supposed to be there but the reality of it is it isn't".

Patel and Kelley (2006: 1) note that, in relation to these groups, "the response from policy makers and service providers is often inadequate" and that: "There is a tendency to view the needs of refugees and asylum seekers within the generic category of 'black and minority ethnic' service users".

Those working with dispersed asylum seekers report that religious needs are rarely given adequate attention and that individuals' difficulties are sometimes heightened dramatically by being required to share cramped accommodation with people of other religions or sects. The refugee and asylum manager who was interviewed emphasised that appropriate places of worship might be too distant for access to be practical. He also cited examples where people had no space for private prayer and where communal resources such as fridges, cookers and televisions became the catalyst for conflict regarding acceptable/unacceptable foods and moral behaviour. Individuals already experiencing considerable stress are required to live with others in the same position with whom they may have no common language and with whom their own faith community may have traditional or current antipathy. He said that:

> ... the Home Office tends to put people of different religions in the same household, so you may end up with a Christian from Iran, a Sunni Muslim from Iraq and another person from a different religion ... so you've got different nationalities, different religions and obviously that in itself is causing a lot of problems. You've got four people thrown together all of a sudden and the reality of it is that it doesn't work.

The experiences of individuals from countries such as Afghanistan, Iran and Eritrea who are applying for asylum on the grounds of a fear of religious persecution in the context of their adherence or conversion to Christianity are relatively well documented. For example, Coton (2007) reports that, in June 2007, the Evangelical Alliance hosted a symposium on the persecution of Christian asylum seekers, at which Simon Hughes MP appealed for an end to what many of those involved view as inappropriate faith-testing questions by immigration caseworkers and a greater recognition of the sensitivities required when interviewing converts. Examples of 'absurd' questions include, "How do you cook a turkey for Christmas?" as a test of the genuineness of a person's Christian faith. Coton (2007: 17) reports that one asylum seeker was asked "What was the forbidden fruit?" and that, subsequently, the reason given by the Home Office for refusing asylum status was that they had failed to identify the fruit as an apple. (In fact there is no reference to any specific fruit in the Book of Genesis.) Coton (2007) also emphasises that poor interpretation services disadvantage appellants – in these cases, both in general terms and because of a lack of understanding of Christian terminology in the appellant's language. In one example, the appellant said that her brother would slit her throat if she returned to Pakistan. The interpreter translated this as "she'd be in trouble" and it was the court clerk who correctly translated her statement for the adjudicator. Coton (2007: 17) suggests that: "Despite a shared language, religious or denominational ignorance frequently produces nonsensical transliterations, instead of coherent translations, of crucial names and Christian terms at hearings and interviews". However, she also notes that, since 2006, and following representations from the Churches' Main Committee (Churches' Legislation Advisory Service) representing 39 Christian and Jewish bodies, the Immigration Nationality Directorate now advises that decision makers should be aware that some biblical terms will not have a direct translation in the languages of some Muslim countries, and that they should check with interpreters before the start of the interview that questions prepared can be translated accurately.

The refugee and asylum worker who was interviewed commented that the Home Office recognises that religious persecution falls under the convention for claiming asylum and that large numbers of Sikhs from Afghanistan have been granted asylum on these grounds. However, he noted that officials frequently argue that, if people are returned to a country like Iran, nobody is going to know their religion and they sometimes make unrealistic requests for documentation, such as baptismal certificates. The people themselves "are very concerned about being picked up by the authorities, imprisoned, tortured and, in some cases, being killed". He said that people are forced to go underground because their cases have been halted by the Home Office, and that, especially where children and expectant mothers are involved, this may lead to serious concerns for their health, welfare and safety. "They may not be able to practise their religion because they are having to move around all over the place just to try and get shelter and accommodation and a place to sleep for the night."

Key themes for practitioners

- Religion is very likely to be significant to all newly arrived migrants.
- Religion is often a source of emotional and psychological support for migrants facing adversity.
- Refugees and asylum seekers may be fleeing religious persecution or face religious-based persecution if returned to their country of origin.
- Refugees and asylum seekers may be followers of religious faiths not generally associated with their country of origin (for example, Sikhs from Afghanistan, Christians from Iran, Muslims from Ethiopia).
- Differing cultural contexts and traditions may result in unexpected, unfamiliar or, at the extreme, unacceptable practices, such as physically violent exorcism of 'evil spirits' from children (see Chapter Six) being presented as parts of otherwise familiar religions, such as Christianity.

Note

[1] Unlike the preceding five chapters, this one does not include individual case examples. This reflects the fact that the professionals available to the authors for interview were dealing with very immediate crises concerning food, housing and immediate safety and were not in a position to discuss religion and belief in the context of individual cases, but did so in terms of this group of service users as a whole.

References

Bates, S. (2006) 'Devout Poles show Britain how to keep the faith', *The Guardian*, 23 December (www.guardian.co.uk/uk/2006/dec/23/religion. anglicanism).

BCA (Birmingham City Archives) (2007) *Migration and settlement in late 20th century Birmingham* ('Connecting histories' project) (www. connectinghistories.org.uk/Learning%20Packages/Migration/migration_ settlement_20c_lp_03a.asp).

Beah, I. (2008) *A long way gone: Memoirs of a boy soldier*, London: Fourth Estate.

Birmingham ILT Services (1987) *Black in Birmingham*, Birmingham: Birmingham ILT Services.

Briskman, L. and Cemlyn, S. (2005) 'Reclaiming humanity for asylum-seekers: a social work response', *International Social Work*, 48(6), 714-24.

Burnett, A. and Peel, M. (2001) 'Asylum seekers and refugees in Britain: health needs of asylum seekers and refugees', *British Medical Journal*, 322(7285), 544-7 (www.bmj.com/cgi/reprint/322/7285/544).

Burrell, K. and Panayi, P. (2006) *Histories and their memories*, London: Tauris Academic Studies.

Butler, A. (2005) 'A strengths approach to building futures: UK students and refugees together', *Community Development Journal*, 40(2), 147-57.

Cemlyn, S. and Briskman, L. (2003) 'Asylum, children's rights and social work', *Child and Family Social Work*, 8(3), 163-78.

Coton, J. (2007) *Altogether for asylum justice. Asylum seekers' conversion to Christianity*, London: Evangelical Alliance (www.eauk.org/public-affairs/ socialjustice/upload/alltogether-for-asylum-justice.pdf).

Council for Racial Equality (2007) *Migration to and from Britain: A timeline of important events* (http://83.137.212.42/sitearchive/cre/diversity/ migrationtimeline.html).

Davis, F., Stankeviciute, J., Ebbutt, D. and Kaggwa, R. (2007) *The ground of justice: The report of a pastoral research enquiry into the needs of migrants in London's Catholic community*, Cambridge: Von Hügel Institute.

Fekete, L. (2005) 'Anti-Muslim racism and the European security state', *Race and Class*, **46**(1), 3-29.

Gerloff, R. (1992) *A plea for British Black theologies: The Black Church Movement in Britain in its transatlantic Cultural and Theological Interaction, Vol 1*, Frankfurt: Peter Lang.

Gorst-Unsworth, C. and Goldenberg, E. (1998) 'Psychological sequelae of torture and organised violence suffered by refugees from Iraq: trauma-related factors compared with social factors in exile', *British Journal of Psychiatry*, **172**(1), 90-4.

Hayes, D. and Humphries, B. (eds) (2004) *Social work, immigration and asylum: Debates, dilemmas and ethical issues for social work and social care practice*, London: Jessica Kingsley.

Herbert, J., Datta, K., Evans, Y., May, J., McIlwaine, C. and Wills. J. (2006) *Multiculturalism at work: The experiences of Ghanaians in London*, London: Department of Geography, Queen Mary, University of London (www. geography.dur.ac.uk/conferences/Urban_Conference/Programme/pdf_ files/Joanna%20Herbert%20et%20al.pdf).

Home Office (2008a) *Asylum statistics United Kingdom 2007*, London: Research, Development and Statistics Directorate (www.homeoffice.gov. uk/rds/pdfs08/hosb1108.pdf).

Home Office (2008b) *Frequently asked questions – asylum* (available online in November 2008. No longer available July 2009).

Hubbard, P. (2005) 'Accommodating otherness: anti-asylum centre protest and the maintenance of white privilege', *Transactions of the Institute of British Geographers*, **30**(1), 52-65.

Humphries, B. (2004) 'An unacceptable role for social work: implementing immigration policy', *British Journal of Social Work*, **34**(1), 93-107.

Institute for Public Policy Research (2007) *The reception and integration of new migrant communities*, London: Commission for Racial Equality.

Irish Studies Centre (2005) *When did you come over? The story of Irish migration to Britain*, London: London Metropolitan University (www.londonmet. ac.uk/irishstudiescentre/archive/exhibition.cfm).

Keitetsi, C. (2004) *Child soldier*, London: Souvenir Press.

MRCF (Migrant and Refugee Communities Forum) and CVS Consultants (2002) 'A shattered world: the mental health needs of refugees and newly arrived communities', London: MRCF (www.harpweb.org.uk/ downloads/pdf/rep1(ref).pdf).

Misra, T., Connolly, A.M. and Majeed, A. (2006) 'Addressing mental health needs of asylum seekers and refugees in a London Borough: epidemiological and user perspectives', *Primary Health Care Research and Development*, **7**, 241-8.

Modood, T. (2005) *Multicultural politics: Racism, ethnicity and Muslims in Britain*, Minneapolis, MN and Edinburgh: University of Minnesota Press and University of Edinburgh Press.

Modood, T. (2006) 'British Muslims and the politics of multiculturalism', in T. Modood, A. Triandafylldou and R. Zapata-Barrero (eds) *Multiculturalism, Muslims and citizenship*, London: Routledge, pp 37-56.

Morris, N. (2007) 'Dispersal policy "put asylum-seekers at risk"', *The Independent*, 16 March (www.independent.co.uk/news/uk/politics/dispersal-policy-put-asylumseekers-at-risk-440442.html).

Nazer, M. and Lewis, D. (2003) *Slave: My true story*, New York: Public Affairs.

Parekh, B. (2006) 'Europe, liberalism and the "Muslim question"', in T. Modood, A Triandafylldou and R. Zapata-Barrero (eds) *Multiculturalism, Muslims and citizenship*, London: Routledge, pp 179-204.

Patel, B. and Kelley, N. (2006) *The social care needs of refugees and asylum seekers*, London: Social Care Institute for Excellence (www.scie.org.uk/publications/raceequalitydiscussionpapers/redp02.pdf).

Pohl, C.D. (2006) 'Responding to strangers: insights from the Christian tradition', *Studies in Christian Ethics*, **19**(1), 81-101.

Small, S. (1994) *Racialised barriers: The Black experience in the United States and England in the 1980s*, London: Routledge.

Statistics Commission (2007) 'Foreign workers in the UK – Statistics Commission briefing note' (www.statscom.org.uk/C_1237.aspx).

Tousignant, M., Habimana, E., Biron, C., Malo, C., Sidoli-Le Blanc, E. and Bendris, N. (1999) 'The Quebec Adolescent Refugee Project: psychotherapy and family variables in a sample from 35 nations', *Journal of the American Academy of Child & Adolescent Psychiatry*, **38**(11), 1-7.

UNHCR (United Nations High Commissioner for Refugees) (2001) 'The wall behind which refugees can shelter: the 1951 Geneva Convention', *Refugees*, **2**(123) (www.unhcr.org/publ/PUBL/3b5e90ea0.pdf).

UNHCR (2006) *Refugees by numbers*, Geneva: UNHCR (www.unhcr.ch/include/fckeditor/custom/File/PublicStatist/Statistiques/RefugeeByNumbers_e.pdf).

UNHCR (2007) *Convention and protocol relating to the status of refugees*, Geneva: UNHCR (www.unhcr.org/protect/PROTECTION/3b66c2aa10.pdf).

Various (2007) *From there to here: Sixteen true tales of immigration to Britain*, London: Penguin.

Valtonen, K. (2008) *Social work and migration: Immigrant and refugee settlement and integration*, Farnham: Ashgate.

Whittaker, S., Hardy, G., Lewis, K. and Buchanan, L. (2005) 'An exploration of psychological well-being with young Somali refugee and asylum-seeker women', *Clinical Child Psychology and Psychiatry*, **10**(2), 177-96.

10

Faith-based social work: contributions, dilemmas and conflicts

> In today's multi-faith society we continue to recognise and respect our Christian foundation, and we also embrace the changing society in which we live. (Narey, 2007)

Faith-based approaches to social work

Gilligan (2009a, forthcoming) explores faith-based approaches to social work and concludes that, while there is no single type, such approaches can be categorised into two broad but contrasting groups: 'fundamentalist or exclusive' and 'liberal or open'. He argues that:

> Fundamentalist–Exclusive approaches begin with the view that the experience of, or adherence to, a faith is an essential starting point, not only for eventual spiritual salvation, but also for a fulfilled and satisfying life in the present. Acceptance of the faith may be seen as an essential component in being able to move on from current difficulties or overcoming past trauma. In such approaches, faith is an integral part of practice which is likely to involve at least an invitation to service users to accept aspects of it. Faith is seen as beneficial, protective and potentially life changing and becomes part of, perhaps fundamental to, practitioners' repertoire of interventions. (Gilligan, 2009a, forthcoming)

He suggests that, in contrast:

> [F]aith-based agencies adopting more Liberal–Open approaches while they usually involve individuals and organizations who profess faith, express the part it plays very differently. Faith is seen as a motivation for action, but not necessarily as an essential part of that action. Practitioners may believe that their faith requires them to act and to provide services, but they will do so without

> attempting to engage those people in their particular faith or any faith other than as beneficiaries of actions motivated by it. In such approaches, faith may sometimes appear almost incidental to face-to-face interventions. (Gilligan, 2009a, forthcoming)

The 'fundamentalist or exclusive' approach is, perhaps, characterised by the Social Work Christian Fellowship (see www.swcf.org.uk/aims.html), which states that it "seeks to develop Biblical thinking, challenge secular assumptions, and promote Christian perspectives in policy-making and practice". Its aims include that of encouraging "Christians working in social work and social care settings to integrate their personal faith with their professional practice". The 'liberal or open' approach, in contrast, is in Britain typified by policy statements from agencies such as Barnardo's and the Children's Society. These acknowledge their faith-based origins, but, also, give explicit emphasis to inclusiveness and, by implication, to the absence of conditionality or proselytising. Barnardo's, for example, tells prospective employees, "We welcome, value and need staff from many world faiths and philosophies, and the diversity and talent they bring" (Narey, 2007).

These are 'Christian' examples, but similar dichotomies are also found to varying degrees among many other faiths and have a similar impact on discussions about faith-based approaches to social work and related activities. For example, there are ongoing debates within youth work around the extent to which 'Muslim youth' does or does not need 'Muslim youth work', and whether this should be seen as a religious exercise (Hamid, 2006; Hussain, 2006; Khan, 2006; Roberts, 2006).

Individuals and organisations who subscribe to religious beliefs (particularly, but not exclusively, Christianity) had a significant influence on the origins of social work in Britain and elsewhere (Guttmann and Cohen, 1995; Bowpitt, 1998, 2000; Payne, 2005; Williams and Smolak, 2007; Prohaska, 2006; Crabtree et al, 2008; Taylor, 2008), although their influence has varied and continues to vary across contexts (see Gray et al, 2008a). In Britain, as elsewhere, faith-based social work and social care agencies provide a significant proportion of services in particular settings, such as work with the homeless or adoption services, where, for example, they account for about 15 per cent of the national caseload. Alongside the rest of the voluntary sector, they may extend the range of interventions available in a specific locality and sometimes provide alternatives that challenge the bureaucratic nature of services offered by statutory agencies, especially in contexts such as social work with asylum seekers and refugees (see Chapter Nine). However, there remains a risk that some faith-based organisations may 'abuse' their position as service providers or be exploited by neo-liberal social policies that charge them with major responsibilities in the absence of adequate resources (Jordan, 2000; De'Ath, 2004). It may sometimes be inappropriate to give faith-based organisations responsibility for particular tasks, most notably risk assessment of clergy suspected of abusing children (see Chapter Six). Some religious organisations may prioritise the religious conversion of service users (see www.caringforlife.co.uk/ or www.teenchallenge.co.uk/content/view/23/49/) or the faith organisation's reputation over the needs of individuals (see Bryant, 2004). They may advocate spirit possession (see Stobart, 2006; Gilligan, 2008) or oppressive views of gay men and lesbian women (see Hicks, 2003; Trotter et al, 2008) or deny the equal rights of women or other groups (see Busuttil and ter Haar, 2002).

Meanwhile, according to Communities and Local Government (2008: 43):

> There are over 23,000 religious charities in the UK and many more faith-based organisations, involving tens of thousands of people motivated by their faith, working at a local and national level to provide support and services to communities.

Secularist pressure groups argue that some of these agencies (those whose primary motivation is to promote their religious beliefs) are likely to discriminate against potential employees and service users (British Humanist Association, 2007) and that the "secular approach to social care" may need defending "against creeping 'faith-based' provision – for example in relation to work with young people and the criminal justice system, mental health, substance misuse and the care of older people" (Atherton/National Secular Society, 2008).

Social workers, beliefs and practice dilemmas

Practitioners may also encounter strong religious beliefs and motivations in relation to those offering to act as carers for vulnerable adults or 'looked after' children. The adoption worker involved with 'Aysha' (Chapter Four), for example, noted her occasional need to challenge religiously based motivations and suggested that their prominence in discussions might indicate the absence of factors that are necessary to ensure that a family will genuinely accept a child. She cited the example of a discontinued application where the prospective adopter had explained their motivation almost exclusively in terms of the statement, "Allah will praise me in Heaven".

There is a wide range of significant issues that may create dilemmas for individual social workers because of their religious beliefs and for agencies because of their faith base. There is also a wide range of resulting behaviours that may require appropriate responses from colleagues, managers or employers, or from funders or accrediting bodies. Issues will vary greatly between individuals and faith communities but may include responses to the following:

- termination of pregnancy/'abortion';
- 'mercy killing'/'euthanasia';
- contraception;
- consumption of alcohol;
- sexual intercourse outside marriage;
- same-sex sexual relationships;
- beliefs in spirit possession (positive or negative);
- religious-based practices such as male infant circumcision;
- use of stimulants such as caffeine;
- blood transfusions;
- use of donor organs;
- corporal punishment/physical abuse of children;
- the authority/rights of children/adults/women/men.

For secular organisations and national accrediting bodies, such as the General Social Care Council (GSCC), the responses and actions of individuals in relation to such matters may raise important questions regarding the extent to which individual 'conscientious objection' can be accommodated. Such issues may also raise significant dilemmas for faith-based organisations where they believe that legislation or government guidance requires them to act in ways that are contrary to their fundamental teachings and against what they see as their duty to their god. For government and legislators, such dilemmas might result in questions around whether agencies that have previously provided acceptable and valuable social work services should be given specific exemptions in legislation.

The issue of the approval of same-sex couples as adopters provides a clear example of the types of issues and dilemmas that may arise.

'Same-sex adoption': conflicting views and values

Gay men and lesbians in England and Wales were already able to adopt as individuals prior to the Adoption and Children Act 2002. However, this legislation, which came into full force on 30 December 2005, allows all couples, regardless of whether or not they are married or in a civil partnership, to adopt jointly. This led to protests by some religious groups, notably Christian fundamentalists and the Roman Catholic hierarchy, who argued against adoption by same-sex couples. They claimed that the care these couples would provide for children would have an adverse impact on their future development (Christian Institute, 2002a, 2002b; Holloway, 2002;

Morgan, 2002). Such claims are vehemently challenged by writers such as Ben-Ari (2001) and Hicks (2000, 2003, 2006). Hicks (2003), in particular, argued that these 'Christian' writers have misused research (for example, Golombok and Tasker, 1996) to construct a mythical version of parenting by same-sex couples.

In October 2002, social workers Norah Ellis and Dawn Jackson were warned by their employers, Sefton Council, that they may be disciplined or dismissed if they acted on their reported comments to colleagues that, as Christians, they thought that same-sex couples could not provide a proper environment for adopted children. Norah Ellis told the press at the time that: "The Government is bending over backwards to accommodate minorities while the Christian majority is being discriminated against". (For contemporary news reports see *Community Care* [2003a] and Harrison [2003].)

Subsequently, it was agreed between them and their employer that they should be transferred to posts in adult services. However, it is perhaps significant that, in this case, the two social workers received their original letters following what one described as "an informal chat over coffee" and before they had discussed their views formally with colleagues or line managers. Their case led to calls in Parliament for the inclusion of a 'conscience clause' in the legislation and such a clause was moved by Baroness Blatch in the House of Lords in June 2003 (see www.publications.parliament. uk/pa/ld200203/ldhansrd/vo030623/text/30623-41.htm). In arguing for this, she cited the examples of section 4 of the Abortion Act 1967, which allows doctors who oppose abortion for moral or professional reasons to refuse to participate in abortions, and section 59 of the School Standards and Framework Act 1998, which protects teachers from being discriminated against because of their religious beliefs. She argued that: "Christianity and the other major world religions believe that sexual activity outside marriage is wrong. Many adherents to Christianity and other religions work in adoption, and they deserve protection for their conscientious views in such instances" (GC 41). She asked: "Will everyone who works with a local authority be compelled to conform to an ideological secularism, despite all the evidence, common sense and deeply held convictions that run counter to it?" (GC 42). Opposing her, Baroness Barker said: "be they Christians or be they not, they have to uphold it without exception ... Many people with strong convictions and religious beliefs work for local authorities and have to uphold laws which they find offensive and repugnant" (GC 43).

A 'conscience clause' was also opposed by groups such as the British Association for Adoption and Fostering (BAAF) and Adoption UK. The deputy chief executive of BAAF, Barbara Hutchinson, said:

> It is not about religious practice, but professional practice and needs of children. People need to look at the requirement of the job – if they really feel they can't do this for religious reasons there are voluntary agencies that make exceptions. (*Community Care*, 2003b)

Community Care (2003c) reports on the comments they received from readers about the issue of a 'conscience clause'. This was clearly an opportunity sample and might not represent the views of others. However, it is arguably indicative of the lack of consensus and polarised opinions within the profession regarding such issues. Comments ranged from:

> A key part of my social work training was instilling a 'non-judgemental attitude'. A conscience clause fundamentally undermines this tenet of social work practice. It seems that here we are being told that these social workers cannot put aside their personal beliefs, and make a judgement on the ability of two adults to provide a good home and upbringing for a child being considered for adoption. If that is the case, then can we trust their judgement in other matters? (*Community Care*, 2003c)

To:

> A religious person who in all conscience cannot agree to an area of work, such as abortion or same sex adoption is discriminated against themselves by the relativist dogma of political correctness. Who is ultimately to say that an individual is wrong to opt out of such work? And who ultimately makes the moral judgement that someone has to do it or lose their job? This slippery road will lead to religious people being increasingly discriminated be they Christian, Muslim, Jewish or whatever. (*Community Care*, 2003c)

The Equality Act 2006 enshrines in law the principle that people must not be discriminated against on the grounds of (among other things) sexual orientation in the provision of public services. The subsequent Sexual Orientation Regulations approved by Parliament in April 2007 caused considerable difficulties for Roman Catholic adoption agencies. As a result, the Roman Catholic Bishops – with some vocal support from the Anglican Archbishops of Canterbury and York – threatened to close down all seven Catholic adoption agencies if they were forced to enable same-sex couples to adopt children. The agencies were given a 21-month exemption, but that expired on 1 January 2009. O'Donoghue (2007: 1) writes that "this legislation contravenes the certain teachings of the Church and our own consciences". The Catholic adoption agencies, supported by the Bishops' Conference, initially, sought permanent exemption from the regulations. They were unsuccessful and, by 2008, had adopted a variety of responses, including cessation of all involvement in adoption and direct defiance of the regulations (Caldwell, 2008a). Some agencies cut all ties with their dioceses and continue to provide adoption services within the regulations and legislation. In at least one case, the non-clerical Catholic social work professionals involved did so, despite the very public opposition of the Diocesan bishop (BBC News Channel, 2008, 2009; Caldwell, 2008b; O'Donoghue, 2008).

Bishop O'Donoghue of the Lancaster Diocese said, in July 2007:

> I favour ... withdrawal from adoption and fostering from December 2008 if all else fails ... we know that what is best for children is to live with married couples. Dilution of that harms children ... children who stay with married parents do by far the best, whilst those with same-sex couples often fare badly, and certainly never as well as a child with a married couple. (O'Donoghue, 2007)

However, the trustees of Catholic Caring Services in the Diocese of Lancaster subsequently decided on an open policy towards all couples in the adoption of children and, in December 2008, its website, far from announcing "a withdrawal from adoption and fostering", included a statement welcoming the Adoption and Children Act 2002 and quoting its Director of Children's Services, Jim Cullen, as saying:

> People who are in a stable relationship, but who are not married, were not previously able to jointly adopt a child. The new law changes this, allowing these unmarried couples to both become a child's legal parent. This will encourage many people to come forward to offer a child a permanent home. (www.catholiccaringservices.co.uk)

He is also clear that he views his agency as remaining "a Catholic charity, operating the same services, with the same staff, same values and same ethos" (Caldwell, 2008b).

Conscience, openness, reflection and social work values

The debate around adoption by same-sex couples reflects a polarisation of opinion and a lack of consensus that can sometimes be found in related contexts such as discussion around religion, belief and child abuse (Gilligan,

2009b). It also serves to emphasise the need for structures, forums and opportunities for social workers to identify, share, reflect on and seek to resolve relevant dilemmas, both individually and collectively. As emphasised in Chapter Three and in many of the case examples in this book, it is essential that social workers address questions around their own religious and spiritual beliefs or the absence of them and their responses to those of others in particular pieces of practice. It is equally important that they have opportunities in supervision and elsewhere to explore the interface between their beliefs and their work in a more general sense and that they are challenged to recognise both the impact (positive and negative) of this interaction on their work and the dilemmas that may arise.

However, this clearly relies on the availability of a 'safe' context in which to do these things. It also raises challenging questions around the day-to-day practical meaning and limits (if any) of the values and principles of 'acceptance' and of being 'non-judgemental', particularly in relation to professional colleagues and student social workers. Indeed, it is telling for the authors of this book to recall that their first conversations about issues relevant to it were in the context of discussions about how to respond to the behaviour of, and the responses of others to, a social work student who had been taught practice by one of them and taught academically by the other (see Inset 1).

Inset 1: 'Thomas'

'Thomas' had recently joined a fundamentalist church, which had helped him to resolve a number of his own issues in the past and which continued as the hub of his spiritual and social life. On placement, he had been very open in supervision about the emotional strength and motivation he drew from his religious beliefs and the pressures that the elders of his church exerted on him to encourage service users of the agency to attend services and other events. He had also been very honest from the outset about his struggle to balance his religious views regarding same-sex relationships, sexual relationships outside marriage and matters such as abortion with the values requirements of the Diploma in Social Work (GSCC, 2002) and the agency's strong commitment to anti-oppressive practice and to anti-heterosexist practice in particular. Thomas accepted that he must follow the policies of the agency and did so. He also accepted that he must meet the values requirements and did so, particularly in relation to demonstrating a student's ability to "Identify and question their own values and prejudices, and their implications for practice" (GSCC, 2002: 16). Indeed this was one of his priorities in supervision and his determination to prevent his religious beliefs impacting adversely on

▶

his practice was thoroughly discussed in the placement report. His practice educator encouraged him, *within supervision*, to be as open as possible about his personal beliefs, values and prejudices and promoted the view that this was an essential starting point to preventing their potential adverse impact on his practice.

Subsequently, Thomas and other students on his DipSW course were invited during a module on values at his university to discuss issues related to same-sex sexual relationships. Thomas began by stating the *personal* belief he had expressed many times in supervision that these were "sinful" and, before he could say more, was vehemently challenged by other members of the class. He made no further contribution to the discussion and subsequently several of his fellow students complained to the DipSW course leader about his expressing "homophobic" views and suggested that his training should be terminated because of this. The matter was investigated and it was established that Thomas saw himself as having begun to express and explore views relevant to his personal life that might potentially create dilemmas for him in practice, not as advocating homophobic policies or practice by social workers. He had initially thought that he was doing this in a 'safe' environment with colleagues who would support him in such an exploration.

In another case, 'Abida', a final-year female Muslim student on a BA Social Work course, was on placement at a voluntary sector, user-led mental health agency (see Inset 2).

Inset 2: 'Abida'

During supervision with her off-site practice educator, Abida explained that, in Islamic culture, symptoms attributed to mental health were in fact *jinns* who had entered the body. She described how her sister, who had been sectioned under the Mental Health Act 1984, had been taken by the family to a healer who had been able to exorcise the bad *jinns*. Her sister had recovered for a few days but had then relapsed. Abida had been working with a Muslim service user who had stopped taking his medication as he and his family all believed that his body had been entered by *jinns* and that there was therefore no point in him taking his medication. Abida also believed that this was the case and had not encouraged him to take his medication. When asked further questions by the practice educator about her beliefs in *jinns*, Abida suggested that these applied only to Muslim service users and that she would work differently with white service users. She did not accept that it was dangerous for the service user not to take medication.

Thomas's and Abida's experiences highlight many issues – in particular, the danger that social work practitioners from a range of faith backgrounds will struggle to resolve dilemmas thrown up by the mismatch between their own values and those of 'social work' or of agencies and may be prevented from even acknowledging these dilemmas, let alone finding ways to explore and resolve them. Without appropriate opportunities to do so, there is a danger that social workers may find themselves in contexts with colleagues and managers that force them to pretend to views that they do not hold and do not act on in their face-to-face practice with service users. Managers, supervisors and employers in fact need to ensure that the opposite is always possible – that is, that social workers facing such dilemmas are free to explore them 'safely' with colleagues, while at the same time acting according to social work values in face-to-face work with vulnerable people, or where necessary changing to a role where their beliefs will not have an adverse impact on practice. More worryingly, if a practitioner (qualified or in training) is not able to recognise and appreciate the consequences of adhering to a particular belief system that is detrimental and potentially dangerous to service users, then their suitability and fitness to practice must be open to question.

In some cases, it may be necessary for individuals to be disciplined, or to have their employment or training terminated for inappropriate actions arising from their beliefs, or for commissions or funding to be withdrawn from organisations that cannot or will not comply with essential requirements. In relation to the Equality Act 2006, the Christian Institute (2006: 1), for example, argues that: "Freedom of religion is not just the freedom to believe things in your head, but to abide by them in your life" and by "life" they presumably mean to include professional practice. However, effectively forcing or allowing individuals to pretend to views they do not genuinely share is likely, in itself, to be extremely counterproductive. Those facing dilemmas because of their beliefs still need opportunities to identify these and their implications for practice, and they need opportunities to resolve them.

Key questions

(1) Which of the social work agencies that you have worked for or alongside have been or are influenced by connections with a faith or faiths?

(2) Does this influence have an impact on approaches to practice and in what ways is this beneficial or disadvantageous to the individuals or groups served by the agency?

(3) How is your approach to practice affected by your personal beliefs and/or your connections with a faith or faiths, or your lack of connections with a faith or faiths?

(4) What dilemmas do you face as a result and how do you resolve these?

(5) Do faith-based agencies have a useful role to play in the delivery of social work? (If so, what is it? If not, why not?)

References

Atherton, S. and the National Secular Society (2008) 'Religion, spirituality and social work – help needed' (www.secularism.org.uk/religionspiritualityandsocialwor.html).

BBC News Channel (2008) 'Church leader in gay adoption row', 6 October (http://news.bbc.co.uk/1/hi/england/lancashire/7655329.stm).

BBC News Channel (2009) 'Agencies obey gay adoption rules', 1 January (http://news.bbc.co.uk/1/hi/uk/7806780.stm).

Bowpitt, G. (1998) 'Evangelical Christianity, secular humanism and the genesis of British social work', *British Journal of Social Work*, **28**(5), 675-94.

Bowpitt, G. (2000) 'Working with creative creatures: towards a Christian paradigm for social work theory, with some practical implications', *British Journal of Social Work*, **30**(3), 349-64.

British Humanist Association (2007) *Quality and equality: Human rights, public services and religious organisations*, London: British Humanist Association.

Bryant, C.C. (2004) 'Collaboration between the Catholic Church, the mental health, and the criminal justice systems regarding clergy sex offenders', in T.G. Plante (ed) *Sin against the innocents: Sexual abuse by priests and the role of the Catholic church*, Westport, CT: Praeger, pp 115-22.

Busuttil, J. and ter Haar, G. (eds) (2002) *The freedom to do God's will: Religious fundamentalism and social change*, London: Routledge.

Caldwell, S. (2008a) 'Cardinal's adoption agency defies Government over gay rights laws', *The Catholic Herald*, 13 June (www.catholicherald.co.uk/articles/a0000300.shtml).

Caldwell, S. (2008b) 'Bishop gives ultimatum to agency over gay adoption', *The Catholic Herald*, 10 October (www.catholicherald.co.uk/articles/a0000389.shtml).

Christian Institute (2002a) *Adoption law – sidelining stability and security*, Newcastle-upon-Tyne: Christian Institute (www.christian.org.uk/html-publications/adoption_briefing2.htm).

Christian Institute (2002b) *Same-sex parenting is bad for kids*, Newcastle-upon-Tyne: Christian Institute (www.christian.org.uk/pressreleases/2002/february_06_2002.htm).

Christian Institute (2006) 'New threat to religious freedom', *The Christian Institute Newsletter*, April (www.christian.org.uk/soregs/sornewsletter_apr06.pdf).

Communities and Local Government (2008) *Communities in control: Real people, real power*, London: The Stationery Office (www.communities.gov.uk/documents/communities/pdf/886045.pdf).

Community Care (2003a) 'Social workers warned not to plead conscience clause in same-sex cases', 15 May (www.communitycare.co.uk/Articles/2003/05/15/40761/social-workers-warned-not-to-plead-conscience-clause-in-samesex.html?key=YOUTH%20OR%20SERVICES).

Community Care (2003b) 'Religious opt out of gay adoptions "should be refused"', 13 May (www.communitycare.co.uk/Articles/2003/05/13/40710/religious-opt-out-of-gay-adoptions-should-be-refused.html).

Community Care (2003c) 'Debate on a conscience opt out clause for social workers', 19 June (www.communitycare.co.uk/Articles/2003/06/19/41155/debate-on-aconscience-opt-out-clause-for-social-workers.html?key=CHILDREN%20OR%20SERVICES).

Crabtree, S.A., Husain, F. and Spalek, B. (2008) *Islam and social work: Debating values, transforming practice*, Bristol: The Policy Press.

De'Ath, E. (2004) 'The historical role of charities in addressing social exclusion', paper presented at the National Evaluation of the Children's Fund online conference, 'Understanding prevention: children, families and social inclusion', 17-24 June (www.ne-cf.org/conferences/show_paper.asp?section=000100010001&conferenceCode=000200080011&id=116&full_paper=1).

Gilligan, P. (2008) 'Child abuse and spirit possession: not just an issue for African migrants', *childRIGHT*, **245** (April), 28-31.

Gilligan, P. (2009a, forthcoming) 'Faith-based approaches', in M. Gray and S. Webb (eds) *Ethics and value perspectives in social work*, London: Palgrave Macmillan, chapter 6.

Gilligan, P. (2009b) 'Considering religion and beliefs in child protection and safeguarding work: is any consensus emerging?', *Child Abuse Review*, **18**(2), 94-110.

Golombok, S. and Tasker, F. (1996) 'Do parents influence the sexual orientation of their children? Findings from a longitudinal study of lesbian families', *Developmental Psychology*, **32**(1), 3-11.

GSCC (General Social Care Council) (2002) *Assuring quality for the Diploma in Social Work – 1. Rules and requirements for the DipSW*, London: GSCC.

Guttmann, D. and Cohen, B.-Z. (1995) 'Israel', in T.D. Watts, D. Elliott and N.S. Mayadas (eds) *International handbook on social work education*, Westport, CT: Greenwood Press, pp 305-20.

Hamid, S. (2006) 'Models of Muslim youth work: between reform and empowerment', *Youth and Policy*, **92** (September), 81-9.

Harrison, D. (2003) 'Christian care workers forced out for opposing gay adoptions',10 May, *Telegraph.co.uk* (www.telegraph.co.uk/news/uknews/1429729/Christian-care-workers-forced-out-for-opposing-gay-adoptions.html).

Hicks, S. (2000) '"Good lesbian, bad lesbian …": regulating heterosexuality in fostering and adoption assessments', *Child and Family Social Work*, **5**(2), 157-68.

Hicks, S. (2003) 'The Christian right and homophobic discourse: a response to evidence that lesbian and gay parenting damages children', *Sociological Research Online*, **8**(4) (www.socresonline.org.uk/8/4/hicks.html).

Hicks, S. (2006) 'Genealogy's desire: practices of kinship amongst lesbian and gay foster carers and adopters', *British Journal of Social Work*, **36**(5), 761-76.

Holloway, J. (2002) *Homosexual parenting – does it make a difference? A re-evaluation of the research with adoption and fostering in mind*, Newcastle-upon-Tyne: The Christian Institute (www.christian.org.uk/html-publications/homosexualparenting.htm).

Hussain, T. (2006) 'Working Islamically with young people or working with Muslim youth?', *Youth and Policy*, **92** (September), 107-18.

Jordan, B. with Jordan, C. (2000) *Social work and the Third Way: Tough love as social policy*, London: Sage Publications.

Khan, M.G. (2006) 'Towards a national strategy for Muslim youth work', *Youth and Policy,* **92** (September), 7-18.

Narey, M. (2007) *Our basis and values*, Ilford: Barnardo's.

O'Donoghue, P., Bishop (2007) 'To all at Catholic caring services and the parishes of the Diocese', letter, 9 July (www.lancasterdiocese.org.uk/admin/Uploads/media/35/caring-services.pdf).

O'Donoghue, P., Bishop (2008) 'Letter to the Trustees of Catholic Caring Services, copied to parishes of the Diocese and the media', 5 October (www.spuc.org.uk/resources/ccs.pdf).

Payne, M. (2005) *The origins of social work: Continuity and change*, Basingstoke: Palgrave Macmillan.

Prohaska, F. (2006) *Christianity and social service in Modern Britain: The disinherited spirit*, Oxford: Oxford University Press.

Roberts, J. (2006) 'Making a place for Muslim youth work in British youth work', *Youth and Policy*, **92** (September), 19-31.

Taylor, C. (2008) 'Humanitarian narrative: bodies and detail in late-Victorian social work', *British Journal of Social Work*, **38**(4), 680-96.

Trotter, J., Kershaw, S. and Knott, C. (eds) (2008) 'Sexualities', *Social Work Education*, Special issue, **27**(2), 117-225.

Williams, M.E. and Smolak, A. (2007) 'Integrating faith matters in social work education', *Journal of Religion and Spirituality in Social Work*, **26**(3), 25-44.

Concluding remarks

11

> Social workers must learn that clients' difficulties often contain an important moral dimension, that clients are often wrestling with the moral aspects of problems in their lives. (Goldstein, 1987, cited in Reamer, 2006: 34)

The idea for this book first arose about five years ago when we were planning a conference entitled 'Shifting sands: developing cultural competence'. We were both convinced that cultural competence was an important element in social work education and training and that it needed to be covered more effectively. However, we also recognised, and still do, that the concept of 'cultural competence' is vague, contended and open to wide interpretation. Indeed, it often feels as if it is built on very loose foundations.

Sundar (2009) examines the links between multiculturalism and 'cultural competence' and cites Abu-Laban (2002) as questioning whether it is "possible for people from diverse groups to experience full economic, political, social and educational inclusion (that is, to be perceived as equals), while at the same time sustaining the traditions and practices unique to their cultural group (that is, to honour their differences)" (Sundar, 2009: 99).

It is now well documented that ethnocentric practices, such as judging a culture by the standards of one's own, have served to legitimise, perpetuate and institutionalise the status and influence of the dominant or majority group by cultivating beliefs about the superiority of 'us' and the inferiority of 'them' (Sue, 2006). In response, cultural relativism – that is, the practice of judging a culture by its own standards – has been identified as an alternative approach that is more in tune with social work values. Although this encourages a better informed and welcome recognition of the very positive aspects of diverse cultures and belief systems, and of the strengths and resilience that they provide to people at times of trauma, crisis and distress, it can also be contentious and difficult to achieve without conscious and active attempts to foster this understanding. As some of the case studies in this book have highlighted, it is also necessary, on occasions, to question and challenge the cultural practices of individuals and groups, including those that arise from religious and other beliefs, and this needs to be done from a well-informed and reflexive standpoint. Too often, a lack of knowledge and awareness, or a fear of being branded as 'racist' or 'judgemental', has led to an unquestioning and unhealthy acceptance of behaviours and actions at the cost of failing to protect vulnerable children and adults from harm and exploitation. It may also be interpreted as endorsing and accepting others' prejudices.

In class, we were discussing the meaning and application of traditional social work values of respect and acceptance. A female African student, who had been working as a care assistant, described how an older, white, English woman refused to let her help with any personal care tasks because she was black. She had been told to accept this by her manager and not to work with this resident. Clearly, this is wrong and should have been addressed by management with the resident. We also discussed the likelihood that some residents might be distressed to have carers of the opposite sex assisting them with bathing and providing other intimate care. Debates about how far to accommodate preferences based on cultural norms continue within mainstream health and social care services. 'Cultural' traditions and 'religious' traditions are often confused and this adds a further complication when trying to ascertain whether a service, intervention or preference is necessary or negotiable.

Our hope is that we have made a compelling case for practitioners and educators to pay attention to matters of religion and belief as part of developing cultural competence. We wish to acknowledge that there are some gaps in our book. We have not been able to pay much attention to the place of different philosophical theories that inform judgements and decision making when dealing with moral and ethical dilemmas. However, readers are urged to consider the role and relevance of ethical theories in their decision making (see Banks, 2006; Hughes and Baldwin, 2006; Parrott, 2006; Reamer, 2006). Deontological theories claim that: "certain kinds of action are inherently right or good, as a matter of principle" (Osmo and Landau, 2006: 865). Religious believers usually have an obligation to uphold and follow certain moral laws in accordance with their religious traditions. Therefore, it is important that practitioners become aware that members of different religions are expected to carry out and comply with certain acts, ranging from doing things that are obligatory to avoiding others that are categorically forbidden. Humanists may reject the divine basis for morality, but will, instead, take into account some key principles such as 'treat others as you would like to be treated' and consider the consequences of actions when making moral decisions (Bowie, 2004). Therefore, it is critical that "social workers actively explore clients' perspectives about what they believe is ethically right or wrong" (Reamer, 2006: 34) and identify the basis of these beliefs in order to locate potential conflicts and aid others (and themselves) to deal with matters of conscience.

Durkheim saw religion as having a positive, beneficial role in society. He identified three main functions of religion in society: first, to promote social cohesion by uniting believers through shared values and norms that also cemented moral and emotional ties; second, to regulate the behaviour of people who identify and associate with them through social conformity, thus legitimising the political system; and, third, to provide meaning and purpose so that people may be comforted in times of need and crisis by a sense of a greater purpose (Macionis and Plummer, 2008: 611-12). Believers of all faiths (and those of no faith) can hold strong convictions that they are truly acting in the best interests of others, and this can generate social conflict and unrest. Social work has a legal mandate and a professional responsibility to protect and to intervene in the lives of those whose best interests and well-being are being overlooked or misinterpreted by those in positions of trust and power over them. Practitioners need to feel equipped with the skills and knowledge necessary to assess and determine the justness, fairness, efficacy and appropriateness of actions attributed to any set of religious or other beliefs or to cultural traditions. As these are not static phenomena, but subject to continual change and individual interpretation, it is also essential that social workers take, and are given, sufficient time to inform themselves about relevant cultures, religions and beliefs as a matter of routine throughout their careers. It is equally essential that they seek, through reflection and discussion, to understand how their own latent (perhaps unconscious) beliefs and biases can contribute to unintended offence, insensitivity, discrimination and oppression.

We have included a series of questions at the end of each chapter to help readers to reflect on past experiences and to avoid the obvious dangers inherent in not listening to service users or behaving as if they "know it" or "have heard it all before". It is also important to recognise that a person's religion or belief can be a very private part of their life, which they may not want to discuss with a worker immediately, or at any time. However, it is equally important to revisit such issues as part of an ongoing assessment. The service user's position may change as the relationship develops and trust is established.

After the 'Shifting sands' conference, we started to explore with students and practitioners what place religion has in their work with others. Working in Bradford, where religion is of central importance in the lives of many people who live, work and study in the city, provided us with many opportunities to research and develop our ideas. Our research and that of others (Furness, 2003; Gilligan, 2003; Furman et al, 2004; Gilligan and Furness, 2006; Gilligan, 2009a) suggests that a large number of British social workers have been brought up with religious or other beliefs and that many continue to draw strength and motivation from them without this bringing them into any conflict with the values of the profession. However, many individual social workers hold views that do and, as a result, practitioners, managers, employers and agencies are likely to find themselves responsible for colleagues whose attitudes and behaviour bring them into direct conflict with their duties and responsibilities as social workers and employees. This inevitably raises fundamental questions about the boundaries between accommodating individual consciences and tolerating unacceptable attitudes and behaviour.

However, some social workers are increasingly confident about using religious or spiritually sensitive interventions in their practice, although the likelihood of their doing so varies between different countries. In a sample of social work students in the US, Sheridan and Amato-von Hemert (1999) found that 31.2% had already recommended participation in a religious or spiritual programme to service users and 79% approved of this practice. Gilligan and Furness (2006) found that 15.5% of a British sample of student social workers had done so, while 34.5% would approve. In general, both qualified social workers and students in Britain were less likely to consider such interventions appropriate than were their counterparts in the US. However, according to Gilligan and Furness (2006: 629), a significant minority of social workers in Britain might approve of such interventions. They report that 60% of the social work students in their sample who held current religious or spiritual beliefs would approve of referring clients to religious or spiritual counsellors (63.5% of Muslims and 53% of 'Christians'), as did 39% of those who did not hold current beliefs.

We believe that it is vital that social work students and qualified practitioners are prepared to work with people for whom religious or other beliefs are of significance, whether these are shared by those practitioners or not – hence, the development of the Furness/Gilligan Framework discussed in Chapter Three.

Such a framework would, we believe, have been helpful to a student such as 'Patricia', who reflected in her learning journal about how she was brought up as a Born Again Christian and about some of the effects this has had on her life and practice (see Inset 1). In particular, she identified that, while on placement, she needed to understand and reflect on her immediate reactions to the behaviour of the young people she was working with.

Inset 1: 'Patricia'

'Patricia' noted that, as a young child, she was brought up to believe that she would go to 'Hell' if she misbehaved. She recalled worrying regularly about things and having to pray a long time for forgiveness. She never swore, always did as she was told and respected adults and people in authority. She was encouraged to believe that anyone who did wrong was a bad person and would go to 'Hell'. Moreover, she recalled that, when she was a teenager, her grandmother had died and this had caused her great confusion. Her

▶

grandmother had not believed in God and therefore, according to the belief system Patricia had been brought up with, her grandmother would burn in 'Hell'. She did not understand how such a loving and caring woman could be punished like this. She had thought that she would be punished for thinking these thoughts, so she had continued to pray, trying to block out or ignore her misgivings.

Her confusion and hurt had continued until she began reading books such as *The God delusion* (Dawkins, 2006), which had persuaded her that she was not alone in having these thoughts and doubts. She had become an atheist and believed that she had seriously questioned and challenged the ways in which her particular religious upbringing had made her think. However, she recognised that such frames of reference still had a powerful influence on her feelings of shock when she observed the way some of the young people talked and acted towards each other, their parents and teachers, and her responses to the lifestyle choices they made. She would, of course, have needed to engage in the same process had she been dealing with a range of other situations where her experiences and her past and current beliefs had a potential impact on her practice – for example, in dealings with service users, carers or colleagues who were Born Again Christians or who had strong religious beliefs entirely different from those that she had been brought up with. Patricia recognised that her past experiences were still potentially significant in shaping her thinking and actions, despite, and sometimes because of, her changed beliefs and the process of change. She needed time and the opportunity to explore them and to reflect on their impact. She will need to continue to do so in order to ensure that her practice remains sensitive, culturally competent and effective.

Our primary aims in writing this book have been to illustrate how religion and belief may have a positive or a negative impact (or both) on people's lives and that they cannot be ignored by social workers or other professionals in their assessment of people's needs and strengths. Religion and belief are complex and sometimes controversial and contended phenomena. Religion may be a fundamental part of, or may profoundly influence, the trauma or difficulties that some individuals experience. Faith can be an essential element in some individuals' resilience and in their survival and recovery in the face of adversity at all stages of the life course. Sometimes, service users may not be aware of the impact of their religion or belief system and the worker can assist them to recognise this process.

Religion must be taken into account if practitioners and their agencies are to comply with the law, statutory guidance and advice, and with professional codes of practice. Practitioners will be faced with dilemmas and conflicts that may stem from religious and/or cultural practices. They need to feel supported by colleagues, managers and their organisations in their actions to tackle discrimination and oppression on religious or cultural grounds. Training and regular team discussions are essential to provide opportunities to develop the knowledge and skills that will allow them to respond appropriately:

> Being open to learn from others, to be challenged by what others are saying or by their experiences, is a prerequisite for an exploration that may lead to greater understanding of myself as well as other people and the issues involved. (White, 2006: 60)

Social workers need to acknowledge the importance of religion and belief in many people's lives to a much greater extent than most have done to date. They also need to respond appropriately when and where religion and belief are important factors. We have been genuinely moved by some of the case studies provided by social workers for this book. Their sense of compassion and concern for others has allowed them to truly see the whole person and to provide help and support in areas which others may not have classed as social work or as being within their remit. They have been able to do this by encouraging the person to speak about their worries and concerns, by listening and by being open and responsive to others' beliefs and fears. For us, social work is about using our communication and interpersonal skills in order to create opportunities and spaces for service users to share their problems and to allow us to help them to improve or alleviate their situations.

We have observed that an increasing number of both our undergraduate and postgraduate social work students demonstrate a strong commitment to their religious beliefs. It has been necessary to provide opportunities for them to explore, reflect on and resolve the relevant dilemmas raised for them by either their own or their service users' religion and beliefs. Part of this work has been to develop the Furness/Gilligan Framework and to share other tools, which can assist them in recognising when and where religion and belief are important. We hope that readers will find this framework useful and easy to apply in their work.

Key questions

We suggest that social workers and others should always ask themselves the following questions:

(1) Are you sufficiently self-aware and reflexive about your own religious and spiritual beliefs or the absence of them and your responses to others?

(2) Are you giving the individuals/groups involved sufficient opportunities to discuss their religious and spiritual beliefs and the strengths, difficulties and needs that arise from them?

(3) Are you listening to what they say about their beliefs and the strengths and needs that arise from them?

(4) Do you recognise individuals' expertise about their own beliefs and the strengths and needs that arise from them?

(5) Are you approaching this piece of practice with sufficient openness and willingness to review and revise your plans and assumptions?

(6) Are you building a relationship that is characterised by trust, respect and a willingness to facilitate?

(7) Are you being creative in your responses to individuals' beliefs and the strengths and needs that arise from them?

(8) Have you sought out relevant information and advice regarding any religious and spiritual beliefs and practices that were previously unfamiliar to you?

References

Abu-Laban, Y. (2002) 'Liberalism, multiculturalism, and the problem of essentialism', *Citizenship Studies*, **6**(4), 459-82.

Banks, S. (2006) *Ethics and values in social work* (3rd edn), Basingstoke: Palgrave Macmillan.

Bowie, R. (2004) *Ethical studies* (2nd edn), Cheltenham: Nelson Thornes.

Dawkins, R. (2006) *The God delusion*, London: Bantam Press.

Furness, S. (2003) 'Religion, belief and culturally competent practice', *Journal of Practice Teaching in Health and Social Care*, **15**(1), 61-74.

Gilligan, P. (2003) '"It isn't discussed". Religion, belief and practice teaching: missing components of cultural competence in social work education', *Journal of Practice Teaching in Health and Social Care*, **5**(1), 75-95.

Hughes, J.C. and Baldwin, C. (2006) *Ethical issues in dementia care*, London: Jessica Kingsley.

Osmo, R. and Landau, R. (2006) 'The role of ethical theories in decision making by social workers', *Social Work Education*, **25**(8), 863–76.

Parrott, L. (2006) *Values and ethics in social work practice*, Exeter: Learning Matters.

Reamer, R.G. (2006) *Social work values and ethics* (3rd edn), New York: Colombia University Press.

Sue, D.W. (2006) *Multicultural social work practice*, Hoboken, NJ: John Wiley & Sons.

Sundar, P. (2009) 'Multi-culturalism', in M. Gray and S.A. Webb (eds) *Social work theories and methods*, Los Angeles, London, New Delhi, Singapore, Washington, DC: Sage Publications, pp 98–108.

White, G. (2006) *Talking about spirituality in health care practice: A resource for the multi-professional health care team*, London and Philadelphia, PA: Jessica Kingsley.

Appendix: A brief guide to religions and beliefs: sources of further information

It is impossible for any book to provide a definitive and comprehensive guide to even the major world religions and we do not claim to do so here. There are, of course, many overlaps in beliefs and perspectives, both between and within faiths. However, sometimes, there appear to be as many (perhaps even more) differences between the views and beliefs of particular groups and individuals within faiths, sects, denominations and so on as there are commonalities. To give just a few examples, many co-religionists place very different degrees of emphasis of matters such as:

- 'predestination'/'free will';
- 'good works'/'faith';
- a personal relationship with God;
- 'peace and justice'/pacifism/'holy war';
- 'spirit possession' (positive and/or negative);
- their holy book as literally the word of God;
- contemporary interpretation of historic scriptures.

At the same time:

- Some faiths have no generally accepted spokesperson who represents their collective viewpoint.
- The 'official' statements of institutional religions do not necessarily reflect the actual views and beliefs of their nominal adherents.
- The governance of organised religions remains immensely varied in its nature.
- Within faiths, some groups exclude other groups from their definition of 'true' believers, while those excluded may include those who have excluded them.

What we do offer here are some very brief outlines of what we, and others, understand to be characteristics and key practices and traditions of the six major world religions that appear most relevant to Britain. We do so with caution, recognising that such 'introductions' can carry with them the risk that readers may be misled into thinking that they have gained sufficient knowledge and understanding when they have not. Such information does not provide an adequate substitute for dialogue with individuals about their actual beliefs and practices or their experience of what aspects of these are significant to them. It can only indicate possible issues. We also provide a brief list of what we have found to be the most useful sources of information regarding religion and belief. We would advise readers to use these to obtain introductory and background information about particular religions and beliefs. However, such a list will never be truly comprehensive, while some of the categorisations of groups are inevitably arbitrary and contentious. Our intention is to be pragmatic, only. Any offence caused is, of course, unintentional and regretted.

We acknowledge that there are many other religions and belief systems. Hence, we would urge readers both to use the resources listed and to develop their own list of similar resources with a view to finding out more about beliefs and practices that may be of particular relevance to their work. However, again, we would stress that third-party information and background knowledge needs to be combined with direct dialogue with the individuals involved.

Christianity

Worldwide, approximately 2.1 billion people describe themselves as Christian. They belong to more than 22,000 different groups (www.adherents.com) and comprise about one third of the global population. In the UK, the 2001 Census reported 41 million people as Christians. This represents nearly three quarters of the total population (National Statistics, 2003). Christ means 'annointed one' or 'Messiah'. Most Christian churches teach that Jesus Christ was the Son of God; that He died to atone for the sins of the world and rose from the dead to eternal life. Christianity emphasises that the values of 'faith', 'hope' and 'charity' should underpin a good life and promises eternal life with God after death to those who lead such lives. Most Christians believe that God is infinite, omniscient and omnipresent. In the concept of the Trinity, they refer to God as three persons in one: God the Father (the creator of mankind), God the Son (Jesus Christ) and God the Holy Spirit (the power of God). Jesus Christ is seen as both human and divine. Babies and young children are usually received into the Christian faith through baptism or dedication rituals, and, in most groups, Christians become full members or 'communicants' following further rites of initiation, including 'confirmation' and adult baptism, during their adolescence or adult lives. Christianity emphasises that individuals should act according to an informed conscience, should serve God and their fellow human beings, and should love their neighbours as themselves. Most Christian churches have communion services as part of their worship, sometimes daily. Communicants usually receive bread (often a thin wafer of unleavened bread; sometimes a small piece of leavened bread) and wine (or similar). These symbolise the body and blood of Christ or are believed to have transubstantiated so that Christ is in them. In this way, Christians share the memory of Christ's death and resurrection. For most Christian groups, the marriage of one man to one woman is important and symbolises the beginning of a new family in God. Prayer is used to praise, thank and petition God, and to ask for forgiveness. Christians' sacred text is the Bible, which is divided into the Old and New Testaments. The Bible is central to much Christian worship and, among some groups, is seen as the only basis for moral teaching or for understanding the world.

Major differences between and within Christian groups originate from different beliefs around Holy Communion (Roman Catholics and members of Eastern Orthodox and Anglo-Catholic Churches believe in transubstantiation, while 'Protestants' do not); from differing views about the role of the Bible; and from different forms of governance and organisation ('Episcopalian' churches, such as the Church of England and the Roman Catholic Church, recognise a hierarchy of bishops, priests and laity, while groups such as Baptists, Congregationalists, Methodists and the Church of Scotland have 'Presbyterian' systems in which churches are governed by elders and all, including ministers, are of equal rank).

Islam

One meaning of the Arabic word 'Islam' is peace and followers believe that they will achieve this through compliance with Allah's divine guidance. 'Allah' is the Islamic name for the One True God and is preferred, by them, to the word 'God'. There are over 1.5 billion Muslims living throughout the world, making up 21% of the total population (www.adherents.com). In the UK, the 2001 Census reported 1.6 million people as Muslims. This represents 3% of the total population (National Statistics, 2003). Islam's holy book is the Koran, which means 'that which is recited'. Muslims believe that the Koran was revealed to Muhammad, as the final Prophet and Messenger of Allah, and that it provides the essential guidance for humanity on how to live their lives. It is central to Islamic faith and it is important to Muslims that they study and learn the teachings of the Koran to help them to understand their role and situation on Earth. All practical, moral and spiritual aspects of life are modelled on the customs and traditions (*Sunnah*) of the Prophet as recounted in the *Hadith*, which provide a major source of Islamic law. The code of conduct for Muslims based on the Koran and *Sunnah* is known as *Shari'ah*. The purpose of *Shari'ah* law is to bring justice to everyone through the enactment of a moral and responsible society. The two main branches of Islam are *Shi'ah* and *Sunni*. The *Sunni* constitute approximately 90% of Muslims. According to *Sunni* understanding, the five pillars of Islam are:

(1) *Shahada*, the declaration of faith that states: "There is no God but Allah, and Muhammad is His Messenger";
(2) *Salah*, the five obligatory prescribed times of daily prayer;
(3) payment of *Zakat*, which is an annual charity tax paid to those who are in need or poor;
(4) a pilgrimage to Mecca during the month of *Hajj* at least once in a lifetime;
(5) fasting during the month of Ramadan.

Most Muslims in the UK have family connections with other countries, notably Pakistan, Bangladesh and India, while Muslims living in one city or town often have family connections with the same region. However, there are likely to be some differences in religious practices, and membership of different mosques will often reflect differences in beliefs and identity. As elsewhere, Muslims in Britain are not one homogeneous group.

Hinduism

Hinduism is one of the world's oldest surviving religions and is deeply rooted in the culture of India. It is based on the sacred texts of *Vedas* (the word of God), *Ramayana* and *Mahabharata* (remembered and written by sages). There are 900 million Hindus worldwide making up 14% of the global population (www.adherents.com). Seven hundred million Hindus live in India. In the UK, the 2001 Census reported 0.5 million people as Hindus. This represents 1% of the total population (National Statistics, 2003). Hindus believe that the soul is born on earth many times. One's actions determine whether the next incarnation will be 'good' or not. This is known as *karma* and the ultimate aim is to escape the cycle of life and rebirth (*samsara*) and to gain liberation (*moksha*) when the soul achieves union with the Ultimate Being, Brahman. Hindus believe that there are three traditional paths to achieve *moksha*. One is the search for spiritual knowledge through meditation, yoga and use of mantras (for example, "om"), a word that is repeated many times. Another path is to perform good works, to fulfil obligations and to carry out one's duty. The third path is *bhakti* or devotion. Worship is usually a daily routine involving purification and prayer. There are three main Hindu representations of God: Brahma, the creator; Vishnu, the preserver (also known as Krishna); and Shiva, the destroyer. Hindus believe that God descends to Earth when there is an increase of evil.

Sikhism

There are 23 million Sikhs worldwide making up 0.36% of the global population (www.adherents.com). In the UK, the 2001 Census reported 0.6 million people as Sikhs. This represents 0.6% of the total population (National Statistics, 2003). Sikhs believe in one God. The founder and first Guru (religious teacher) of Sikhism was Guru Nanak. The Sikhs' sacred text is *Guru Granth Sahib*, which contains much of their religious teaching. Sikhs believe that God cannot be represented in human or physical form and therefore does not belong to any one particular faith. They teach that God can be experienced only through meditation, worship and service to others. The *langar* is a communal meal that is shared after a service by men and women. The sharing of a meal in this way signifies to Sikhs the equal status of all. Sikhs believe in reincarnation but emphasise that only in human incarnation can someone experience the love of God. *Khalsa* Sikhs commit themselves to a life of discipline, following their initiation (often called "baptism") with sweetened water (*amrit*). Sikhs refer to this rite as "taking *amrit*" and when they speak of "proper Sikhs" they usually mean *amritdhari* ("baptised") Khalsa Sikhs. Their uniform is referred to as the "five Ks" or *panj kakke*. These signs are required of both men and women. They are: *Kesh* (uncut hair); *Kangha* (wooden comb); *Kirpan* (miniature sword), *Kara* (steel wristband); and *kach* or *kachehra/kachchahira* (knee-length shorts).

Sikhism originates in the Punjab, but many Sikhs now live outside of the Punjab, which was partitioned by the British in 1947 when India and Pakistan gained independence. Sikh communities often maintain their culture through educational and social activities based at their temple or gurdwara. Almost all Sikh men have and use the name *Singh* (lion) and all Sikh women the name *Kaur* (princess).

Judaism

There are 18 million Jewish people worldwide making up 0.3% of the global population (www.adherents.com). In the UK, the 2001 Census reported 0.27 million people as Jewish. This represents 0.5% of the total population (National Statistics, 2003). Jewish people believe that they are descended from a Semitic tribe that originated in the land of Canaan and their earliest ancestor was the prophet Abraham. Many Jews believe that their Scriptures (often referred to by others as the Old Testament) give a record of their early history and demonstrate that God promised they would become a great people and the rightful owners of the Land of Canaan. The Scriptures and particularly the first five books (Genesis, Exodus, Leviticus, Numbers and Deuteronomy) contain laws that are the basis of the Jewish way of life. Each week texts from the first five books (the *Torah* or *Pentateuch*) are read in the synagogue. The whole cycle of readings takes a year. Debate and study of the *Torah* are an integral part of Jewish life and the Scroll of the *Torah* is treated with great reverence. For 'religious' Jews, the *Torah* is the ultimate guide to conduct and devotion to it is seen as essential.

Jews are not homogeneous in their beliefs or practices, which range from the strictly Orthodox – who are most visible and believe that the books of the *Torah* were dictated directly by God and must, therefore, be obeyed in every particular – to the completely secular. In the UK, Orthodox Jews accept the Chief Rabbi as their spiritual leader. The much less visible Reformed or Liberal groupings, in contrast to the Orthodox, accept the possibility of human error in the *Torah* and adopt cultural relativism. They have their own synagogues. Many Jews in the UK are descended from people who fled from Polish and Russian pogroms during the 19th century or from refugees from Nazi Germany in the 1930s. The vast majority of Jews live in London, but there are also large communities in Leeds, Manchester, Glasgow and Brighton.

Buddhism

There are 350 million Buddhists worldwide making up 6% of the global population (www.adherents.com). In the UK, the 2001 Census reported 0.15 million people as Buddhist. This represents 0.3% of the total population (National Statistics, 2003). Buddhism teaches that all life is interconnected and that compassion is, therefore, both natural and important. It focuses on individual spiritual development and attainment of insight into the true nature of life. It was founded in India, 2,500 years ago. Buddhism originates from Siddhartha Gautama's quest for Enlightenment. Buddhists do not believe in a personal God, but believe that nothing is fixed or permanent and, therefore, change is always possible.

There are two main Buddhist sects: the Theravada Buddhists and the Mahayana Buddhists. However, there are several other Buddhist groupings. Buddhists worship at home or at temples and believe that the path to Enlightenment is through the practice and development of meditation, morality and wisdom.

Non-religious

It is estimated that there are about 1.1 billion people worldwide who describe themselves as agnostic, atheist or secular humanist, or as having no religious preference (www.adherents.com). They make up 16% of the global population. In the UK, the 2001 Census reported 9.1 million people had no religion and that 4.3 million people had refused to state their religion in their census return. These figures represent 15.5% and 7.3% of the total population (National Statistics, 2003). More recent research conducted in a different way by Tearfund (Ashworth and Farthing, 2007) found that 32.2 million people in the UK (66%) had no connection with any religion or church.

Further information

- The British Broadcasting Company (BBC) provides very useful introductory and background information online at www.bbc. co.uk/religion/religions/. The religions featured are: atheism, Baha'i, Buddhism, Candomhlé, Christianity, Hinduism, Islam, Jainism, Jehovah's Witnesses, Judaism, Mormon, paganism, Rastafari, Santeria, Shinto, Sikhism, Taoism, Unitarianism and Zoroastrianism. Links are provided to information about matters such as the beliefs, history, rites and rituals, festivals and worship of each religion.
- The Commission for Racial Equality provides *A guide to religion and belief in Britain* at http://83.137.212.42/ sitearchive/cre/diversity/religion.html. This offers introductions to six religions and to humanism, which it defines as "either the non-belief in religion, or the holding of beliefs that are non-religious in nature".
- The Higher Education Council's Subject Centre for Philosophical and Religious Studies provides *Faith guides* to Christianity, Hinduism, Judaism, Islam and Sikhism. They include sections on debunking common stereotypes, contact details for relevant organisations and suggestions for further reading. The guides are available as hard copies from the Subject Centre or can be downloaded via links at http://prs. heacademy.ac.uk/publications/faith_guides.html.
- Mark Chandler provides information and links regarding religions in Britain at www.ukstudentlife.com/Personal/ Religion.htm. This information is aimed primarily at people

who come to the UK from other countries and provides straightforward and brief introductions to six world religions.

- The Wabash Center at Wabash College in Indiana, US provides a very wide-ranging and eclectic Internet Guide to Religion, available at www.wabashcenter.wabash.edu/resources/ guide_headings.aspx. It offers a "selective, annotated guide" to electronic resources about a wide variety of religions and aspects of and issues within religion, including matters such as apocalyptic thought and millennialism, death and dying, abortion and feminist theology.

- Ansari, H. (2002) *Muslims in Britain*, London: Minority Rights Group International.

- Beckford, J., Gale, R., Owen, D., Peach, C. and Weller, P. (2006) *Review of the evidence base on faith communities*, London: Office of the Deputy Prime Minister.

- British Humanist Association (BHA) (2007) *Quality and equality: Human rights, public services and religious organisations*, London: British Humanist Association.

- Institute of Community Cohesion (2008) *Understanding and appreciating Muslim diversity: Towards better engagement and participation*, Coventry: Institute of Community Cohesion (www.sheffieldfaithsforum.org.uk/resource/114).

- Mirza, M., Senthikumaran, A. and Ja'far, Z. (2007) *Living apart together: British Muslims and the paradox of multiculturalism*, London: Policy Exchange.

- Open Society Institute (2004) *Muslims in the UK: Policies for engaged citizens* (www.eumap.org/topics/minority/reports/ britishmuslims).

- Parekh, B. (2000) *The future of multi-ethnic Britain*, London: Profile Books.

- Purdam, K., Afkhami, R., Crockett, A. and Olsen, W. (2007) 'Religion in the UK: an overview of equality statistics and evidence gaps', *Journal of Contemporary Religion*, **22**(2), 147-68.

- Weller, P., Feldman, A. and Purdam, K. (2001) *Religious discrimination in England and Wales* (Home Office Research Study 220), London: Home Office.

References

Ashworth, J. and Farthing, I. (2007) *Churchgoing in the UK: A research report from Tearfund on church attendance in the UK*, Teddington: Tearfund (www.tearfund.org/webdocs/Website/News/Final%20churchgoing%20report.pdf).

National Statistics (2003) *Census 2001: National report for England and Wales*, London: The Information Management Company (www.statistics.gov.uk/census2001).

Index

Also available from The Policy Press

Social welfare and religion in the Middle East
A Lebanese perspective
Rana Jawad

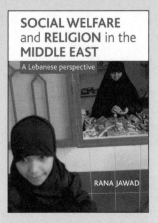

For a region which usually occupies media headlines and academic enquiry with concerns over global security and the supply of petroleum oil, the Middle East would appear averse to any talk of progressive social policy. But below the hard-hitting headlines, what do local Middle Eastern populations think of social welfare, equality and solidarity?

The original analysis in this book presents a new and comprehensive narrative of social welfare in the Middle East through an examination of the role of religious welfare. Religion is, arguably, the longest and most dynamic surviving force of social and political action in the region. Based on an in-depth study of the major Muslim and Christian religious welfare organisations in Lebanon (including Hezbollah), and drawing on supplementary research conducted in Iran, Egypt and Turkey, the book argues that religion – whether through the state apparatus, civil society organisations or populist religious movements – is providing sophisticated solutions to the major social and economic problems of the Middle East.

As religion continues to regain its centrality in both academic and policy circles around the world, this book presents a new framework which examines the complex social and political dynamics shaping social welfare in the Middle East. It also opens up broader debate on the role of faith-based welfare in the changing social policy landscape.

HB £65.00 US$89.95 **ISBN** 978 1 86134 953 8
240 x 172mm 328 pages July 2009

Islam and social work
Debating values, transforming practice
Sara Ashencaen Crabtree, Fatima Husain and Basia Spalek

Encouraging greater cultural competence, this unique book enables social work practitioners to gain a deeper understanding of how Islamic principles inform and influence the lives of Muslim populations and illustrates how this can be translated into professional practice.

This is the only book specifically on social work with Muslim communities and describes the basic tenets of Islam and the daily practices and rituals of the faithful Muslim community. It contextualises the historical legacy of Islam, examining the disparity between universal Islamic precepts and traditional practices and focuses specifically on family welfare, health, Islamophobia and crime as primary issues for practice. The book includes case studies which help the reader explore and develop ideas for culturally congruent social work practice.

PB £18.99 US$29.95 **ISBN** 978 1 86134 947 7
234 x 156mm 208 pages July 2008

To order copies of these publications or any other Policy Press titles please visit **www.policypress.co.uk** or contact:

In the UK and Europe:
Marston Book Services, PO Box 269,
Abingdon, Oxon, OX14 4YN, UK
Tel: +44 (0)1235 465500
Fax: +44 (0)1235 465556
Email: direct.orders@marston.co.uk

In the USA and Canada:
ISBS, 920 NE 58th Street, Suite 300,
Portland, OR 97213-3786, USA
Tel: +1 800 944 6190
(toll free)
Fax: +1 503 280 8832
Email: info@isbs.com

In Australia and New Zealand:
DA Information Services,
648 Whitehorse Road Mitcham,
Victoria 3132, Australia
Tel: +61 (3) 9210 7777
Fax: +61 (3) 9210 7788
E-mail: service@dadirect.com.au